Paul in Syria

T0346459

Paul in Syria

The Background to Galatians

Paul W. Barnett

20 19 18 17 16 15 14   7 6 5 4 3 2 1

First published 2014 by Paternoster
Paternoster is an imprint of Authentic Media Limited
52 Presley Way, Crownhill, Milton Keynes, MK8 0ES.
www.authenticmedia.co.uk

British Library Cataloguing in Publication Data

A catalogue record for this book is available from the British Library

ISBN 978-1-84227-853-6
978-1-78078-334-5 (e-book)

Cover Design by David Smart
Printed and bound by CPI Group (UK) Ltd., Croydon, CR0 4YY

For
Allan and Sandy
Peter and Elizabeth
Fellow-travellers in Syria

Contents

Abbreviations

ABD	Anchor Bible Dictionary
ESV	English Standard Version
ET	English Translation
JBL	Journal of Biblical Literature
JSNT	Journal for the Study of the New Testament
NTS	New Testament Studies
NovT	Novum Testamentum
RTR	Reformed Theological Review (Melbourne)
TDNT	Theological Dictionary of the New Testament ()
WJT	Westminster Theological Journal

Preface

Although I had travelled extensively in the Middle East it had not been my privilege to visit Syria, a truly beautiful country with amazing historical sites. My eventual visit occurred shortly before the outbreak of the tragic civil war in 2011.

As often happens, exposure to the landscape and its settlements excited questions about the biblical text. For me that meant a rush of questions about Paul's visits to Damascus and his journey to 'Arabia' in between.

I had long been curious about Paul's fourteen 'unknown years', the first three to four of which were in Damascus–'Arabia'–Damascus. Inevitably my mind turned to the remaining decade in which Paul was preaching the faith 'in the regions of Syria and Cilicia' (Gal. 1:21). At the time Paul wrote Galatians, Damascus was not part of the Roman province of Syria–Cilicia, although it may have been in the recent past.[1]

One of the mysteries about Paul is that we don't really know what he was doing throughout that decade. The mystery is difficult to penetrate since there are few biblical references and correspondingly few modern studies. Nonetheless, by pursuing a linear approach to such texts as we have I was surprised at the detail that emerged about Paul in Syria–Cilicia AD 37–47.

It was at this point I felt that Galatians would be helpful to cast light back on Paul's activities in Syria and Cilicia. Since I had long believed that Galatians was written soon after the mission in Galatia it seemed likely that the letter would be especially helpful.

Of course, the dating of Galatians is much debated with many arguing for a later dating, whether from Corinth (50–52) or from Ephesus (52–5). In the end, though, I didn't think it mattered materially if Paul wrote Galatians later since 'the regions of Syria and Cilicia' would have been firmly in Paul's mind whenever he wrote the letter. He would probably have worked out the biblical apologetic that appears in Galatians during the Syria–Cilicia decade 37–47.

Broadly speaking, what emerged from my review of those years was that Paul had been preaching to Jews in synagogues and to the Gentile churches he established in Syria and Cilicia. The evidence points to his circumcision-free message to Gentiles focused on faith in the crucified Christ as the means to 'life' with God. That message was expressed in terms of Paul's own radical conversion *from* attempting to 'live' to God through law *to* 'living' to God through his faith-union with the Crucified One. That One who had loved Paul and died for him was now alive, and Paul was alive in and with him and, indeed, indwelt by him.

This Damascus conversion drove Paul to re-examine the Scriptures and to reformulate the key promises of the Old Testament. In consequence Paul highlighted the faith of Abraham by which God credited 'righteousness' to him. Consistently, Paul radically diminished the role of Moses and law and its covenantal adjunct, circumcision. He identified the 'present' Jerusalem, the Jerusalem that is 'below', with Mt Sinai (= law), and which he blamed as a potential agent of the slavery of both Jews and Gentiles.

MAP OF GALATIA AND SURROUNDING AREAS

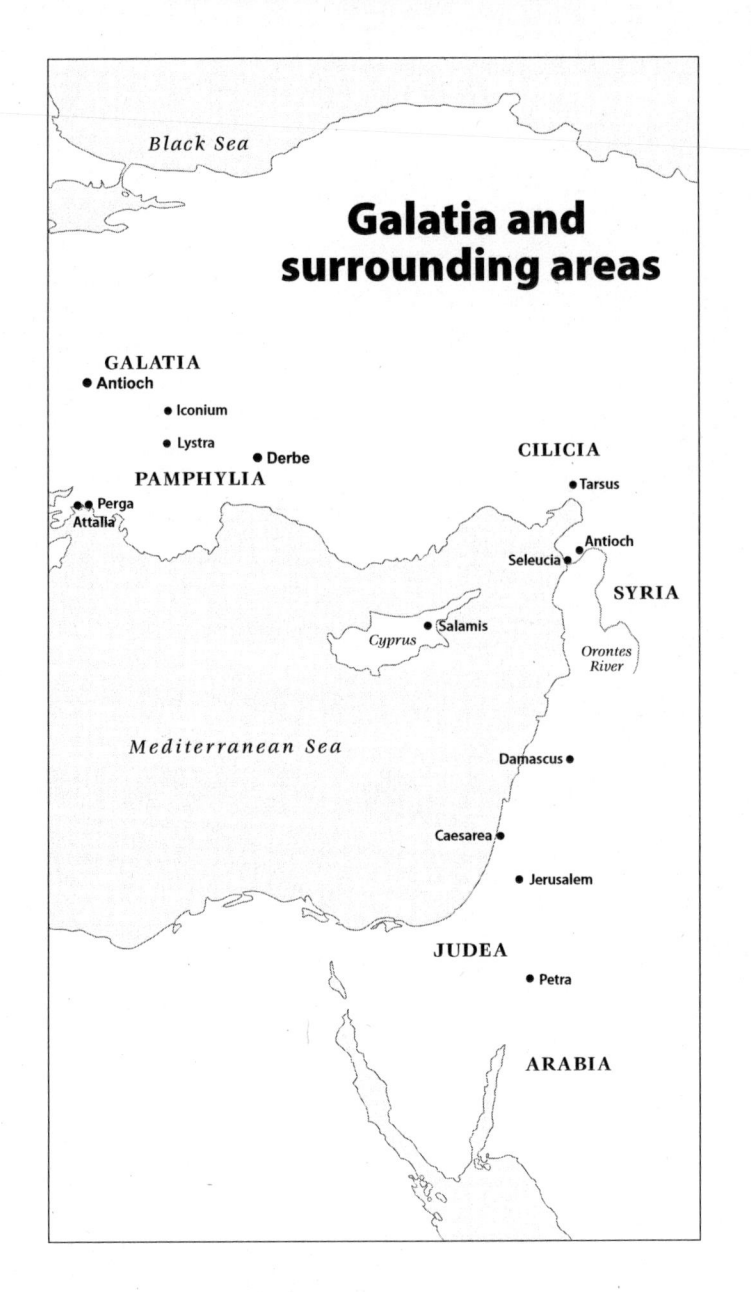

1

Paul in Syria and Cilicia (AD 37–47)

It is clear from Galatians that Paul spent the years between his
first and second return visits to Jerusalem in 'Syria and Cilicia'[1] a
period of about a decade. This calculation is based on the simple
subtraction of 'three years' from 'fourteen years' (Gal. 1:18; 2:1).

Of the various dates for Paul's second visit to Jerusalem 'after
(*dia*) fourteen years', the year 47 seems most likely.[2] Accordingly,
Paul was in the province of Syria–Cilicia between *c*.37 and 47.
Despite the word order *Syria and* Cilicia, Paul spent the greater
part of that decade in the region of Cilicia.

Texts

It is noteworthy that such a lengthy period in the apostle's life has
so few textual references.[3]

Then I went into the regions (*ta klimata*) of *Syria and Cilicia*.
And I was still unknown in person to the churches of Judea that are in
Christ. They only were hearing (*akouontes ēsan*) it said,
'He who used (*pote*) to persecute us
is now (*nun*) preaching the faith (*tēn pistin*) he once tried to destroy.'
And they glorified God because of me. (Gal. 1:21–4, our italics)

I . . . set before them . . . the gospel that I proclaim among the Gentiles
. . .
I had been entrusted with the gospel to the uncircumcised . . . he
[God] . . . worked also through me for [my apostolic ministry] to the
Gentiles. (Gal. 2:2,7–8)

Then it seemed good to the apostles and the elders, with the whole church [who sent] . . . with Paul and Barnabas . . . Judas called Barsabbas, and Silas . . . with the following letter: 'The brothers, both the apostles and the elders, to the brothers who are of the Gentiles in Antioch and *Syria and Cilicia*, greetings.' (Acts 15:22–3, our italics)

And [Paul] went through *Syria and Cilicia*, strengthening the churches. (Acts 15:41, our italics)

In Galatians 1:21–4 Paul does not indicate who the people were to whom he preached, whether Jews, God-fearers or Gentiles. From Galatians 2:2,7–8 and Acts 15:22–3,41, however, we infer that during his decade in ministry in Syria and Cilicia he preached to Gentiles and established Gentile churches.[4] However, as we note below, Luke gives the clear impression that Paul did not engage with the Gentiles until he reached Cyprus and Antioch in Pisidia, until *after* the period in Syria and Cilicia (Acts 13:46).

Scholarly References

The relatively small number of scholarly works devoted to this period coincidentally matches the paucity of textual references to Paul's decade in Syria–Cilicia.

One exception is the classical work of M. Hengel and A.M. Schwemer, *Paul Between Damascus and Antioch: The Unknown Years*, which asserts that ' "Syria and Cilicia" . . . become the most important sphere of activity for the apostle for the next thirteen years'.[5] Their major achievement, however, was to establish the fact of such activity with little discussion about its character.[6]

Useful, but rather brief, are the contributions of F.F. Bruce, R. Riesner, U. Schnelle, E. Schnabel, and J.D.G. Dunn.[7] This is no criticism, however, since there are few texts that form a basis for historical reconstruction.

Significance of This Period

A lengthy period

A decade is a lengthy timespan and 'Syria and Cilicia' is a large region. Thus the question arises: where in the province did Paul spend his time during that decade? Both Galatians and Acts indicate that Paul was located in Antioch in the latter year or years of the decade (Gal. 2:1; Acts 11:25) while the book of Acts points to Tarsus as the place to which Paul went initially and where he devoted most of his time during those years (Acts 9:30; 11:25).

It is significant that the 'Syria and Cilicia' period was as long as the period Paul the missionary traveller spent in AD 47–57 establishing congregations in Galatia, Macedonia, Achaia and Asia, as narrated in Acts 13 – 20. For this earlier, equally long span of years, however, we have only the few references (noted above), and Paul's more general claim: 'from Jerusalem and all the way round to Illyricum I have fulfilled the ministry of the gospel of Christ' (Rom. 15:19). The sheer length of time Paul spent in 'Syria and Cilicia' invites more attention than has been given.

A period in which there are issues to resolve

The most significant issue is the divergence of emphasis between Paul and Luke over the ethnicity of Paul's mission in those regions. As noted, Luke states that it was at Antioch in Pisidia that Paul declared, 'We are turning to the Gentiles' (Acts 13:7,46–7), implying that only there did he begin his mission to the non-Jews.

From Paul's own pen, however, we learn that he had preached to Gentiles from the time of his conversion at Damascus (Gal. 1:16; 2:2,7–8). The presence of the uncircumcised Titus accompanying Barnabas and Paul to Jerusalem in *c.*47 (Gal. 2:3) implies that he had been preaching the gospel to *Gentiles* in Syria and Cilicia in the years between his first and second return visits to Jerusalem.

In Chapter 2 we will address this question further. For the moment, it is sufficient to say that Paul's account is the one to follow, rather than Luke's. This is not because Luke's as a 'secondary' source is less reliable than Paul's, but because Luke has shaped his narrative in a particular way.

Luke was concerned to narrate the progress of the gospel from Jerusalem to the 'ends of the earth', that is to say, to the centre of the Gentile world, Rome. The conversion of the *Roman* centurion Cornelius by Peter[8] was a primary pointer in that direction, which was followed years later by Paul's arrival in Cyprus and his conversion of the *Roman* proconsul. This was followed by his arrival in Antioch in Pisidia, a *Roman* colony (Acts 13:14). Luke passed over the events between Cornelius (*c.*40) and Sergius Paulus (*c.*48), including Paul's ministry in Syria and Cilicia, despite the fact that these events were separated by so many years. In short, it was not that Luke was inaccurate in his narrative,[9] but rather that he was highly selective about the events he chose to make prominent and those he chose to pass over.

A period in which some details emerge indirectly

Although the texts that apply directly to Paul in Syria and Cilicia are few, there are several references in 2 Corinthians that cast light on Paul's activities there.

The fivefold synagogue beatings referred to in 2 Corinthians 11:24 probably occurred within the period between Paul's conversion in Damascus and his second return visit to Jerusalem fourteen years later. Luke's extensive accounts of Paul's westward missions in Acts 13 – 20 are silent about such beatings, suggesting that they had occurred earlier, within the 'unknown years' between Damascus and Antioch. We can envisage one synagogue beating occurring in Damascus (cf. Acts 9:22) but since Paul spent the greater part of 'the three years' in 'Arabia' (Gal. 1:17–18) it seems more likely that the remaining beatings occurred in Syria and Cilicia. In our view it was Paul's law-free teaching to Gentile God-fearers in the synagogues that brought these punishments upon him.

Paul's rapture into paradise seems also to have occurred while Paul was in Syria and Cilicia, as also chronicled within the same *peristasis* in 2 Corinthians 12:2–3 and is discussed at greater length in Chapter 3.

The years in Syria and Cilicia would have provided Paul with the opportunity to develop skills of letter-writing, that will become evident in such a powerful epistle as Galatians which we will argue was written immediately after his missionary tour of

Galatia.[10] This letter was, in effect, a speech to be read aloud to the congregations of Galatia. Following the arguments of H.D. Betz many scholars have adopted the view that Paul employed the rhetorical formats of political speech-makers of that era. Did Paul undergo some kind of rhetorical training during these Cilician years, perhaps in the academies of Tarsus? In Chapter 3 we will argue against this suggestion. For now it is enough to contend that Paul's letters developed out of his homiletic practices in the churches of 'Syria and Cilicia' AD 37–47.

Although Paul explicitly locates the years between his first and second return visits to Jerusalem in 'the regions of Syria and Cilicia' many scholars effectively ignore 'the regions . . . of Cilicia' and focus all attention on 'the regions of . . . Syria', by which they mean *Antioch*. The history-of-religions school believed that Antioch was a centre of Gnosticism and the mystery cults and that Paul developed his distinctive *Kyrios* theology in the Syrian capital. In Chapter 3 we will point out that we know almost nothing about the religious culture of Antioch in the first century and that the suggestion that Paul was subject to such syncretistic influence is unlikely to be true.

It can be agreed, however, that Paul's eventual migration to Antioch did influence him in other ways. Although he had been preaching the faith of Christ crucified to Gentiles since his 'call' outside Damascus, it seems to have been at Antioch that he reached the painful conclusion that God was 'hardening' the Jews to this message, but at the same time increasingly opening the hearts of the Gentiles to it. Among other reasons it may have been his encounter with the Jew–Gentile 'mixed' congregation in Antioch that directed his heart to westward (i.e. Rome-ward) missionary enterprise, which in turn directed him and Barnabas (accompanied by Titus) to travel to Jerusalem seeking the 'fellowship' of the 'pillar' apostles for such a venture. The journey to Cyprus, Pisidia and Lycaonia was the consequence of that meeting in Jerusalem (Gal. 2:1–10).

A period that is early within Christian history

Paul's so-called 'unknown years' (AD 34–47) were at the same time the earliest years of Christian history, immediately following the crucifixion and resurrection of Jesus in Jerusalem (in AD 33). It was, however, a decade and a half from which nothing written has survived; the letters of the New Testament only begin to appear in the mid-to-late forties.[11]

Be that as it may, there can be no doubt that oral statements of Christian faith were formulated very soon after the first Easter, evidence for which is found in Paul's twofold reminder to the Corinthians about the 'traditions' that he 'delivered' to them in AD 50. One concerned the death and resurrection of Christ (1 Cor. 15:3–7), the other the words and actions of the Lord on 'the night he was betrayed' (1 Cor. 11:23–5). Paul 'received' these 'traditions' either at Damascus in *c.*34 or Jerusalem in 36/7. Two observations may be made about these 'traditions'. One is that each was carefully pre-formatted and the other is that Paul was not their author.

These observations point to what might be called a 'rabbinic' culture within the community of the first Christians in Jerusalem. The letters of the New Testament generally are marked with the terminology of rabbinic transmission, whether by Paul (1 Thess. 4:1; 1 Cor. 11:2; Col. 2:7; Rom. 6:17; 16:17; 2 Tim. 2:2), by the author of Hebrews (Heb. 3:1; 4:2,12–13; 5:11–12; 6:1; 10:23.), by John (2 John 9:10), or by Jude (Jude 3).

Such a conclusion is not surprising. The first apostles were located in Jerusalem, the home of the academies of the Pharisees whose culture of precise oral transmission was well established.[12] Furthermore, Jesus was a 'rabbi' who had instructed his 'disciples' by repetition of parables, poetic oracles and aphorisms.[13] The formation of a 'rabbinic' society in Jerusalem employing rabbinic modes of transmission was a natural development for the first Christians in the Holy City.[14]

In Chapters 6 and 7 we will propose that James and Peter were active in formulating traditions during the years Paul spent in Syria and Cilicia, traditions that would become the basis for much of the literature of the New Testament in the ensuing years. Their respective engagements with Paul are a critical part of earliest Christian history.

The Aims of This Book

The objectives in writing are threefold. First, we seek to cast further light upon the sparsely documented but lengthy period of

Paul's years in Syria and Cilicia. These were early and formative years in the life of Paul the apostle of Christ and they represent the immediate precursor to Paul's first steps westward in his mission to the Gentiles. The mission to Galatia in 47/48 in turn immediately preceded his letter to the Galatians.[15]

Accordingly, a second objective is to consider Paul's theological reflections during the decade-long span in Syria and Cilicia. This was the period in which Paul worked out the theology he would subsequently preach to the Galatians and that he would reapply in his letter to their churches.

Third, since Galatians refers to Peter and James (in 36/7 and 47) we are inevitably drawn to consider the theological understanding of these noted leaders during Paul's years in Syria and Cilicia, 37–47. Paul's doctrines can be measured alongside those of Peter and James. As we will argue, Paul identified with Peter's general emphasis on atonement through union with the crucified but risen Christ, but James articulated doctrines that sharply differed from Paul's, whether they were a true or distorted view of Paul's understanding. Consequently, Paul's years in Syria and Cilicia coincide with the period of the formation of the Petrine and Jacobean traditions that would assume written form in later decades.

Procedure

The approach taken is chronological and contextual. It is the attempt to think oneself into the time span and the place involved, that is, where Paul was between 37 and 47, what he was doing and what his thinking was at that time, but also – so far as we are able – to attempt to discern the thinking of other key players like Peter, James and the 'circumcision' advocates.

This approach is to be distinguished from a merely theological approach that organizes Paul's texts under various headings, without taking account of time, place and circumstance. It is possible, in the example of his letter to the Galatians, that Paul so passionately states his argument that we cannot neatly assemble doctrinal texts from this epistle alongside others in his more coolly written letters. The actual, dynamic context is all-important.

Since Galatians is such a passionate letter, one whose author-ship or undivided unity is not doubted, it is important to locate it chronologically and contextually. It does not matter that scholars are divided about the date of writing, whether immediately after the mission in Galatia in *c.*48, or from Corinth in *c.*50–52, or from Ephesus in *c.*52–5. The point is that letter reflects Paul's thinking as from the years in Syria and Cilicia, as reflected throughout the letter, not least in Galatians 1:21–24; 2:1–21. Having said that, however, in our opinion the case for Paul having written from Antioch in *c.*48 remains the strongest.[16]

2

The Problem: Paul's Mission Audiences

In his apologetic autobiography embedded within Galatians Paul states that at Damascus God called him to proclaim his Son 'among[1] the Gentiles' (Gal. 1:15–16).

Our problem is that it was only fourteen years later in Jerusalem that he received the agreement of the 'pillars' James, Peter and John to 'go to the Gentiles' (Gal. 2:9).

For its part, the book of Acts also implies that Paul did not preach to Gentiles during these fourteen years. Luke describes Paul preaching to *Jews* in Damascus (Acts 9:20) but makes no mention of Paul visiting 'Arabia' and describes Paul preaching to *Jews* in Jerusalem, including Hellenistic Jews (9:28–9). Only when Paul came to Syrian Antioch is there any hint of Paul's engagement with 'Greeks'[2] (11:20). Based on Acts 13:46 we would conclude that Paul only began preaching to Gentiles in Antioch in Pisidia in *c.*47. Did Paul only begin to proclaim Christ to Gentiles on his first missionary journey following that meeting in Jerusalem (Acts 13 – 14)? What was Paul doing in those fourteen years between the Damascus 'call' and the Jerusalem 'agreement'?

Details are relatively few for the fourteen years between the Damascus event and the Jerusalem agreement.[3] Nonetheless, it is possible to recover an approximate chronology for these so-called 'unknown years'. The book of Acts[4] is broadly consistent with the sequence in Paul's survey of his career in Galatians.

Date[5]		Galatians		Acts	
34	1:13	Paul attempted to destroy the church of God	8:3	Paul ravaged the church in Jerusalem	
	1:16	God revealed his son in Paul	9:3	A light from heaven . . . a voice	
	1:17	Paul in Damascus	9:8	Paul in Damascus	
	1:17	Paul in Arabia			
	1:17	Paul in Damascus			
36	1:17	Paul in Jerusalem	9:26	Paul in Jerusalem	
	1:21	Paul in Syria	9:30	Paul in Tarsus	
		[Antioch and Tarsus]	11:25	Paul in Antioch	
47	2:1	Paul in Jerusalem	11:30	Paul in Jerusalem	

Did Paul confine his evangelism to Jews during the fourteen 'unknown' years, or did he also preach to Gentiles?

Varying Opinions

Biblical historians have not been slow to notice this problem and to offer solutions. Francis Watson, for example, concludes that Paul did in fact limit his preaching in Damascus to fellow-Jews.[6] By contrast, Martin Hengel and Anna Maria Schwemer argue that (Gentile) God-fearers would have been among Paul's hearers in the synagogues in Damascus where Paul preached following his baptism.[7] As well, they assert that when Paul went to 'Arabia' he began to fulfil the Damascus 'call' by preaching Christ to the Gentiles.[8]

Nicholas Taylor, however, thinks that Paul went to Arabia before Damascus and only later was integrated into the Christian community through baptism, which 'brought about a reduction in his post-conversion dissonance'.[9] Taylor argues that Paul's conversion seriously disorientated him. His discussions with Peter in Jerusalem would have 'further reduced his post-conversion dissonance and therefore further development in Paul's theological thinking'.[10]

In fact, he argues that 'Paul's apostolic formation was the product of his association with the church at Antioch, and was subsequently and radically transformed into the apostolic self-conception reflected in his letters'. It was only at Antioch that Paul 'was fully integrated into the life of the Christian community and became one of its leaders'.[11] According to Taylor, 'Acts 13:4 represents the commencement of Paul's apostolic ministry, as the delegate of the Christian community in Antioch, accompanying Barnabas on the outreach of the community.'[12]

In pursuit of this thesis Taylor rejects Paul's references to missionary work among Gentiles during the fourteen years. He regards the autobiographical aspects of Galatians 1:11 – 2:14 about early mission work among Gentiles (e.g. Gal. 2:8) as 'anachronistic', a back projection from later activities.[13]

In sharp contrast, Hengel and Schwemer contend that Paul's theological universe radically changed at Damascus, when he understood himself to be no longer a man 'in law' but a man 'in Christ' and when he was dramatically given a prophet's vocation to take the message of the crucified *Christos*, who is now the *Kyrios*, to the nations.[14]

Taylor's line of thought, however, is not sufficiently sensitive to Paul's precarious situation when he wrote Galatians. He was the object of suspicion in Jerusalem (from the 'false-brothers' – Gal. 2:4), in Antioch (from Peter, Barnabas and 'rest of the Jews' – Gal. 2:11–14), and in the churches of Galatia (whose members regarded Paul as their 'enemy' – Gal. 4:16). His autobiography in Galatians while passionate is, at the same time, precise as to time and place and carefully expressed. Paul was aware that his critics would seize any error of fact. The 'anachronism' argument directed to the nature of Paul's autobiography in Galatians is unconvincing.

Taylor's reconstruction raises another issue. It is that he passes over with little comment Paul's period of activity in Tarsus and the wider region of Cilicia during these years. Instead he focuses his attention on Paul's visit to Antioch, metropolis of Syria. He writes, 'Paul states that he went from Jerusalem to Syria and Cilicia. However, Paul's principal base during this period of his life was Antioch where he worked in association with Barnabas.'[15] Taylor and many others leap from Jerusalem to Antioch, effectively ignoring Paul's mission activities in Tarsus and wider Cilicia.

Paul's Apostolic Ministry to Gentiles during the Fourteen Years

As noted above, exegesis of both Galatians and Acts points to their historical agreement about the broad outline of Paul's 'unknown years', *c.* AD 34–47.[16] That agreement points to Paul's radical about-face near Damascus followed by a sojourn in that city, an escape to Arabia, a return to Damascus and a visit to Jerusalem. From Jerusalem Paul went to the regions of Syria and Cilicia before returning to Jerusalem for a second time.

Damascus[17]

When Paul was first in Damascus 'immediately he proclaimed Jesus in the synagogues, saying, "He is the Son of God"' and he 'confounded the Jews living in Damascus by proving that Jesus was the Christ' (Acts 9:20,22).

For two reasons it is likely that there were Gentile God-fearers attending the synagogues. First, according to Josephus a majority of Gentile women in Damascus had converted to the Jewish religion,[18] explaining perhaps the Damascenes' dislike of the Jews.[19] Second, one of Paul's motives in coming to Damascus may have been to arrest Hellenists who had fled from Jerusalem in order to prevent them making converts from the God-fearers who attended the synagogues of Damascus.

Thus it is reasonable to think that there were God-fearers in the synagogue congregations where Paul had argued that 'Jesus was the Christ'. Nonetheless, although Paul did have 'disciples' in Damascus (Acts 9:25) there is no way of knowing whether they were Jews or God-fearers.

The Jews of Damascus sought to kill Paul (Acts 9:23). Was it because he preached Christ as an alternative to the law as the means to 'life'? Was he telling God-fearers that faith in Christ obviated the necessity for circumcision? Was Paul flogged in the synagogue before he fled to Arabia (cf. 2 Cor. 11:24)?

'Arabia'

By 'Arabia' Paul means the desert kingdom of the Nabateans, whose ruler was the long-serving King Aretas IV (cf. 2 Cor. 11:32).[20] Why did Paul go 'into Arabia' (Gal. 1:17) and not elsewhere, for example, north to Palmyra, south to the Hellenistic cities of the Decapolis, or west or to the Hellenized coastal cities of Phoenicia? The probable answer is that Nabatea was a major kingdom nearest Eretz Israel and home to the descendants of Ishmael, a kindred tribe to the descendants of Isaac. At the same time, the Nabateans were 'Gentiles' and a part of Paul's newly mandated missionary vocation.

Paul does not indicate where he travelled in Arabia or the people whom he addressed.[21] We reasonably assume that once more he went to synagogues to argue from the Scriptures that the long-awaited Christ had now come in the person of the crucified and risen Jesus, where he sought to influence *Gentile* God-fearers as well as Jews.[22]

It appears that Paul was as unwelcome in Arabia as he had been in Damascus, though for a different reason. Paul arrived in Nabatea at a singularly inopportune time. Some years earlier Aretas IV had given his daughter Phasaelis in marriage to Herod Antipas, tetrarch of Galilee–Perea, doubtless to help secure friendly border relationships. During the late twenties, however, Antipas committed adultery with Herodias, prompting the Nabatean princess to return home.[23] Simmering hostilities were reaching boiling point between Aretas and Antipas at the very time Paul the Jew was preaching in the synagogues in Arabia, *c.*34/35.

The only light thrown on this period in his life is Paul's own comment that Aretas' governor (*ethnarchēs*) in Damascus sought to seize him after he returned to the city (2 Cor. 11:32; cf. Gal. 1:17). Prior to AD 34 Damascus had either been part of the province of Syria–Cilicia[24] or, alternatively, had been an independent city-state as part of the Decapolis.[25] Equally inconclusive is information about the rule in Damascus during the years 34–40. It is possible that Antipas, tetrarch of Galilee–Perea, had been assigned the city in 34, but that Aretas had gained the control by 37.[26] If Paul returned to Damascus in 36 it would have been during Antipas' tenure of the city when the tetrarch of Galilee–Perea had allowed Aretas to have a 'consul' representing Nabateans who were living in the city. If, however, Paul returned in 37 Damascus would by then have been part of Aretas' kingdom. Either way, Paul's preaching in 'Arabia' (Nabatea) had come negatively to the attention of the king who had been unhappy with Paul's activities in his kingdom. Some time after Paul returned to Damascus he must flee from 'the city of Damascus' to escape Aretas' governor.

Jerusalem

Luke states that Paul 'went in and out among them all at Jerusalem', that is, among the apostles. He 'went in' among the apostles for fellowship and support, but he 'went out' into wider Jerusalem – as the text of Acts proceeds to say – 'preaching boldly in the name of the Lord'. This is further elaborated as, 'he spoke and disputed against the Hellenists; but they were seeking to kill him' (Acts 9:28–9). Paul, the persecutor become preacher, was himself now the one persecuted – and in Jerusalem!

There was more involved in this visit to Jerusalem than we would conclude from Galatians 1:18–19 and Acts 9:26–30. Twenty years later Paul testified to King Agrippa II that his recent ordeal in Jerusalem was due to his earlier preaching in Jerusalem and Judea. 'I . . . declared first to those at Damascus then *at Jerusalem and throughout all the country of Judea*, and also to the Gentiles, that they should repent and turn to God and perform deeds worthy of their repentance' (Acts 26:20, our italics). This more comprehensive and extensive[27] character of Paul's ministry in Judea is also to be inferred from Paul's reflections to the Thessalonians: 'For you, brothers, became imitators of the churches of God in Christ Jesus which are in Judea; for you suffered the same things from your own countrymen as they did from the Jews, who killed both the Lord Jesus and the prophets, and drove us out, and displease God and oppose all men' (1 Thess. 2:14–15).

Paul is referring to a five- or six-year period of persecution from 'the Jews' that was directed

(i)   to Jesus himself (29–33), and subsequently
(ii) to the churches in Judea (from 34), and
(iii) to Paul himself (36/37).

Neither in Jerusalem nor in the province of Judea is there any hint that Paul preached to Gentiles, including to God-fearers.

Tarsus and Cilicia

Paul's temporal markers '*then* after three years I went up to Jerusalem . . . *Then* I went to the regions of Syria and Cilicia . . . *Then* after fourteen years I went up again to Jerusalem' make it clear that Paul spent about ten of his fourteen years as a Christian in 'the regions of Syria and Cilicia' (Gal. 1:18,21; 2:1, our italics).

Luke, however, implies that Paul passed the greater part of this decade in Tarsus. He states that Paul was 'sent' from Caesarea *to* Tarsus (Acts 9:30, our italics) and that later (he does not say how long) Barnabas brought Paul *from* Tarsus and 'for *a whole year* they met with the church' (Acts 11:26, our italics). This implies that Paul spent only one or two years in Antioch so we reasonably conclude that he was in and around Tarsus for most of the intervening years. Even if some adjustment needs to be made we must conclude that for the greater part of the decade after Paul left Jerusalem it was Tarsus and not Antioch that was his base.[28] This chronology needs to be taken seriously based on Luke's specific reference to a 'whole year' spent in Antioch, the more so if, as some think, Luke was from Antioch and well placed to know these details.

Why did Paul allow himself to be 'sent' to Tarsus? There was probably more than one reason:[29]

(i)   After perilous times in Damascus and Jerusalem, Tarsus, his city of origin, with its relatives and friends, would have been a safe haven for the fiery preacher;
(ii) As a major city in a Roman province Tarsus afforded Paul a degree of protection as a Roman citizen;
(iii) Paul was a 'citizen' of Tarsus (Acts 21:39), a citizenship he would have inherited from his father;[30]
(iv) Tarsus had a Jewish community,[31] providing him opportunities for ministry, both to Jews and God-fearers;

(v) Tarsus was located on a main road from Antioch and the east
      that passed through the Taurus Mountains leading to Cappa-
      docia in the north and Asia in the west.

There is compelling evidence from Galatians and Acts that Paul
preached to Gentiles in Tarsus and Cilicia.

Galatians

Following his visit to Jerusalem three years after the Damascus
event (Gal. 1:18) Paul states that he went into the regions of Syria
and Cilicia: 'Then I went into the regions of *Syria and Cilicia*.
And I was still unknown in person to the churches of Judea that
are in Christ. They only were hearing it said, "He who used to
persecute us is now preaching the faith he once attempted to
destroy." And they glorified God because of me' (Gal. 1:21–4, our
italics). He does not state whether his preaching in Syria–Cilicia
was directed to Jews or Gentiles. In the next passage, however,
Paul makes clear that his preaching audiences in that province
included Gentiles.

Paul's *own* words in Galatians about his visit to Jerusalem fourteen years after the Damascus 'call' are decisive.

> I . . . set before them [James, Peter and John] . . . the gospel I proclaim
> *among the Gentiles* in order to make sure I was not running or had not
> run in vain. (Gal. 2:2, our italics)

> On the contrary, when they saw that I had been entrusted with the
> gospel to the *uncircumcised,* just as Peter had been entrusted with the
> gospel to the circumcised (for he who worked through Peter for his
> apostolic ministry to the circumcised worked also through me for
> mine to the *Gentiles*). (Gal. 2:7–8, our italics)

Since the words immediately preceding Galatians 2:1,7–8 refer to
Paul's preaching in 'the regions of Syria and Cilicia' we conclude
that Gentiles were among those to whom Paul preached.

To clinch his point with James, Peter and John about his circumcision-free gospel Paul calculatedly brought along Titus, an uncircumcised Gentile (a 'Greek'), a beneficiary of Paul's apostolate to

the Gentiles. We assume Titus came from the 'regions of Syria and Cilicia'. As a consequence of meeting Titus the 'pillars' of the Jerusalem church 'saw that [Paul] had been entrusted [i.e. by God] with the gospel to the uncircumcised' and that '[God] had worked through [Paul's] apostolic ministry (*apostolē*) . . . to the Gentiles' (Gal. 2:7,8).

Acts

Events following the meeting of the Jerusalem Council (AD *c.*49) cast light upon Paul's activities in Syria and Cilicia during his decade-long ministry there.

> the apostles and the elders, with the whole church [in Jerusalem] . . . [sent] to Antioch . . . Paul and Barnabas . . . with the following letter:
> 'The brothers, both the apostles and the elders,
> to the brothers who are of the *Gentiles* in *Antioch* and *Syria* and *Cilicia*, greetings. (Acts 15:23, our italics)
>
> [Paul] went through *Syria* and *Cilicia*, strengthening the churches. (Acts 15:41, our italics)

References in Acts to Gentile churches in Syria and Cilicia are congruent with Paul's own words about 'preaching the faith' in 'the regions of Syria and Cilicia' (Gal. 1:21–3). These texts from Galatians (2:1,7–8) and Acts (15:23,41) overturn the assertion that Paul did not begin to preach to Gentiles *until* the first missionary journey. The letter from Jerusalem was addressed to 'brothers who are of the *Gentiles* in . . . *Antioch* and *Syria* and *Cilicia*'. Luke's narrative that Paul went from Antioch through Syria and Cilicia, strengthening the *churches*, demands that these (or some of them) were *Gentile* churches. In short, Luke indicates – contrary to alternative views – that Paul preached to *Gentiles* in Syria and Cilicia and that there were Gentile *churches* in these regions established by him during the decade he spent in this province.[32]

Conclusion

The view that Paul did not begin preaching to Gentiles until the first missionary journey is understandable. Were we to depend only on the book of Acts we would appear justified in taking this view. However, this would require us to pass over the information from Acts 15:23,41 as discussed above which, when considered alongside Galatians 1:21 – 2:8, provides pretty clear evidence that Paul's ministry during the fourteen 'unknown years' was directed to Gentiles as well as to Jews. While the basis for a Gentile engagement in Damascus and 'Arabia' is inferential the case for it in 'the regions of Syria and Cilicia' is strong. In particular, this would apply to Tarsus and the region of Cilicia where Paul spent the greater part of the decade between his first and second return visits to Jerusalem.

It is likely that the Gentiles Paul influenced throughout these years were mostly synagogue-connected God-fearers and not Gentile idolaters. We will argue in the next chapter that it was at Antioch in Syria that Paul came to understand that the Damascus 'call' meant a more intentional approach to Gentiles who were outside the orbit of the synagogues. This would mean that Paul's involvement with Gentiles in Tarsus and Cilicia was primarily with God-fearers in the synagogues and not rank idolaters.

While Paul's experience in Antioch was critical for the new direction Paul would take, he was there for a relatively brief period. By contrast, the years in Tarsus and greater Cilicia were also very significant. We will argue in Chapter 9 that it was in Tarsus (and wider Cilicia) and Antioch (and its hinterland) that Paul would have developed his apologetic exegesis justifying his circumcision-free inclusion of Gentiles.

One reason among others for the importance of Galatians is that we encounter these patterns of exegesis in this letter. This importance is strengthened if Paul wrote to the Galatians shortly after his return from his missions there (as recorded in Acts 13 – 14). If this chronology is correct it would mean that his Galatians letter was back-to-back with his decade-long ministry to Gentiles that would have involved him in vigorous exchanges with the rabbis in Syria and Cilicia. The fruit of those exchanges is found in the exegesis in Galatians 3 – 4 (see Chapter 9).

While the 'fourteen' years overall were important in forming and shaping Paul's theology in his earliest (extant) letter,[33] his engagement with Jews and Gentiles in 'the regions of Syria and Cilicia' in particular formed the immediate background to Galatians. This is the argument of this book.

3

Paul in Tarsus and Cilicia (*c.* AD 37–45)

Our calculations suggest that Paul spent about a decade in 'the regions of Syria and Cilicia' between his first and second return visits to Jerusalem (Gal. 1:18 and 2:1).

It further appears that Paul spent about eight of those years in the 'region' of Cilicia, Tarsus[1] in particular, before joining Barnabas in Antioch (Acts 11:25–6). Curiously scholars tend to pass over these Tarsus years and direct their attention to Paul's sojourn in Antioch in Syria.[2] This is understandable because Antioch was the biggest city in the region and the centre of what became the second most important centre of Christianity after Jerusalem, and a rival to that city's influence. Nonetheless, without minimizing the significance of Antioch it does appear that the years in Tarsus and Cilicia were significant in the formation of Paul's theology, in particular his identification of key Scriptures for apologetic purposes in his debates with the Jews.

Synagogue Beatings

Writing in AD 56 Paul informed the Corinthians of his missionary sufferings ('weaknesses') including repeated punishment within the synagogues: 'Five times I received at the hands of the Jews the forty lashes less one' (2 Cor. 11:24). Many authorities locate these synagogue beatings in Paul's early period following the Damascus event,[3] which the book of Acts narrates in sparse detail. Since Luke describes Paul's later westward missions in detail we would have expected him to mention these floggings had they occurred then.

According to Deuteronomy 25:1–3 this punishment was for the wrongdoer in a dispute, on the verdict of a judge. Writing during the New Testament era, Josephus observed that this public punishment, which was most disgraceful to the offender, was for someone who had acted 'contrary to the law'.[4]

The Mishnah tractate *Makkot* ('Stripes'), though compiled later, probably reflects rules and procedures that would have applied in the apostolic era. The forty lashes less one were for various breaches of the law, including the bearing of false witness (*Makk.* 1:1–10), sexual misdemeanours (*Makk.* 3:1), ritual impurity (*Makk.* 3:2,8), abuse of sacrificial offerings (*Makk.* 3:3) and misuse of a Nazarite vow (*Makk.* 3:7). It is unlikely, however, that Paul would have been guilty of these transgressions. He was a leading younger Pharisaic scholar (Gal. 1:13–14) who (later) when in the presence of fellow-Jews conducted himself as if 'under the law' (1 Cor. 9:20).

It is more likely that Paul was deemed to have committed one or more of the thirty-nine grievous transgressions done with a 'high hand' that warranted being 'cut off from among his people' (Lev. 18:29; Num. 15:30–31), as set out in the tractate *Kerithoth* ('Extirpation'). Among the sins that would have applied to Paul were *blasphemy* and transgression of the law of *circumcision* (*Ker.* 1.1). To anticipate our argument below, it seems:

(i)   Paul's *blasphemy* was to deny the saving power of the law, and that

(ii) his breach of the law of *circumcision* was to deny its necessity to Gentile proselytes.

Fundamental to Paul's post-Damascus understanding was his denial that law is the source of 'life' and his positive assertion that this salvation ('life') was only to be found in the crucified Messiah, Jesus (cf. Gal. 3:11,21). Such teaching was antithetical to Jewish theology. Mishnah *Aboth* 6:7 asserts that 'Great is the Law, for it gives *life* to them that practice it both in this world and in the world to come'. Within this same tractate R. Hananiah b. Akasya says, 'The Holy One, blessed is he, was minded to grant merit to Israel; therefore hath he multiplied for them the Law and commandments, as it is written, *It pleased the Lord for*

his righteousness' sake to magnify the Law and make it honourable'
(*Makk.* 3.16; cf. Isa. 42:21).[5]

Paul, however, was dismissive of law-keeping as a basis for
'life', commenting, 'Cursed be everyone who does not abide by
all things written in the Book of the Law, and do them' (Gal. 3:10
citing Deut. 27:26; cf. Lev. 18:5). It would not be a problem if Paul
wrote these words from Galatians later, during the westward
mission phase; his views on the law were most likely constant
throughout his ministry, from the time of the Damascus event. In
any case Paul's mission in Southern Galatia occurred immediately
after his ministry in Syria and Cilicia, and was in geographical
extension of that ministry.[6]

For Paul 'Christ crucified' was the *'soteriological* alternative' to
the Torah.[7] This message was a *skandalon* for Jews (1 Cor. 1:23), for
two related reasons. If

(i)   it was blasphemous to dismiss the law as the source of 'life', it
      was no less so to assert
(ii) that the messianic son of David, who was the crucified victim
      of the Gentiles he was expected to conquer, was the source of
      that 'life'.[8]

According to Paul salvation ('life') was not found 'under' or 'in'
the Torah but only 'in Christ crucified'. Again, it scarcely matters
if in fact these views were written some years later (see Gal. 6:2; 1
Cor. 9:21; 2 Cor. 3:3; Rom. 7:6; 8:2).

It appears then that Paul argued from the Scriptures in the synagogues of Syria and Cilicia that Christ crucified not the law was
the means to 'life'. For that he was accused and found guilty of
blasphemy, warranting his 'extirpation'. Nonetheless, remarkably
Mishnah *Makkot* provided relief from 'extirpation' if the accused
offender submitted to the scourging of the forty lashes less one.
The tractate decreed, 'when he is scourged then he is thy brother'
adding, 'and his soul shall be restored to him' (*Makk.* 3:15). In other
words, the Mishnah mandated this beating in order to enable
the violator of the law to be accepted back within Judaism.[9] The
beating effectively absolved the perpetrator from 'extirpation'.[10]

This prompts the question why Paul repeatedly submitted
himself to such violent treatment in the synagogues 'at the hands

of the Jews'. The short answer is that Paul was determined to remain a Jew. But why did he resolve to continue a Jew when many of his fellow-Jews would have preferred that he de-convert from the covenantal faith?

There is one main reason for Paul's determination. It was his sense that God had elected Israel as his people and had not rejected them notwithstanding the current (temporary) 'hardening' towards the Christ who had come (Rom. 10:14–21; 11:2a,25–32). Paul was passionately concerned for their eventual salvation, to the point of being prepared, as he said, to be 'accursed and *cut off* from Christ for the sake of my brothers, my kinsmen according to the flesh' (Rom. 9:3, our italics). His submission to the five beatings showed that Paul, on the one hand, was not willing to be cut off from Israel, such was his commitment to his people and their salvation, yet on the other he was even prepared for their sake to be cut off from the very Christ he was proclaiming. In short, as A.E. Harvey observed, Paul allowed the synagogue to administer this punishment, 'in order to maintain his Jewish connections'.[11]

Paul expressed his passion for Israel by a principled preaching to 'the Jew first' (Rom. 1:16; 2:9; cf. 1 Cor. 9:20). Luke's narrative confirms Paul's own stated policy in his account of Paul's travels where he chose cities that had a Jewish presence and where he routinely began his ministry in the synagogue (Acts 13:14 – Antioch in Pisidia; 14:1 – Iconium; 16:12 – Philippi; 17:1 – Thessalonica; 17:13 – Berea; 17:17 – Athens; 18:4 – Corinth; 19:8 – Ephesus). Paul's practical priority in ministry to Jews must be regarded as historically secure. Furthermore, this priority should not be regarded as merely pragmatically strategic, but based on deep theological reflection on the divine promises to Abraham (Rom. 15:8–9).

If, as seems likely, the five synagogue beatings were confined within the fourteen 'unknown' years they would indicate that Paul engaged in synagogue ministry throughout those years. Furthermore, since Paul also established Gentile churches throughout those years (Acts 15:23,41) it raises the question whether there was a connection between those beatings and the creation of these Gentile churches. Did the synagogues beat Paul because he preached a circumcision-free gospel to synagogue-based God-fearers? Were those beatings the painful evidence to Paul of the 'hardening' that, he said, had fallen upon Israel (Rom. 10:16,18–21; 11:7–10,25)?

Caught up to the Third Heaven[12] and Its Consequence, the Thorn

In AD 56 Paul wrote:

> I know a man in Christ who fourteen years ago was caught up to the third heaven – whether in the body or out of the body I do not know, God knows. And I know that this man was caught up into paradise – whether in the body or out of the body I do not know, God knows – and he heard things that cannot be told, which man may not utter. (2 Cor. 12:2–3)

It appears, then, that this revelation to Paul occurred in *c.*42, during his time spent in Cilicia.

An earlier passage in 2 Corinthians should be read alongside this one.

> Therefore, knowing the fear of the Lord, we persuade others. But what we are is known to God, and I hope it is known also to your conscience. We are not commending ourselves to you again but giving you cause to boast about us, so that you may be able to answer those who boast about outward appearance and not about what is in the heart. For if we are beside ourselves, it is for God; if we are in our right mind, it is for you. (2 Cor. 5:11–13)

The key to this passage is the word 'answer'. Paul is helping the Corinthians 'answer' those who boast in 'outward appearance', in this instance the new preachers ('peddlers'/'super-apostles'/'false apostles') in Corinth who boasted that they were often 'beside' themselves. This probably refers to the bizarre religious manifestations by which they presented themselves as 'superior' to Paul.[13] Paul matches their boast about 'visions and revelations' but debunks it by speaking of it in the remote past ('fourteen years ago'), vaguely ('I know a man'), and in uncertain terms ('whether in the body or out of the body, I do not know'). Moreover, this highest of experiences was succeeded by the lowest of experiences, the onset of a 'thorn' that was not removed, despite repeated prayer.

These men, like Paul, were Jews (probably Pharisees by background) who would not have been strangers to trances induced by extended fasting, after which they would speak in incoherent ways to demonstrate that they had been in the presence of the Almighty in paradise.

One such Jew from an earlier generation was the author of 2 Baruch who spoke of his fasting-induced experiences: 'I went . . . and sat in the valley of Kidron . . . I sanctified my soul there, and ate no bread . . . and I drank no water, and I was there till the seventh day . . . it came to pass that my soul took much thought, and I began to speak in the presence of the Mighty One' (2 Baruch 21:1–3).

Paul the ex-Pharisee wrote of a similar experience 'fourteen years ago', when he was transported to paradise where he heard 'things that cannot be told' (*arrēta rhēmata* – 2 Cor. 12:4). Unlike the 'super-apostles' who pointed to 'visions and revelations' as evidences of their superiority to Paul, Paul will not engage in this competition. He does not even want to talk about it and only does because the rivals have forced him to. In any case, it is old news, occurring *fourteen* years ago. Paul will make no claim for his ministry based on 'outward appearance', about being 'beside himself' in religious ecstasy or bizarre speech, as it seems his rival ministers are doing.

This rapture to paradise points to two realities. First, it identified him as a Jew by background and culture, more specifically as a Pharisee for whom such mystical experiences were not uncommon.[14] Second, however, it occurred to Paul as a 'man in Christ', a Christian (2 Cor. 12:2).[15] Paul's 'vision' and 'revelation' in 'paradise' was of 'the Lord', that is, the Lord Jesus Christ. This was not the same as the Damascus 'revelation', but it was consistent with and continuous with that revelation.

Speaking as a 'fool', even as a 'madman' (2 Cor. 11:23), Paul provided the Corinthians with an extended catalogue of his missionary sufferings, 'weaknesses' that ironically displayed his inferiority to the super-apostles. The climax of his sufferings was the 'thorn for the flesh' (*skolops tē sarki* – 2 Cor. 12:7) that was given to him as a direct consequence of his rapture to paradise.

Although he mentions the 'thorn' (or 'stake') last in his list, it probably occurred soon after the rapture to the third heaven, that is, in AD 42 or 43. It may have been one of the earliest of the sufferings Paul sustained. He does not identify it and there have been numerous guesses. It is tempting, however, to link it to the 'bodily ailment' (Gal. 4:13) that was the occasion for his initial preaching to the Galatians in AD 47 just a short time after the onset of the thorn. Although his condition was a 'trial' to the Galatians, they received him as 'an angel of God, as Jesus Christ' (Gal. 4:14). In other words, it seems that the effects of the 'thorn'[16] (as the sequel to the rapture that occurred in Cilicia) were soon noticed in nearby Pisidia and Lycaonia.

Preaching the Faith in Syria and Cilicia

Paul refers to vigorous preaching in Syria and Cilicia during the years 37–47: 'Then I went into the regions of *Syria and Cilicia*. And I was still unknown in person to the churches of Judea that are in Christ. They only were hearing it said, "He who used to persecute us is now preaching the faith he once attempted to destroy." And they glorified God because of me' (Gal. 1:21–4, our italics).

The effects of Paul's preaching in 'the regions of Syria and Cilicia'[17] came to the attention of 'the churches of Christ in Judea' (Gal. 1:21–3). By 'Judea' Paul meant the Roman *province* of Judea, that is, not merely the region of Judea but including also Galilee, Samaria, Perea and the coastal cities (also Acts 8:1; 9:31). Paul was 'unknown' to many members of those churches because they were created as a result of and in the years following his persecutions of the church in Jerusalem: 'So the church throughout all Judea and Galilee and Samaria had peace and was being built up. And walking in the fear of the Lord and in the comfort of the Holy Spirit, it *multiplied*' (Acts 9:31, our italics).

'The regions of Syria and Cilicia' refer to the Roman *province* of Syria–Cilicia, the province adjoining Galatia.[18] As well, however, Paul may have intended to convey that these 'regions'[19] represented their two major cities where Paul spent the greater part of his time during the decade between his first and second visits to Jerusalem. It was in *Tarsus* (and wider Cilicia) and *Antioch* (and its immediate surroundings in the region of Syria?) that Paul lived during these years.[20] When Paul visited the Galatians he would have told them his dramatic life story, including the events of the 'fourteen' years since Damascus. These present words merely serve as a brief reminder. That Paul proclaimed 'the faith' throughout 'the regions of Syria and Cilicia' is evidence that Paul did not merely *take refuge* in Tarsus.

The verb tenses in Gal. 1:22–3 point to the extensive period in which Paul was preaching in 'the regions of Syria and Cilicia'. Paul '*remained* unknown' to the churches of Judea but they '*kept* hearing' that the former persecutor was now proclaiming the faith he had been attempting to destroy.[21] Paul wanted the Galatians to know that he was proclaiming the Son of God (1:16) *throughout* the fourteen years, including for the duration of the decade in Syria and Cilicia.[22]

Speech Rhetoric and Paul's Letters

In recent decades some scholars have proposed that Graeco-Roman rhetorical traditions of that era had shaped the format of Paul's letters. Paul wrote his letters to be read aloud to congregations so – according to this viewpoint – they should be regarded as 'speeches'. In his influential commentary H.D. Betz proposed that Galatians was an 'apologetic' letter written as a speech for a courtroom situation with a jury (the addressees), an accuser (Paul's opponents) and a defendant (Paul). Thus understood the structure of the letter consists of an epistolary prescript (1:1–5), an *exordium* or *prooemium* (1:6–11), a *narratio* (1:12 – 2:14), a *propositio* (2:15–21), a *probatio* (3:1 – 4:31), an *exhortio* (5:1 – 6:10), and a *conclusio* (6:11–18).[23]

If, as I believe, Paul wrote Galatians in c.48[24] it would make this his earliest extant letter, written immediately after his years in 'the regions of Cilicia and Syria'. In turn, this could mean that Paul had become acquainted with and competent in the use of this kind of rhetorical tradition during that decade, in particular during his eight years in Cilicia (Tarsus).

It is difficult to think of another period in Paul's life that would have afforded him the opportunity to become accomplished in this form of letter-writing, as argued by Betz and others.[25] Paul's boyhood years (AD 5–16) were indeed spent in Tarsus, but in a strictly orthodox Jewish family who probably shielded him from exposure to Gentile thought by educating him at home with private tutors.[26] His years of youth and early adulthood were spent in Jerusalem (AD 17–34), where he was educated as a Pharisee and in the scholarship of the Greek Bible.[27] His decade of westward missions (AD 47–57) were so intense that it is difficult to see how there could have been time to devote to learning the rhetorical crafts in view of his constant travelling, tent-making and preaching.

So was Tarsus in Cilicia the 'school' in which Paul learned how to write letters as 'speeches' in the manner of the rhetorical speeches of those times? The Tarsus years represent the best possibility for this kind of education.

A considerable length of time in Cilicia, however, is not evidence in itself that Paul became skilled in such rhetorical techniques. First, his fame as preacher of 'the faith he had previously attempted to destroy' that reached Jerusalem over a sustained period (Gal. 1:21–4) implies that Paul was fully committed to this preaching while in Cilicia. Second, references to synagogue beatings (most of which occurred in Cilicia) on one hand, and to Gentile churches in Cilicia (Acts 15:23,41) on the other, imply that Paul both preached in synagogues (2 Cor. 11:24) and established Gentile congregations in Cilicia. In short, he was busy! Third, in consequence of his high profile as a Christian it is likely that many of his (Jewish) family in Cilicia disowned him (Phil. 3:8 – 'For his sake I have suffered the loss of all things'), making it necessary to labour as a tent-maker. Fourth, Galatians 3 – 4 reveals a writer skilled in polemical arguments from the Old Testament texts, in the manner of a rabbi, but also as a naturally gifted preacher. There are no clear echoes from Graeco-Roman literature in Paul's Letter to the Galatians.[28] Not least, fifth, the rhetorical structure for Galatians proposed by Betz finds no historical parallel. In his review article, W.A. Meeks comments that Betz is forced to refer 'almost exclusively to rhetorical and epistolary *theory* rather than to specific examples of real apologies and real letters from antiquity', and is unable to offer 'a single instance of the apologetic letter with which we can compare Galatians'.[29]

If brief, the Cilician years provided the theoretical opportunity for Paul to learn the techniques of rhetorical speech-writing, but there is no evidence that he did.

To the contrary, the *Letter* to the Galatians reflects homiletic techniques Paul would have developed in teaching in the synagogues and churches of Cilicia. These included:

(i)   Paul's own memoir (as in 1:11–17),
(ii) the apologetic use of Old Testament texts (as in 3:6 – 4:7; 4:21–31), and
(iii) the paraenesis related to the Spirit, church discipline and support of the teacher (as in 5:16 – 6:10).

The absence of parallels to the rhetorical structure that Paul is said to have employed by Betz and others tells against this hypothesis. On the other hand, Paul's employment of his personal story, his distinctive adaptation of Old Testament texts and the paraenetic elements in the epistle are readily imaginable as arising from his homiletic approach in synagogues and churches throughout the years of ministry in Cilicia.

Conclusion

Of Paul's fourteen 'unknown' years between the Damascus 'call' and the agreement to 'go' to the Gentiles, his time spent in Cilicia was the longest, about eight years. Nonetheless, we are dependent on tiny details in Luke's narrative in the book of Acts and Paul's in Galatians, along with snippets of information in 2 Corinthians and the Letter of James, to give us fleeting glimpses of Paul's years in the city where he was born and its wider region.

From Acts we learn of Gentile churches in Cilicia and conclude that Paul must have been their founder. The synagogue beatings imply that Paul taught in the synagogues and was punished for heretical teaching, most probably that Gentile God-fearers' baptism in the name of the crucified Christ, rather than adherence to the Torah, was their source of 'life' with God. It is reasonable to conclude that subsequent to his beatings Paul gathered these God-fearers into separated Gentile congregations.

James' letter to Jews of the Diaspora by its reference to 'justify', 'faith', 'saved' and 'works' (Jas 2:14–26) seems to be correcting (a version of) Paul's teaching that had come to the attention of the writer in Jerusalem.[30]

Paul's Second Letter to the Corinthians also records the highest of Paul's 'experiences', the rapture to paradise that was followed by the lowest of his experiences, the onset of the unremoved thorn (or stake).

Paul's years in Tarsus in Cilicia are significant since they are the almost immediate precursor of Paul's and Barnabas' mission to Cyprus, Pisidia and Lycaonia that was followed (we believe) soon afterwards by his Letter to the Galatians. Our argument is that such an understanding of Paul's Cilician years materially assists our understanding of that letter.

4

Paul in Antioch-on-the-Orontes and Syria (c. AD 45–7)

During the middle-to-late thirties a church was established in Antioch,[1] to which Paul was to attach himself as one of the leaders, and from which, with Barnabas, he would be sent forth westward towards the heart of the Roman world.

According to Luke, the message of the Christ of Israel came to Antioch in two waves. First, there were Hellenists displaced by Paul's assaults in Jerusalem who had migrated to Antioch (Acts 11:19). There is no reason to doubt that this occurred from AD 34 as an immediate consequence to Paul's persecutions in Jerusalem. Some Hellenists went inland to Damascus perhaps with the intention of returning later to Jerusalem. Others travelled north along the coast, some settling in Phoenicia, others going offshore to Cyprus, others again coming to rest in the northern metropolis of Antioch (Acts 11:19). These, however, directed their preaching of the Christ to the Jews in the synagogues, possibly with limited response.

A second wave also composed of unnamed men who came to Antioch is more closely identified as 'men of Cyprus and Cyrene' (Acts 11:20; cf. 6:4 – 'the synagogue of the Cyrenians'). The date of their arrival is not known, but it may have been as early as the late thirties. These took the bold step of preaching the Christ to 'Greeks', that is, to Gentiles, 'a great number of whom . . . turned to the Lord' (Acts 11:21). The question, however, is which 'Greeks' does Luke mean, the Gentile God-fearers in the synagogues or rank outsiders? On balance, it is more likely that Luke intends to mean the God-fearers in the synagogues rather than those idol-worshipping Gentiles who were outside the orbit of the synagogues.

Then, however, Luke makes an easily unnoticed but critical first reference to 'the church' in Antioch (Acts 11:26), provoking the question, *when* did these disciples, 'Jews' and 'Greeks from the synagogues also[2] form a distinctive 'church' assembly? Most likely it was this new and different congregation that attracted the attention of the people of Antioch – perhaps the officials – causing them to name these people *Christianoi* / 'Christians'[3] (Acts 11:26). This was 'the church of the *Christianoi*', historically the first 'church' defined as 'Christian'.

Did this dramatic development happen before or after Barnabas arrived from Jerusalem? Again on balance, it seems that the establishment of a discrete 'mixed' church in Antioch occurred as the result of the preaching of these Cypriots and Cyreneans, that is, in the late thirties and it was this new development that attracted the attention of the leaders in Jerusalem and their dispatch of Barnabas to Antioch.

Critical Questions about Paul's Years in Syria and Cilicia

The considerable length of Paul's years in the 'regions of Syria and Cilicia', which are recorded with sparse detail, prompts two important questions.

Was Paul's Christology pre-formed in Jerusalem or Antioch?

As noted, the sequence of Paul's movements between Damascus and Antioch (*c*.34–47) find agreement in our sources, Paul's own writings (chiefly Galatians) and the book of Acts. Furthermore, we are able to date Paul's location in the various places – Damascus, Arabia, Damascus, Jerusalem/Judea, Tarsus/Cilicia and Antioch – with reasonable confidence.

The question, then, arises about the origin of Paul's theological understanding as revealed in Galatians, his earliest surviving letter. Broadly speaking there are two viewpoints as to the time and place where Paul's Christology was 'formed', in Damascus and Jerusalem in the mid-thirties or in Antioch in the mid-forties.[4]

The latter view is associated with Bousset and Bultmann and the 'history-of religions school' who argued that Paul was influenced by the 'atmosphere' of Graeco-Oriental religious syncretism (mystery cults and gnostic beliefs) that were said to characterize Antioch in Syria. This would help explain Paul's preoccupation with Jesus in such terms as 'Lord'/*Kyrios* and 'Son'/*Huios* in 1 Thessalonians and 1 Corinthians (see e.g. 1 Thess. 1:10; 1 Cor. 1:9; 8:5).

So: do Paul's Christology and mission preaching originate from Damascus and Jerusalem in the mid-thirties or from Syria and Cilicia in the late thirties to mid-forties? The evidence for the origin of Paul's normative Christian thought points conclusively to 'the Damascus event', dated *c*.34.

This is not to demand that Paul's *expressions* of his Christology and mission preaching became fixed in all details at Damascus. His letters are at some points dialectical, even emotional, such was his personal and pastoral sensitivity to the circumstances of the people and the churches of his mission.[5] Nonetheless, his varying responses are anchored to critical core beliefs that he came to hold at the *beginning* of his years as apostle and minister.

A dominant reason for this conviction is the central place Damascus occupies in Paul's thinking, whether in regards 'direct references' or 'identifiable allusions' to the radical change that occurred in Damascus.[6] Damascus was the hinge around which Paul's life turned, separating his 'former life in Judaism' (as persecutor) from his new life 'in Christ' (as preacher) – see Galatians 1:13–14 and 1:21–4.

Damascus was the place – and his arrival there the time – when everything changed for Paul, whether in regards his relationship with God (as one now 'justified' in Christ crucified and risen – Gal. 2:16,21; 3:24–5) or his new vocation (as apostle to the Gentiles – Rom. 11:13; Gal. 1:15–16). It was from that time Paul became conscious of change *within* him. God revealed 'his Son' *in* Paul (Gal. 1:16; 2:20). Like those to whom he preached the Crucified One, Paul had become aware of the life-changing presence of the Spirit of God's Son within him (Gal. 3:1–5; 4:6; 5:16–24). Paul frequently employs contrastive verb tenses[7] to indicate the radical 'before and after' nature of the various changes of his beliefs and life-direction.

This fundamental Damascus 'conversion' appears consistently within Paul's writings. True, Paul had visions and revelations subsequent to Damascus[8] but none of these is ever cast in terms of the sharp 'before-and-after' life-changing contrasts that characterize the Damascus event.

Furthermore, critical to the question of Paul's Christological 'formation' is the central place Paul attributes to Jerusalem and the leaders of the Jerusalem church, especially in his letter to the Galatians. True, Paul insists that his Damascus 'call' to preach the Son came from God (Gal. 1:11,15–17) and not people. Yet it is equally true that Paul looked to the *endorsement* of the leading apostles in Jerusalem, at both his first and second return visits.[9]

Of special interest is Paul's meeting with the 'pillar' apostles James, Peter and John in Jerusalem that effectively concluded these fourteen years. Paul 'laid before (*anethemēn*) them . . . the gospel which I preach among the Gentiles' (Gal. 2:2, RSV) seeking the favourable verdict of these leaders. He asked rhetorically whether he had been 'running in vain' during the years since his Damascus 'call' when he abandoned his 'former life in Judaism' to 'preach [to the Gentiles] the faith he had [previously attempted] to destroy' (Gal 1:12–13,23). To the contrary, these leaders endorsed the message he had been preaching in Damascus, Arabia and Syria–Cilicia and agreed to a further 'going' with his circumcision-free message to the Gentiles (Gal. 2:8–9). The Jerusalem leaders would not have endorsed Paul had he been corrupted by religious syncretism.

Paul's vindication in Jerusalem, however, was reversed in Antioch. When James' delegates arrived there Peter, Barnabas and 'the rest of the Jews' took sides against Paul over the question of eating with Gentile believers (Gal. 2:11–13). Paul's insistence on the circumcision-free message to Gentiles was the underlying point of division. It appears that James, Peter and Barnabas were retreating from their more liberal attitudes expressed earlier in Jerusalem. The new preoccupation with circumcision of Gentiles and Jewish table-fellowship with them and other matters related to Jewish ritual demonstrates that the issue of syncretism in Antioch, as contended by the 'history-of-religions' proponents, was not their concern.

What part, then, in Galatians (and other writings) does Antioch play in Paul's 'formation' or possible new departures in his view of Christ or the direction of his ministry? The answer is: none at all. Antioch was merely the last phase of that fourteen-year span of his ministry begun in Damascus (Gal. 2:1), and a brief one at that (Acts 11:26). Paul's Christology and mission preaching were well formed, tried and tested by the time he arrived in Antioch.

Moreover, and in any case, the presuppositions about the syncretistic 'atmosphere' in Antioch, on which the 'history-of-religions' school based its reconstructions, is without foundation.[10] It is true that Antioch was a deeply pagan metropolis, and remained so for centuries into the Christian era. Yet little evidence of Antioch's religious life from the New Testament era survives, whether in literary, numismatic or archaeological sources.[11] This is not to suggest that first-century Antioch was not pagan or indeed syncretistic; it probably was.[12] But most of our evidence comes from later centuries.[13] This means that the 'history-of-religions' advocates must engage in conjecture, giving little basis for historical confidence.

In this regard, we remember that the first disciples (from the mid-thirties) in Antioch were Jews (Acts 11:21–2). They were fugitive Hellenist Jews from Jerusalem for whom pagan religious life in the Diaspora would have held few surprises. The elderly Paul writing to the Philippians from Rome many years after his childhood in Tarsus still remembers how conservatively Jewish his family life in the Diaspora had been (Phil. 3:4–5). There is no reason to doubt that the original Jewish Jerusalem disciples in Antioch were as resistant to syncretism as Paul's parents had been. In turn, these Jewish disciples would have held in check any gnostic or cultic tendencies in the Gentiles who began to belong to the emerging church. In any case, the majority of incoming Gentiles were probably God-fearers (Jewish 'sympathizers') who had already turned their backs on pagan ways to belong to Diaspora synagogues.

Finally, the centre-point of Paul's world-view was Jerusalem and not Antioch. It was in Jerusalem (for the twelve and 'all the apostles') and in Damascus (for Paul) that God initiated the worldwide preaching of Christ crucified and risen (1 Cor. 15:9–11). Whatever their differences of emphasis and emotion concerning circumcision of Gentiles, Paul and the Jerusalem leaders were in agreement about the scripturally based message of the vicarious death and resurrection of Christ (1 Cor. 15:11).

Jerusalem was the point of departure from which Paul's apostolate to the Gentiles 'encircled' the eastern Mediterranean (Rom. 15:19) and it was *to* Jerusalem as the point of return that Paul went back with the collection from the Gentile provinces (Rom. 15:25–31). In Paul's references Antioch is merely one dot among others in that 'circle'.

Why did Paul wait for so long before his westward missions?

While Paul and Luke agree about the sequence of Paul's movements during the years between his Damascus 'call' and the Jerusalem 'agreement' (*c.*34–47) their respective perspectives of Paul's activities throughout those years are different. Luke passes over this span so briefly that some refer to these as Paul's 'unknown' years. Luke may have unintentionally contributed to the impression that Paul was 'unknown' throughout this lengthy period.

It is not that Luke's perspective is inaccurate. Initially as Paul's travelling companion and later as his chronicler he enjoyed unparalleled access to the apostle's life story.[14] Rather, Luke wanted to acknowledge the prior contributions of Peter, Stephen and Philip bringing the gospel to the Samaritans and the Gentiles. Only then does the author of Acts resume his interest in Paul when he becomes the sole focus of the remainder of his narrative. Once Paul's precursors have run their respective courses the spotlight falls on Paul alone (Acts 13 – 28).

Furthermore, Luke does intend us to understand that Paul had been active during those years, as implied by the reference to Gentiles in churches in Antioch, Syria and Cilicia (Acts 15:23,41). The existence of those churches and their Gentile members must have been due to Paul's ministry in Tarsus and Cilicia and in Antioch and Syria during this sparsely documented period (*c.*37–47).

Paul's letters, however, provide a different perspective on his activities in 'the regions of Syria and Cilicia'. It is clear in Galatians that from Damascus and throughout the fourteen years he preached God's Son to the Gentiles that the 'pillars' of the Jerusalem church retrospectively recognized his God-given apostolate to the uncircumcised *throughout that period* (Gal. 1:15–16,21–3; 2:2,8–9).

How, then, can we explain the length of time Paul stayed in the region of the Syria and Cilicia before beginning his westward missions to the Gentiles? Was he disobedient to the heavenly 'call', or somehow undiscerning of its missionary intent? We have argued against the proposition that he preached only to Jews during this period.

One possible element limiting Paul's movements may have been the crisis in the cities of the eastern Mediterranean created during the principate of Gaius (AD 37–41). A near civil war erupted between Greeks and Jews in Alexandria and also in Antioch (though the sources are inferior[15]). Did the turbulent state of affairs in Antioch keep Paul in Syria and Cilicia for the moment?

Greater weight, however, should be given to the view that Paul interpreted the Damascus 'call' to preach 'among the Gentiles' as already being fulfilled in his ministry to *the God-fearers in the synagogues*. It seems unlikely initially that Paul thought he should seek Gentile converts outside the orbit of the synagogues. As Hengel and Schwemer have argued, there were significant numbers of the Gentile 'sympathizers of Judaism' in the synagogues of the cities Paul visited during these years.[16] As well, his five synagogue beatings (2 Cor. 11:24) seem to have occurred during these early years, suggesting a concentration on *synagogue-based* ministry to God-fearers.

Why, then, did Paul seek the agreement of the 'pillars' of Jerusalem to 'go' with a circumcision-free message to the Gentiles (Gal. 2:1–10)? What is the explanation of a dramatic change of modus operandi whereby Paul became the travelling missionary with a new focus on the Gentiles, including those who were outside the synagogues?

Why Paul Went to the Gentiles

Apocalyptic ferment

In this regard we note, first, the importance of Paul's ministry in Antioch, which he shared with Barnabas, as his junior associate. Upon arriving in Antioch in the early-to-mid forties Paul discovered that numerous 'Greeks' had already 'turned to the Lord' (Acts 11:21).

When Barnabas arrived from Jerusalem to Antioch and Paul from Tarsus they came upon a vibrant and entirely new phenomenon. Here for the first time was a mixed congregation of the circumcised and the uncircumcised acknowledging but also likely proclaiming Jesus as 'the Christ', attracting the name *Christianoi* attached to them by the people of Antioch (Acts 11:26). It is likely that Paul was influenced by what he saw in Antioch, a vision for mixed congregations of Jews and Gentiles worshipping the crucified and resurrected *Christos*.

A second factor that probably contributed to Paul's decision to seek the approval of the 'pillar' apostles in Jerusalem for a more intentional 'going' to the Gentiles was the stability of Claudius' era. The chaos and near civil war between Greeks and Jews in Alexandria and the cities of the eastern Mediterranean including Antioch during the Gaius' years (AD 37–41)[17] had been replaced by the greater stability of Claudius' rule. This may have encouraged Barnabas and Paul to travel to the west to bring the message of Christ to the Gentiles.

A third observation is that Judea at that time was in the grip of apocalyptic fervour. While Claudius brought greater political stability to the empire at large, the same cannot be said for Judea during the forties where his policies inspired a burst of apocalyptic preaching and activity.

In AD 44 the untimely death of King Herod Agrippa I brought his brief rule over a united Israel to an end to the disappointment of the Jews. Worse still, Claudius reannexed Judea, and Galilee for the first time, so that the borders of the land of Israel under Roman rule were considerably extended. Compounding this problem Claudius appointed as governors 'procurators',[18] administrators with a more explicitly tax-gathering function than their predecessors, the military 'prefects' appointed under Augustus and Tiberius.[19] It might have been expected that the first such procurator would have been both sensitive and judicious. Cuspius Fadus (AD 44–6), however, proved to be neither wise nor competent. He attempted to seize the vestments used by the high priest, unsuccessfully as it turned out,[20] and he put down a regional uprising with unnecessary force.[21]

During Fadus' tenure a significant apocalyptic event took place. Theudas, a self-styled prophet, marched from Jerusalem to the

Jordan accompanied by a multitude where he attempted to part the waters of the Jordan in the manner of Joshua (or Moses).[22] The governor's violent suppression of Theudas' 'enacted prophecy' is a measure of the seriousness with which he viewed it. Yet Theudas' attempted miracle-sign signalled the hope of a Joshua-like reconquest of the land and the expulsion of the Roman occupying forces.[23]

The sense of apocalyptic urgency was likely heightened by the severe famine (and the accompanying civil unrest) that gripped the eastern Mediterranean from the mid forties. This, too, might have been viewed as a supernatural portent, a signal to take the gospel message to the Gentiles.

Israel 'hardened'

The final and most important 'apocalyptic' element to have influenced Paul's explosion of missionary activity among the Gentiles was his conviction that Israel had entered a period of divine 'hardening'. It appears that Paul had come to understand that the people of Israel (both in Palestine and the Diaspora) had comprehensively rejected the claims of the Messiah, Jesus. The five synagogue beatings were tangible and painful evidence of this hardening.

Paul and others had been 'sent' to 'preach' to the people of Israel (Rom. 10:14–15). There was little positive response and considerable resistance.

> But they have not all obeyed the gospel. For Isaiah says, 'Lord, who has believed what he has heard from us?' . . . But I ask, have they not heard? Indeed they have; for 'Their voice has gone out to all the earth, and their words to the ends of the world.' But I ask, did Israel not understand? First Moses says, 'I will make you jealous of those who are not a nation; with a foolish nation I will make you angry.' Then Isaiah is so bold as to say, 'I have been found by those who did not seek me; I have shown myself to those who did not ask for me.' But of Israel he says, 'All day long I have held out my hands to a disobedient and contrary people.' (Rom. 10:16–21)

Paul refers to this rejection as the 'mystery' of the 'hardening [that] has come upon Israel, until the fullness of the Gentiles has come in' (Rom. 11:25; cf. 11:7 – 'the rest [of Israel, apart from the elect] were hardened'). This is no passing observation, however, but a direct appeal to scriptural fulfilment. God had sent Isaiah to 'make the heart of this people fat and their ears heavy and [to] shut their eyes' until they are reduced to a tiny 'stump' (Isa. 6:9–13). Paul cites that oracle (which he combines with LXX Deut. 29:4 – 'God gave them a spirit of stupor') to establish that God was now fulfilling that promise of his 'hardening' upon Israel.[24]

This in turn gave Paul the signal that the moment had arrived for the 'coming in' of the Gentiles (Rom. 11:25), an idea that picks up Jesus' own references to people 'coming into' the kingdom of God or 'coming into' life.[25] Paul probably also saw the fulfilment of many prophetic oracles promising the nations' 'coming' to Jerusalem, for example:

> For I know their works and their thoughts,
> and the time is coming to gather all nations and tongues.
> And they shall *come* and shall see my glory. (Isa. 66:18, our italics)[26]

> Many peoples and strong nations shall *come*
> to seek the LORD of hosts in Jerusalem,
> and to entreat the favour of the LORD. (Zech. 8:22, our italics)[27]

In short, it was against this political, apocalyptic and prophetic background and under the conviction that God had 'hardened' Israel that Paul decided to leave Syria–Cilicia and strike out Rome-wards,[28] bringing the message of Jesus the Messiah and his impending return in salvation and judgement.[29]

Summary

It seems that from the time of his ministry in Antioch Paul began to consider that God wanted him to seek out Gentiles who were *outside the synagogues*. On the one hand, the large intake of Gentiles in Antioch (including perhaps some idolaters) may have pointed towards a more purposeful mission towards Gentiles who were outside the synagogues. On the other hand, however, Paul may have realized that an eschatological 'hardening' of Israel had begun because the rejection of Christ by

Jews everywhere was now apparent. The time had now come to bring in the Gentiles.

As we will see, however, this radical new direction was to have serious consequences for Paul. It provoked a vigorous reaction in some quarters in Jerusalem that issued in Jerusalem-based counter-mission that would seek to overturn Paul's circumcision-free basis of divine righteousness and covenantal equality. Eventually it created tension between Paul and the Jerusalem leadership, the end of Paul's working relationship with Barnabas, and the end of his formerly close associations with the church in Antioch. From that time Paul must make new friends in new places, westward towards Rome.

Conclusion

Despite the relatively few references in Galatians and the Acts to Paul's decade-long ministry in 'the regions of Syria and Cilicia' our argument is that these years were deeply formative for Paul. No letter from Paul survives these years, if indeed there was one. Nonetheless, his Letter to the Galatians was written soon after this obscure period when at last we hear from Paul himself about what he believed. Elements in the letter probably reflected his apologetic teaching in the synagogues and his pastoral teaching in the newly formed Gentile churches. This view, of course, depends significantly on our argument that Galatians was written soon after his mission to the Galatians and the Incident in Antioch.[30] That being so, however, we find from this early letter that Paul's theology was fully formed and that, in particular, his exegesis of biblical texts was comprehensive and integrated to his conviction that 'life' and the power of the indwelling Spirit was to be found only in the crucified Messiah and not in the 'works of the law'.

5

Paul in Jerusalem, Antioch and Galatia (AD 47–8)

Paul spent the latter decade of the 'fourteen' years in the 'regions of Syria and Cilicia'.[1] These years are relatively poorly documented in contrast with the next three years. The sequence of events seems to have been:

Date		Galatians	Acts
47	Barnabas, Paul and Titus travel to Jerusalem	2:1	11:29–30
	The Jerusalem agreement	2:7–9	
47/48	The mission to Cyprus and Galatia		13:1 – 14:25
	Paul and Barnabas return to Antioch		14:26–8
48	The counter-mission in Galatia		
	Paul hears of the counter-mission in Galatia	1:7; 3:1; 5:10,12	
	Peter arrives in Antioch	2:11	
	The 'circumcision' party arrives in Antioch	2:11	15:1
	The incident in Antioch	2:13–14	15:2
	Paul writes Galatians		
49	The Jerusalem Conference		15:4–21
	The Jerusalem letter to Antioch, Syria and Cilicia		15:22–9

Triumph in Jerusalem

The view taken here is that Galatians 2:1–10 and Acts 11:29–30 describe the same visit to Jerusalem by delegates from Antioch. Each source directs our attention to separate objectives by the Antiochene leaders Barnabas and Paul in making this journey. According to Luke their mission was to deliver financial 'relief' (*diakonia*) to the 'brothers who lived in Judea' in view of the impending famine. Paul, however, indicates that their mission was to secure the 'fellowship' (*koinōnia*) of the 'pillar' apostles for him and Barnabas to 'go to the Gentiles'.

Paul's gospel and mission (Gal. 2:7–8)

Paul sought and received the affirmation from James, Peter and John that he had 'not run in vain (*eis kenon*)' in his preaching of the gospel among the Gentiles during the previous fourteen years (Gal. 2:3).[2] The Jerusalem apostles 'added nothing (*ouden prosanethento*)' to the circumcision-free message Paul had preached throughout that time (Gal. 2:6). On the contrary, they 'saw that [Paul] had been entrusted (*pepisteumai*) with the gospel to the uncircumcised' and that God had 'worked also through (*enērgēsen kai*)' Paul 'to the Gentiles' (2:7,8).

Paul's words in Galatians 2:7–8 provide an exceptional window into earliest Christian missions, following the resurrection of Jesus in AD 33, until the meeting in Jerusalem in AD 47.

Peter	Paul
Peter was entrusted (i.e. by God) with the gospel to the circumcised	Paul was entrusted (i.e. by God) with the gospel to the uncircumcised
(God) worked through Peter for his apostolic ministry to the circumcised	[God] worked also through [Paul for his apostolic ministry] to the Gentiles

Luke confirms Paul's reference to Peter's mission to the circumcised (= the Jews) in the land of Israel: 'So the church throughout all *Judea* and *Galilee* and *Samaria* had peace and was being built up. And walking in the fear of the Lord and in the comfort of the Holy

Spirit, it multiplied. Now as Peter went here and there among them all . . .' (Acts 9:31–2, our italics).

Due to Paul's persecution the disciples from the Jerusalem church were 'scattered' throughout the three regions of Israel 'preaching the word' (Acts 8:4). They 'took root' as congregations in Judea, Galilee and Samaria where Peter went among (*dierchomenon*) them as a travelling pastor and evangelist (Acts 9:32 – 10:48). Meanwhile throughout the fourteen years since God's Damascus revelation Paul was preaching his circumcision-free gospel 'among the Gentiles' in Damascus, Arabia and – in particular – in 'the regions of Syria and Cilicia' (Gal. 1:21; 2:2; cf. Acts 15:23,41).

Titus (Gal. 2:3)

It appears that Paul planned carefully this visit to Jerusalem 'after fourteen years'. He sought the 'fellowship' with the 'pillars' for a new initiative in 'going' to the Gentiles, but it must be on the basis of his long-standing practice of declaring a circumcision-free gospel for Gentiles.

That Paul was *with* Barnabas (Gal. 2:1) indicates that for the moment Barnabas and not Paul was the leader in the church in Antioch. All Paul's attention, however, is directed to the third member of the party, the uncircumcised Greek (= Gentile), Titus, whom he had *taken along with* him. Titus (Paul's 'true child in a common faith' – Titus 1:4) was the physical embodiment of the doctrine Paul was insisting on in Jerusalem. Taking Titus to Jerusalem was a test case that the gospel is based on the grace of God and is circumcision-free. Paul brought this Gentile believer to Jerusalem to force the issue.

Since Paul had been most recently in 'the regions of Syria and Cilicia' (Gal. 1:21) it is reasonable to suppose that Titus came from those 'regions', a prime example of a Gentile convert of Paul's who had been won by the apostle's Christ-centred preaching of 'the faith' (Gal. 1:23). The churches in Judea continually heard reports of Paul's preaching of 'the faith', but now they saw with their own eyes the tangible effects of that preaching.

Paul would not be content for this 'fellowship' in Jerusalem to be based on words alone. The ex-Pharisee probably anticipated the reaction of those he calls 'false brothers'. Although absent from

Jerusalem for many years he would have known how things were among the disciples in the Holy City, just as those in Jerusalem would have known about the believers in the church in Antioch.

The 'false brothers' (Gal. 2:4–5)

'False brothers' were 'secretly brought in' to this 'private' meeting between the leaders from Jerusalem and Antioch (or maybe at some other meeting in Jerusalem), though Paul does not say by whom. Paul accuses them of subterfuge because they were 'brought in secretly . . . to *spy out our freedom* [to] *bring us into slavery* [and] *submission*'. Evidently they were less than candid in gaining access to the meeting.

Their concern was directed at the uncircumcised Titus. The 'false brothers' apparently sought to have Titus circumcised as the basis for table-fellowship between him and everyone else present, who were all *Jews*. Paul successfully resisted their demands[3] – which were tantamount to 'slavery' – and the 'pillars' acquiesced in this, probably with some reluctance.

Who were these 'false brothers' in Jerusalem? Clearly they were in some sense fellow-disciples, yet whom Paul condemns as *pseudo*, 'false' or 'pretended' brothers.[4] In Galatians Paul refers to 'false brothers' in Jerusalem (2:4–5), as 'those of the circumcision' in Antioch (2:12), and as 'agitators' in Galatia (1:7; 5:10). Were these different people or the one group (or outlook) described in varying ways?

It seems they were the one group, or at least they were people united by a common objective, the circumcising of male Gentile believers. Most likely they were extremist members of the Jerusalem church who advocated a continuing expression of Jewish practices – notably circumcision – among the Gentile followers of the Messiah, Jesus. Are we able to be more precise? Luke tells us that they were 'believers who belonged to the party of the Pharisees' (Acts 15:1,5; cf. 21:20 – 'Jews . . . who have believed . . . zealous for the law').[5]

The truth of the gospel (Gal. 2:5)

Yet Paul was equally determined to preserve *our freedom*, by which he meant the freedom of Gentiles like Titus not to have to submit to the *slavery* of the *necessity* of circumcision. The *truth of the gospel* (v. 5) must not be compromised which it would be once the note of *necessity* is sounded.[6] The only *necessity* is to commit by faith to Jesus Christ crucified and risen. To add any necessity to that is to corrupt the 'truth of the gospel', and to invite spiritual servitude. '*Truth* of the gospel' stands in stark contrast with '*false* brothers'.

The presence of the Gentile Titus 'flushed out' the 'false brothers' who attempted to 'force' circumcision on Titus.[7] In this they were unsuccessful. The verbal agreement by the 'pillar' apostles about the circumcision-free nature of Paul's gospel found physical proof in their fellowship with the uncircumcised man. Paul had deliberately forced the issue and had come away from Jerusalem having achieved 'fellowship' with the 'pillars' for an onwards 'going' to the Gentiles with a circumcision-free message.

So ended the critical journey to Jerusalem. Soon enough Paul and Barnabas would set out from Antioch for Cyprus, accompanied by John Mark. Is it possible that Paul had intended to take Titus on this journey? Was that part of Paul's original plan in bringing Titus to Jerusalem? Had Paul calculated the advantages of having an uncircumcised Gentile with them on their projected mission, a man whose *uncircumcision* proved to be no barrier to table-fellowship with the highest authorities in the Jerusalem church? Did the Jerusalem 'pillars' suggest that John Mark should go instead? Peter's faction in Jerusalem met in the home of Mary, the mother of John Mark (Acts 12:12), so that Peter could rely on John Mark's report about the proposed mission of Barnabas and Paul to Cyprus, Pisidia and Lycaonia. Moreover, John Mark was the cousin of Barnabas (Col. 4:10), whose allegiance to Jerusalem was more secure than Paul's.

After Jerusalem

Paul's visit to Jerusalem with Barnabas 'fourteen years' after the Damascus event was encouraging (Gal. 2:1–9). The 'false brothers' did not succeed in *compelling* the circumcision of Titus the 'Greek' (presumably) as the basis for table-fellowship in Jerusalem. The three 'pillar' apostles acknowledged that in his circumcision-free approach to Gentiles throughout the fourteen years that Paul had not 'run in vain'; they 'added nothing' further to Paul's Christ-based message.

Rather, they recognized that, indeed, Paul had been 'entrusted (i.e. by God)' with the 'mission' (*apostolē*) of 'the gospel to the uncircumcised', just as Peter had been for the mission to the circumcised. Accordingly, the three leaders gave Paul the 'right hand of fellowship' in his plan to 'go' to the Gentiles.

This agreement was the catalyst for Paul's new thrust into the Gentile world that in turn provoked passionate reaction in the form of a counter-mission to 'the churches of Galatia' and in Antioch and beyond Antioch into the province of Syria and Cilicia.

Mission in Galatia

Fortified by the agreement of James, Peter and John, Paul and Barnabas, with John Mark, set out for their mission to Cyprus and the colony-cities on the Roman road network in Pisidia and Lycaonia – Antioch, Iconium and Lystra.[8] It is clear from Paul's Letter to the Galatians that significant numbers of his readers were Gentiles. He reminds them, 'Formerly, when you did not know God you were enslaved to those that by nature are not gods' (Gal. 4:8; cf. 'idolatry' – 5:20). These Gentiles were 'baptized into Christ' without the necessity of circumcision (Gal. 3:27).

A changeover in leadership appears to have happened during this journey. Paul went '*with* Barnabas' to Jerusalem (Gal. 2:1), which was appropriate since Barnabas was the first named of the five leaders of the church in Antioch (Acts 13:1). Yet, from Paul's account it seems he took centre stage in the discussions with the 'pillars' (Gal. 2:2,7,10). In Luke's account of the journey Paul is the 'chief speaker' (14:12); Barnabas is Paul's 'companion' (Acts 13:13) whose voice is only heard along with Paul's (13:46).

Did John Mark withdraw from the mission because, as Barnabas' cousin, he objected to Paul's assumption of leadership? Or did the conversion of the Gentile proconsul of Cyprus (Acts 13:12) give John Mark the unwelcome signal that Paul's mission would be so clearly directed at the uncircumcised?

Counter-mission in Galatia

Who were the 'agitators' and where did they come from? Paul does not identify those he calls the 'agitators' in Galatia or indicate

where they had come from. Clearly they were *Jews*. Their mission
for the circumcising of Gentiles says as much (Gal. 5:2–12; 6:12–13)
as does Paul's response to their appeal to the primacy of law and
their biological descent from Abraham (Gal. 3:7–18; 4:21–31).

At the same time we conclude that they were *Christian*, at least
in their own eyes. This is evident from their 'preaching of the
gospel' which, however, Paul said was a 'distortion' of the true
gospel, in fact, a 'contrary' gospel (1:6–9). That distortion lay in
its demands that to faith in Christ must be added 'works of the
law', ritual acts like circumcision, the observance of the calendar
(4:8–11), and the food laws. 'Faith operating through love' (5:2–6)
was not sufficient.

Dunn is correct in saying, 'the letter makes clearest and fullest
sense if we see it as a response to a challenge from *Christian-Jewish*
missionaries who had come to Galatia to correct or improve Paul's
gospel.'[9]

But where had they come *from*? The answer, almost certainly,
is from Jerusalem. Otherwise, how else can we explain the prominence Paul gives to Jerusalem throughout the letter (1:17,18; 2:1;
4:25,26)? Paul's non-dependence on the authority of Jerusalem
and its leaders James and Peter dominates his personal memoir
(1:11 – 2:14). Furthermore, the 'false brothers' were in Jerusalem;
the 'agitators' who were imposing circumcision on Gentiles in
Galatia almost certainly came from Jerusalem; and 'those of the
circumcision' who came from James to Antioch were from Jerusalem (2:11–12). This is precisely because of the appeal the counter-mission in Galatia made to the authority of Jerusalem. Paul's
apologetic whereby he points to the authority of Christ and not
Jerusalem is in direct answer to those whose appeal was to the
primacy of Jerusalem and her leaders.

Likewise, Paul's allegory of Abraham's two wives, Hagar and
Sarah, is his thinly veiled repudiation of 'the present Jerusalem'
who is a source of slavery but also of persecution in Galatia (4:21–
31). Paul writes so negatively of Jerusalem because his circumcising opponents appeal so strongly to Jerusalem. In itself the
allegory does not identify Jerusalem as the place of origin of the
counter-mission, but it does when read alongside Paul's relega-
tion of the authority of Jerusalem in his memoir.

When did they travel to Galatia?

The mission of the 'agitators' from Jerusalem was to overturn or correct Paul's teachings in Galatia. Their goal, apparently, was to make Paul's Gentile converts acceptable in table-fellowship with Jews (both believing and unbelieving Jews) and to achieve this fellowship by the Gentiles fulfilling the 'works of the law', circumcision in particular. In short, their aim was to make Jewish proselytes of Gentile Christians.

When and how did they know of Paul's mission in Galatia? Here we must speculate since neither Galatians nor the book of Acts tells us directly. Had Paul signalled his proposed journey to Galatia while in Jerusalem? Did John Mark report back from Pamphylia to Jerusalem in negative terms about Paul's non-requirement for the circumcision of Sergius Paulus? Had Galatian Jews sent messages to Jerusalem following Paul's mission there?

Whatever, their source of information a counter-mission went out from Jerusalem to the Galatian churches. We do not know the route they followed. But the most likely option is that they travelled by ship to Tarsus and then overland up through the Cilician Gates to the network of Roman roads that would take them from Lystra through Iconium to Antioch in Pisidia, and then by a reverse route back to Tarsus. Presumably the Galatian synagogues were their first port of call where they would have found the whereabouts of the church meetings established by Paul.

They came to these small communities as 'Christian' missionaries claiming the authority of Jerusalem with a 'gospel' message that complemented (added to) the message of Paul. It would not have been difficult to portray Paul as idiosyncratic, a maverick self-authenticating figure who had come to them independently of the authority of the Jerusalem church, and whose doctrines were significantly deficient.

Their mission and their message in turn came in some detail to the attention of Paul (by whom we do not know) sometime after his return to Antioch prompting him to write his explosive letter to the Galatians.[10]

Defeat in Antioch (Gal. 2:11–14; Acts 15:1–2[11])

We will discuss this situation in greater detail later (see p. 79–83) but we need to mention it briefly since it forms the immediate background to the Letter to the Galatians.

Some time after Paul and Barnabas had returned to Antioch from their Galatian mission Peter also arrived in the Syrian capital. At first Peter shared table-fellowship at the common meal with Gentile believers in the church in Antioch, including (presumably) the Lord's Supper (Gal. 2:11–12).

Then, however, 'certain men came from James' who appear to have attacked Peter about this practice. This was ultimately to force the Gentiles to embrace circumcision as a condition of that table-fellowship. If Peter withdrew from Gentile believers in the common meal it would send the clear message to male Gentile believers that they *must* be circumcised to qualify as covenant brothers with whom Jewish believers could eat.[12]

Peter's behaviour is difficult to understand. Paul had stayed with him for fifteen days a dozen years earlier (1:18) and doubtless explained the gospel he had received from Christ and which he had preached to Gentiles, without objection. Two years ago Peter with James and John did not insist on Titus' circumcision, saw no need to 'add' anything to Paul's gospel and gave his 'right hand of fellowship' to Paul.

Most disturbing of all Paul tells the Galatians *even Barnabas was led astray by their hypocrisy.* The Galatian Gentiles owed their spiritual freedom to Barnabas as much as to Paul. But now first Peter, then the Jewish believers and finally *even* Barnabas have fallen like a row of dominoes under the impact of the 'men who came from James' to Antioch.

In the final analysis it appears that the authority of James and the mother church, Jerusalem, prevailed and that Paul was defeated by the weight of these Jerusalem envoys and their influence over Peter, Barnabas and the Jewish members. In the first missionary journey Paul had been a missionary sent from Antioch, but that relationship was coming to an end.

The schism in Antioch and Paul's defeat was to have far-reaching consequences.

Paul's Letter to 'the Churches of Galatia'

It is reasonable to assume that the key events – Paul's and Barnabas' return from Galatia, the arrival of Peter in Antioch, the arrival of 'certain men from James', Paul's dispute with Peter and the abandonment of Paul, and the news of the counter-mission in Galatia – occurred in quick succession. These events came as an unwelcome sequence of hammer blows that would have shattered Paul's confidence following his triumph over the 'false brothers' in Jerusalem and the encouraging responses of Gentiles in Cyprus, Galatia and Pamphylia.

These exceedingly negative circumstances help us comprehend the sometimes bitter tones we encounter as we read his letter to the churches in Galatia. Nonetheless, as we will argue, despite its volatility that letter is carefully structured and coherently argued. In broad terms it consists of:

(i)   Paul's invective against the 'agitators'' 'other' gospel (1:6–10);
(ii) Paul's memoir explaining his independence from Jerusalem (1:11 – 2:14);
(iii) his text-based theological arguments rebutting the agitators (2:15 – 5:15; 6:11–16);
(iv) his appeal to the Galatians' experience of the Spirit (3:1–5; 5:16–25); and
(v)   his pastoral exhortations to the Galatians (6:1–10).

The Jerusalem Church's Letter to Churches in Syria and Cilicia (Acts 15:23–9)

After the Incident in Antioch (Gal. 2:11–14; Acts 15:1–2) the Antioch delegates travelled to Jerusalem where they met with 'the apostles and elders' in a meeting at which James presided. At the conclusion of the meeting 'the brothers, both the apostles and elders' in Jerusalem wrote to 'the brothers who are of the Gentiles in Antioch and Syria and Cilicia' (Acts 15:23):

> Since we have heard that some persons have gone out from us and troubled you with words, unsettling your minds, although we gave

them no instructions . . . it has seemed good to the Holy Spirit and to us to lay on you no greater burden than these requirements: that you abstain from what has been sacrificed to idols, and from blood, and from what has been strangled, and from sexual immorality. If you keep yourselves from these, you will do well. Farewell. (Acts 15:24–9)

This letter tells us, first, that 'certain men' who 'came from James' to Antioch, whom Paul also calls 'those of the circumcision' (Gal. 2:12), must also have disseminated their message further afield beyond the Syrian capital. A later reference to 'Gentiles' in the 'churches' in 'Syria and Cilicia' (Acts 15:41) confirms the existence of such churches. In short, the visit by these emissaries from Jerusalem was more territorially ambitious than their journey to Antioch as implied by Galatians 2:12 / Acts 15:1.

In fact, when all the pieces of evidence are considered we begin to see a comprehensive counter-mission against Paul that reached into Galatia, Antioch the capital of Syria, and beyond Antioch into the wider province of Syria and Cilicia.

- From Jerusalem a circumcision mission in Galatia
  Gal. 5:2; 4:25
- From Jerusalem a circumcision mission in Antioch
  Acts 15:1; Gal. 2:12
- From Jerusalem a circumcision mission in Syria–Cilicia
  Acts 15:23–24,41

Because these anti-Paul activities occurred at more or less the same time and in adjoining provinces (Galatia and Syria and Cilicia) it is difficult to escape the conclusion that they were more or less coordinated. As noted, Paul uses differing terms like 'false brothers', the 'agitators', and 'the circumcision party' but he is referring to those who held similar, conservatively Jewish views and who sought to impose their practices on Gentiles who had been influenced by Paul's circumcision-free message.

Second, the encyclical from Jerusalem was in response to reports that 'some persons have gone out from us and *troubled* (*etaraxen*) you with words, unsettling your minds' (Acts 15:24). The striking thing here is that Paul also uses the verb 'to trouble' or to '*agitate*' (*tarassō*) in Galatians to describe the counter missionaries in

Galatia (1:7 – *hoi tarassontes*; 5:10 – *ho . . . tarassōn*). It is difficult to think this common usage is coincidental. The Jerusalem-based counter-mission 'troubled' the Gentiles in Galatia and the emissaries from Jerusalem 'troubled' the Gentiles in Antioch, Syria and Cilicia. And the source of the 'trouble' was their demand that Gentiles submit to 'works of the law' as the basis for fellowship with Jews (believing as well as unbelieving Jews).

Why did the Jerusalem leaders decide to use the word 'to trouble'? It is likely that Paul suggested the word. It was his way of describing the 'troubling' of Gentiles in his churches in Galatia and it was equally appropriate to describe the 'troubling' of Gentiles in his churches in Syria and Cilicia.

Third, however, we note the different reactions of Paul (in Galatians) and the Jerusalem leaders (in Acts 15:19–21,23–9) to those who sought to impose circumcision on Gentiles. In Galatians Paul rejects absolutely circumcision (5:1–10; 6:11–16), the observance of the Jewish calendar (4:8–11), in fact, all and any 'works of the law' (2:16; 3:2,5,10). So far as Paul is concerned Gentiles who commit to Christ crucified are free to remain Gentiles. 'Faith working through love' is a sufficient response to the gospel (5:6).

By contrast the Jerusalem encyclical, while not mentioning circumcision, implies that circumcision is a not a 'burden' to be expected of Gentiles. On the other hand, however, that meeting expected Gentiles to observe various dietary strictures, specifically the eating of food sacrificed to idols (*eidōlothutōn* – Acts 15:20,29) and animals that had been strangled (*pniktōn* – Acts 15:20,29). James imposed these restrictions for the sake of Jews, whether believing or unbelieving Jews (Acts 15:21).

It is not altogether clear if these restrictions applied absolutely or only to occasions when Gentiles and Jews shared table-fellowship. Either way it is doubtful that this request would have healed the rift in Antioch. So far as we can tell the church remained divided along Jew and Gentile lines.

What is clear, however, is that Paul did not apply these provisions to Gentiles in his continuing mission, in Corinth (see e.g. 1 Cor. 10:23 – 11:1). What is also surprising is that the Jerusalem meeting and its encyclical did not address the situation in Galatia, but only in Antioch and Syria–Cilicia. Did the Jerusalem church regard Antioch and Syria and Cilicia as an extension of Jerusalem, her 'daughter', as it were? The church in Antioch was founded by former members of the Jerusalem church and then led by Barnabas who was sent from Jerusalem. Did they think Galatia belonged in a different category, being founded by a mission from Antioch and led by the independently minded Paul?

Conclusion

The 'fourteen years' that separate the Damascus event and the Jerusalem agreement are not well documented (Gal. 1:15–21; 2:1–2,7–8). That is not to say that these years were uneventful. To the contrary we have argued that Paul had been very active wherever he had been during those years, whether in Damascus, Arabia, Judea or in 'the regions of Syria and Cilicia'. The reasons for sparse documentation are, first, that no letter by Paul survives from this period and, second, that Luke chooses not to expand on Paul's travels until the beginning of Paul's westward missions.

By contrast the next three years are well documented. Luke extensively narrates the missions in Cyprus, Pisidia and Lycaonia. In Galatians Paul provided considerable detail about the agreement in Jerusalem, the impact of the agitators in Galatia, and the schism in Antioch.

Those were years of fierce disputes. Paul provocatively brought the uncircumcised Titus with him to Jerusalem to put pressure on the 'pillar' apostles to agree for Paul to 'go' to the Gentiles with a circumcision-free gospel. Despite the strong opposition of the 'false brothers' in Jerusalem Paul prevailed, at least for the moment. But no sooner had Paul and Barnabas returned from their travels in Galatia than two groups set out from Jerusalem to overturn Paul's teachings among Gentile Christians.

One group, whom Paul calls 'the agitators', reached the Galatian churches and sought to complement Paul's grace-based gospel by calling on Gentiles to fulfil 'the works of the law', including circumcision and the Jewish calendar. Another group, 'the circumcision party', came to Antioch and coerced Peter, Barnabas and the Jewish believers to separate from table-fellowship with Gentile Christians. By this they attempted indirectly to force Gentiles to become Jewish proselytes. This group did not confine their activities to Antioch but sought to impose circumcision on Gentiles in the churches in Syria and Cilicia. It is difficult to escape the conclusion that these counter-missions from Jerusalem to adjacent provinces (Galatia and Syria and Cilicia) were in some way coordinated. Paul observed that the counter-mission in Galatia 'troubled' (or 'agitated') the Gentile believers (Gal. 1:7; 5:10) and the 'official' letter from the Jerusalem meeting said that those who travelled to Antioch and Syria and Cilicia 'troubled' the Gentiles (Acts 15:24).

Since, as we argue, Paul wrote Galatians soon after news reached him about the agitators in Galatia, it means this letter is very significant. It indicates Paul's immediate reaction to these attempts to overturn the gospel he preached to Gentiles.

Beyond that, however, as his earliest extant letter, Galatians reveals Paul's 'mind' at the end of his initial fourteen years as a Christian. Galatians is our earliest window into his thinking about 'the faith' he began to hold as from the Damascus event. Those fourteen years had been years of conflict, in particular with fellow-Jews (both non-Christian and Christian). Paul's grace-based theology and his understanding of scriptural texts had been hammered out during those years. His letter to the Galatians allows us to see into the thinking of this passionate man, whose life had been so deeply affected by the Christ who died for him and who lived within him (Gal. 2:20).

6

James and Paul (AD 34–49)

We are fortunate to have access to information about three leaders who were present from the beginning of Christian history, Peter, James[1] and Paul. In this chapter we direct our attention to James, brother of the Lord, and Paul. Significantly, James like Paul was not a follower of the historical Jesus.

James and Paul: Christian Contemporaries

James in Jerusalem

James had been a member of the church in Jerusalem from the time his resurrected brother appeared to him in 33. By 37 he was known as 'an apostle' and with Peter one of the key people Paul must meet on his first visit to Jerusalem as a now baptized Christian (Gal. 1:18–19). Following the flight of Peter from Jerusalem to 'another place' in c.42 James became de facto the leader of the church in the Holy City (Acts 12:17). After Peter's return in c.44 (following Agrippa's death) James was the first[2] named of the three 'pillars' of the Jerusalem church, with Peter as the second 'pillar' (Gal. 2:9). In c.48, however, Peter went to Antioch leaving James as the sole leader in Jerusalem as evident

(i)   in his dispatch in c.48 of his envoys to Antioch to direct Peter and the Jewish believers to separate from Gentile believers (Gal. 2:12; cf. Acts 15:1); and
(ii) in his undisputed leadership in c.49 at the Jerusalem Council (Acts 15:13–21).

James, Peter and Paul (AD 33–49)

It is noteworthy that James and Paul were contemporaries as disciples of Christ, James from 33 and Paul from 34, about a year later.

It is clear from Table 6.1 that from AD 33 James remained in Jerusalem where he became progressively more influential whereas Peter became correspondingly less influential and Paul was mostly absent.

Table 6.1 The Rise and Rise of James in Jerusalem

Date	James	Peter	Paul
29–33	Not a disciple of Jesus	The leading disciple of Jesus	Not a disciple of Jesus
33	Witness of resurrection	Leader in Jerusalem	
34		Mission in land of Israel	'Called' at Damascus
35		Mission in land of Israel	Arabia
36		Mission in land of Israel	Arabia
37	Called an 'apostle'	Mission in land of Israel	Damascus/ Jerusalem/Syria and Cilicia
38		Mission in land of Israel	Syria and Cilicia
39		Mission in land of Israel	Syria and Cilicia
40		Mission in land of Israel	Syria and Cilicia
41		Mission in land of Israel	Syria and Cilicia
42	Sole leader	To 'another place'	Syria and Cilicia
43		To 'another place'	Syria and Cilicia
44		To 'another place'	Syria and Cilicia
45		Return to Jerusalem	Syria and Cilicia
46			Syria and Cilicia

47	1st named 'pillar'	2nd 'pillar' in Jerusalem	Jerusalem->Antioch -> Galatia
48	Sole leader – sent envoys to Antioch	To Antioch	Antioch
49	Sole leader; presided at Jerusalem Council	Jerusalem	Jerusalem

From at least 37 James was called an 'apostle' and probably from the early forties possessed such prominence as head of the Jerusalem church that he had the authority to direct the affairs of churches that extended beyond the borders of the land of Israel, including Antioch in Syria.[3]

James and Paul (AD 36/7–48)

Paul only refers to James in two letters.

First Corinthians

In *c*.55, in his citation of the gospel he had 'received', Paul writes that the resurrected Christ 'appeared to James' (1 Cor. 15:7). Paul includes James with other resurrection 'witnesses' and himself as declaring the common apostolic message: 'Whether then it was I or they, so we preach and so you believed' (1 Cor. 15:11). In short, Paul here writes approvingly of James.

Earlier within the letter he mentions 'the brothers of Lord and Cephas' (1 Cor. 9:5) implying that they had visited the Achaian capital. We infer that these men represented the interests of the Jewish mission, as agreed in *c*.47 in Jerusalem. Most likely 'the brothers of the Lord and Cephas' concentrated on winning *Jews* for the faith of the Messiah Jesus. There is no reason, however, to believe that James was among these 'brothers of the Lord'; he seems to have remained in Jerusalem.

Paul's reference to these men is not negative – at least not at this stage in Paul's dealings with the Corinthians. The Jewish 'super-apostles' who arrived in Corinth later in 55 probably validated their mission there on account of the earlier visit from leaders of the Jewish mission, 'the brothers of the Lord and Cephas'.[4] Had

Paul written 1 Corinthians a year later he might not have thought so positively about them.

Galatians

Paul wrote to the Galatians – his earliest extant letter – in c.48, from Syrian Antioch.[5] He refers to James three times.

(i) Paul 'saw' James in Jerusalem in 36/37 (1:19)

Three years after the Damascus christophany, Paul returned to Jerusalem to 'visit' Peter and to 'see' James. Pointedly, following that Damascus 'revelation', Paul did not 'consult' with 'flesh and blood', that is, these Jerusalem leaders, but 'went away into Arabia' (Gal. 1:17).

In this memoir Paul is reinforcing with the Galatians the fact that he was dependent on God for his 'call' to him and for the authority to preach the Son of God to the Gentiles. Paul pointed to God and not the 'flesh and blood' leaders in Jerusalem.

At the same time, however, Paul indirectly makes it clear that Peter and James were the two prominent leaders in the community of faith in the Holy City. This is quite remarkable in so short a time between the resurrected Christ's appearance to James (in 33) and Paul's return to Jerusalem (in 36/37). James had risen to significance above the original disciples of Jesus, except Peter.

(ii) Paul's private meeting with James, Peter and John in c.47[6] (2:1–10)

It is obvious that Paul came to Jerusalem seeking the endorsement of the 'pillars', James, Peter and John, for a more intentional mission to the uncircumcised.

First, Paul presented the gospel he had been preaching to the Gentiles during the past fourteen years. James, Peter and John 'added nothing' to Paul, confirming that he 'was not running in vain and had not run in vain' in respect of this gospel message (vv. 6,2).

Second, James, Peter and John supported Paul against the 'false brothers' who attempted to 'force' the circumcision of the 'Greek' Titus as the basis for covenant fellowship in Jerusalem (v. 3). The

uncircumcised Titus was a concrete example of Paul's circumcision-free preaching to Gentiles during the previous fourteen
years. By the presence of Titus, Paul effectively forced the 'pillar'
apostles to make up their minds, one way or another.

Third, James and the other 'pillars', having recognized that
God had already 'worked through' Paul's mission to the Gentiles
throughout those years, just as he had 'worked through' Peter in
the mission to the circumcised throughout a parallel period, gave
to Barnabas and Paul 'the right hand of fellowship' for them to
'go' to the Gentiles with a message that did not require circumcision of Gentile males (Gal. 2:8–9).

(iii) James' envoys to Antioch c.48: the Incident in Antioch (2:11–14)

The events following the Jerusalem meeting proved to be epochal
in the history of early Christianity and in the life of Paul.[7]

The sequence that makes best sense of the data in Galatians and
the book of Acts is:[8]

47	Jerusalem: Titus not 'forced'; gospel recognised; mission agreed (Gal. 2:10)
47/8	Mission to Galatia (Acts 13 – 14). News reaches Paul of the counter-mission to Galatia. James' envoys arrive in Antioch (Gal. 2:11; Acts 15:1).
48	Paul writes to the Galatians.

The striking thing here is James' volte-face in sending 'certain
men' to Antioch who applied pressure on Peter the Jew to stop
eating with Gentile believers in the church in Antioch. Various
suggestions have been offered to account for James' behaviour:

- This action in Antioch reveals James' true intention. He was
  insincere at the meeting in Jerusalem.[9] It is unlikely, however,
  that Paul would have lied about the meeting in Jerusalem since
  he knew his words in Galatians would be subject to rigorous
  and critical scrutiny.
- James regarded Antioch as part of 'the land of Israel' so that it
  was consistent for him to urge Gentiles to comply with Jewish
  dietary practices, but not necessarily to demand circumcision.[10]

So far as Paul was concerned the demand for dietary compliance was one and the same as the demand for circumcision.[11] Both overturned the 'truth of the gospel', the way of grace not necessity (Gal. 2:5,14).

- James' envoys exceeded his instructions. This may be inferred from the words of the letter from 'the apostles and the elders, with the whole church' in Jerusalem who wrote to 'the brothers who are of the Gentiles in Antioch and Syria and Cilicia': 'we have heard that some persons have gone out from us and have troubled you with words, unsettling your minds, *though we gave them no instructions*' (Acts 15:24, our italics). This opinion is consistent with Gal. 2:12 which identifies 'certain men . . . from James' (*tinas apo Iakōbou*) as 'the circumcision party' (*tous ek peritomēs*). Luke's account confirms this: 'some men came down from Judea and were teaching the brethren, "Unless you are circumcised . . . you cannot be saved"' (Acts 15:1). These envoys from Jerusalem represent the same pro-circumcision viewpoint as those whom Paul calls 'false brothers' in Jerusalem who sought to force Titus to be circumcised (Gal. 2:3–4).
- The ingathering of Gentiles during the journeys of Paul and Barnabas in Cyprus and Galatia far exceeded the expectations of James and the church in Jerusalem. This is speculative, but not unreasonable. Prior to the agreement in Jerusalem in *c.*47 between the delegates from Antioch and Jerusalem, Paul had already created a significant network of Gentile churches in Syria and Cilicia. But now, following the journeys into Pisidia and Lycaonia, further circumcision-free congregations had been added and when considered next to those in the adjoining province now comprised a sizable land mass occupied by the congregations in the Pauline mission. Bockmuehl, Dunn and others may be correct in believing that Jerusalem held that since Syria was subject to the hegemony of Jerusalem, the same held true for Galatia, the adjoining province.[12]
- The political situation had changed in Jerusalem between *c.*47 (when James agreed with Paul's circumcision-free emphasis) and AD 48 (when he now disagreed with it). The meeting in Jerusalem in AD 47 would have occurred in the early part of Tiberius Alexander's tenure as procurator of Judea. The procurator Claudius appointed after the death of Agrippa (44) was Cuspius Fadus (44–6) who proved to be inept but also inflammatory of Jewish

scruples. It may have been to ease a volatile situation that Claudius appointed as governor the Alexandrian Jew, Tiberius Alexander, who however 'did not stand by the practices of his people'.[13] These were turbulent times. The effects of the great famine were deeply felt with consequent social upheaval. Tiberius Alexander hunted down, captured and crucified James and Simon, sons of the famous patriot Judas the Galilean. It is reasonable to suppose that the incumbency of an apostate Jew who crucified Jewish heroes in times of extreme financial difficulty would stimulate a conservative reaction among the Jews in Jerusalem that flowed over into James' circle of believers and cause him to change his mind.[14]

- Closely related is the suggestion that the 'circumcision party' in Jerusalem had gained the upper hand, so that James was to a new degree subject to their will. The church in Jerusalem was to a significant degree a microcosm of the temple-city, the capital of world wide Jewry. The church was embedded in the city and there were significant numbers who also belonged to the sect of the Pharisees (Acts 15:5; cf. 21:20–21). When present at the private meeting with the three 'pillars' Paul was able to resist the pressure to have Titus circumcised, such was the force of his personality and the strength of his scholarship as a former Pharisee.

But now Paul had returned to Antioch and from there travelled towards the west with his law-free message, and the 'pillars' were exposed to the full force of the Pharisaic believers. Representatives of that viewpoint set out to Antioch, and Syria and Cilicia as well to Galatia to 'correct' Paul's doctrines and bring them to completion by making Gentile believers become Jewish proselytes.

Under these circumstances James succumbed to the pressure of 'Jerusalem' and sent envoys to Antioch to apply pressure to Peter to lead the Jewish believers out of table-fellowship with the Gentile brothers.

Did James Intend to Make Proselytes of the Gentiles Who Believed?

Some scholars think James' action regarding separation at meals was, in effect, his attempt to force Gentiles to be circumcised to make them acceptable as covenant brothers with the Jewish believers.[15]

This would have meant that James was either quite the captive of the 'circumcision party' or that he was personally and aggressively committed to proselytizing Gentile believers through the imposition of circumcision, the calendar, and dietary and purity requirements.[16]

For a number of reasons this hypothesis is unlikely. First, it leaves unexplained Paul's narrative of his visit to Jerusalem where James supported Paul regarding Titus and circumcision, did not 'add anything' to the circumcision-free gospel Paul had preached to the Gentiles since the Damascus 'call', and agreed that Paul should 'go' with that message to the Gentiles. Second, it does not account for Paul's subsequent visits to Jerusalem – for the council in *c.*49 (Acts 15:6–14), after his sojourn in Corinth (Acts 18:22), or his final visit bringing the collection that had been such a source of anguish (1 Cor. 16:1–4; Rom. 15:25–8).

From this distance it is not possible to identify the parties and dynamics within the body of believers ('Christian Jews') in Jerusalem in the forties and fifties. True, the church was embedded within a totally Jewish matrix in the Holy City. The members probably remained members of the synagogues. Nonetheless, Paul distinguishes clearly between believers and unbelievers in Jewish Jerusalem, and prays for deliverance from the latter (Rom. 15:31).

Rather than seeing James as positively and aggressively a proselytizer, the evidence suggests a more nuanced appreciation of James in what was an increasingly volatile situation in Judea as the war with Rome drew closer by the day.

Accordingly, there is another possible or even probable way of viewing James, brother of the Lord. It is that he fully subscribed to the decisions and agreements reached in Jerusalem in *c.*47, decisions and agreements reached regarding Paul's law-free gospel for Gentiles. Consistent with this, James – along with others to whom the Lord appeared – proclaimed the message centred in the death, resurrection and appearances of Christ (1 Cor. 15:11).

To secure this freedom for Gentiles it seems that James envisaged separate and parallel congregations of Jews and Gentiles. The Jews who believed would continue to live as Jews and the Gentiles who believed would not be required to fulfil the works of the law.

In short, James saw the future in the segregation of congregations along ethnic lines. James' encyclical letter and the decision of the Jerusalem Council are consistent with the 'segregation' policy.

James' Letter and the Decision of the Jerusalem Council

James' encyclical[17]

James' worldwide encyclical is addressed to the 'twelve tribes of the Diaspora'. It does not mention Gentiles and is pastorally directed to Christian 'synagogues' (Jas 2:2). While James echoes negatively key Pauline words and ideas like 'faith', 'works', 'saved' and 'justified' (Jas. 2:14–26) – which he does not appear to understand – he implies that such words and ideas have no place among his readership. For his part, Paul argued precisely that Jews like Peter and himself were 'sinners' who needed to be justified by faith of/in Christ (Gal. 2:15–16). James, however, is dismissive of these Pauline doctrines although – as noted – it is doubtful by what he says that he understood them.

In sum, James' letter points to a discrete mission among Jews and networks of exclusively Jewish congregations.

The Jerusalem Council c.49

In addition to James' encyclical to 'the twelve tribes of the Dispersion' (RSV) he also presided at the Jerusalem Council where the 'apostles and elders' on his behalf wrote to 'the brothers who are of the Gentiles in Antioch and Syria and Cilicia' (Acts 15:23–29).

This letter acknowledges that 'some persons have gone out from us and troubled (*etaraxen*) you with words', where the word 'troubled' picks up Paul's complaint about those who have 'troubled' the Galatian Gentiles (Gal. 1:7; 5:19). As noted (p. 52–53), it seems too much of a coincidence that the same word 'troubled' should be employed regarding those who 'troubled' the Gentiles in Galatia and those who 'troubled' the Gentiles in Antioch and Syria and Cilicia. It is likely that the similarity of language points to an anti-Paul mission to put pressure on ('trouble') Gentile disciples in both Syria–Cilicia and Galatia.

This 'other' letter is silent on the issue of the circumcision of Gentiles, though presumably it leaves the matter open as a matter of freedom for Gentiles. Rather, it calls for Gentiles to abstain from idolatry, eating the meat of strangled and blood-undrained animals, and sexual immorality, as if they were 'residential aliens' within Israel.[18]

The reason for these provisions was to avoid giving offence to Jews, that is, *Jews in general* and not Jewish *Christians* specifically. In other words, this letter is addressed to Gentiles to conduct themselves appropriately in the presence of Jews in the Diaspora, including both believing and unbelieving Jews.

Consistent with James' evident authority in Jerusalem *c*.49 we find elements in the encyclical of James that also appear in James' other letter, addressed to Gentile churches in Antioch, Syria and Cilicia.

	James	Acts
The epistolary 'greeting' (*chairein*)	1:1	15:23
'Listen my brothers"	2:5	15:13
'the honourable name by which you are called'	2:7	15:7 (?)
'keep himself unstained from the world'	1:27	15:29 (?)

The similar elements, while insufficient in themselves to prove commonality between James the writer of the encyclical and James the president at the council are, nonetheless, consistent with it.

Thus, in effect, we have two letters from James, one to Jews and the other to Gentiles. This supports the view that in James' mind there were two parallel and unintegrated mission groups, one Jewish and the other Gentile.

James' letter	to *the twelve tribes* of the Diaspora	James 1:1	mid-to-late forties

James' letter	to the brothers who *are of the Gentiles in* Antioch and Syria and Cilicia	Acts 15:23	*c*.49

James adopts a liberal attitude to these Gentile churches. He appears content with the theological foundations Paul had laid, based on the message of Christ crucified with no requirement to fulfil 'works of the law' like circumcision. His only stipulations were to avoid certain practices for the sake of good relationships with the Jews. On the other hand, however, the extremists from the church in Jerusalem, whom Paul calls 'false brothers' and 'those of the circumcision' (Gal. 2:4,12), who seem to have been 'Pharisees who believed' (Acts 15:1,5), demanded the circumcision of Gentiles and compliance with the 'works of the law'. James was painfully situated between two powerful viewpoints, Paul's and that of the 'circumcision party'.

James, Paul and Jerusalem

Paul displays a degree of ambivalence towards James throughout his writings. His name only appears four times (1 Cor. 15:7; Gal. 1:19; 2:9,12; cf. 1 Cor. 9:5 – 'brothers of the Lord') whereas Paul refers ten times to Peter (1 Cor. 1:12; 3:22; 9:5; 15:5; Gal. 1:18; 2:7,8, 9,11,14).

Paul writes sarcastically about the three 'pillars', of whom James was pre-eminent ('those who seemed to be influential' – Gal. 2:2,6). James, Peter and John only *seemed* to be influential, suggesting perhaps that the 'false brothers' were indeed influential. As well, Paul's reference to James as the sender of envoys to Antioch to force Jewish believers away from table-fellowship with their Gentile brothers (Gal. 2:12) was implicitly negative. Furthermore, Jerusalem – which was identified with James' leadership in Paul's 'allegory' – is explicitly negative ('Hagar is Mount Sinai in Arabia; she corresponds to the present Jerusalem', a Jerusalem that symbolizes 'slavery' and 'persecution' – Gal. 4:25,29).[19]

In Paul's mind James would have been inseparable from the counter-missionaries from Jerusalem who sought to impose 'works of the law' upon Gentile believers. Although he doesn't mention it, it is likely that Paul would have regarded Jerusalem as the source of the letters of commendation of the counter-mission that had intruded into his 'field' of mission in Corinth (2 Cor. 3:1; 10:15).

At the same time, however, Jerusalem remained critically important to Paul. He saw his mission as having begun in Jerusalem and not, for example, from Damascus or from Antioch-on-the-Orontes (Rom. 15:19). For all its problems the Gentile churches owed a spiritual debt to Jerusalem that they were duty-bound to repay in material terms (Rom. 15:27). Paul's ambitious and exhausting collection from the Gentile churches was inspired by this sense of indebtedness to Jerusalem, which in Paul's mind would have been inseparable from its leader, James.

How are we to explain this ambivalence towards Jerusalem, the source of so much pain for Paul? One likely explanation is that its leader, James, was 'the brother of the Lord'. Doubtless James had many positive attributes as a leader of the large messianic community in Jerusalem (Acts 21:20), yet Paul's respect for him probably arose in particular from his service to the One who was the brother of James.

The Wisdom of Jesus in the Letter of James

Let me anticipate the fuller discussion in Appendix 4: James' Encyclical to the 'Twelve Tribes of the Diaspora'. Many rightly see a close connection between James' encyclical to the 'twelve tribes of the Dispersion' and the collected teachings of Jesus in the synoptic tradition. There seems to have been a special relationship between (a version of) the Sermon on the Mount and James' epistle to the 'twelve tribes'.

It would make sense of the data if James and 'the brothers' (i.e. his siblings; cf. Acts 12:17) were significant in collecting, digesting and shaping those teachings of Jesus from the early thirties in Jerusalem, though it is uncertain whether these were in oral or written form.[20]

James has much to say about the 'word' in his epistle. It was a 'word' that brought about the new birth among his readers and which is not merely to be 'heard' but 'done' (Jas 1:16–21). The question is: what was the content of that 'word'? Since so much of the epistle echoes the synoptic teaching of Jesus, it is likely that the 'word' was some version of the collected teachings of Jesus.

Conclusion

James, the brother of the Lord, provides an interesting point of contrast with Paul. Neither man was a disciple of Jesus of Nazareth but was converted soon after his historic lifespan. The resurrected Christ 'appeared to James' (1 Cor. 15:7) and this seems to have been when he became a disciple. Paul the Pharisee and persecutor was 'called' to be an apostle outside Damascus about a year later and then baptized inside or near the city. In other words, both men became followers of Christ at about the same time, at the beginning of Christian history.

Paul passed most of the period 34–49 away from Jerusalem. He was in Damascus–Arabia–Damascus 34–36/7, in Syria–Cilicia 37–47, and in Galatia 47/48. Paul only visited Jerusalem twice within the decade and a half after his apostolic 'call', once in 36/7 and once in *c*.47. Nonetheless, the reports during 37–47 of Paul's preaching in Syria–Cilicia of 'the faith he had once tried to destroy' found their way to the churches of Judea, including presumably to James in Jerusalem (Gal. 1:22–4). It was during this decade in Syria–Cilicia that Paul established a number of Gentile churches in that province (cf. Acts 15:23,41).

The various glimpses we catch of James over the next decade and a half indicate a man who was regarded as an 'apostle' in *c*.36/7 (Gal. 1:19), as de facto leader *c*.42–4 in the absence of Peter (Acts 12:17), as first of the three 'pillars' in Jerusalem by *c*.47 (Gal. 2:9), and as sole leader by *c*.48 (Gal. 2:12; Acts 15:13–21). Such was James' prominence by the mid-forties that he alone of the men named James had the authority to send an encyclical to 'the twelve tribes of the Diaspora' (Jas 1:1). On balance, I believe James sent this epistle during the mid-to-late-forties, making it the earliest extant document of Christianity.[21]

The disturbing question remains: why did James endorse Paul's circumcision-free gospel to the Gentiles in Jerusalem in *c*.47 (Gal.

2:1–10) and about a year later apply pressure to Peter in Antioch not to eat with Gentile believers (Gal. 2:11–13)? Of the various suggestions offered the most likely is that James had come under new pressure from the 'circumcision party' in Jerusalem who were under pressure from Jewish nationalism in a very volatile situation in Roman-occupied Judea. In those circumstances, James may have sought a way through the impasse by forcing a separation of Jewish from Gentile churches. In that way he was able to support Paul's law-free gospel for Gentiles and recognize the validity of a network of Gentile churches.

Such a solution was unacceptable to Paul, for at least two reasons. First, it may have implied that Jews were not equally sinners with Gentiles and not in need of the saving work of Christ so as to be justified by faith alone, without the works of the law (Gal. 2:15–16). The other was that Paul's gospel envisaged ethnically mixed congregations where 'there is neither Jew nor Greek . . . for you are all one in Christ Jesus' (Gal. 3:28).

7

Peter and Paul (AD 34–49)

The two opening chapters of Galatians provide the earliest written window into the critical first decade and half of Christian history. In the previous chapter we set James alongside Paul for the decade Paul was in Syria and Cilicia (37–48), based on Galatians 1 – 2, along with James' encyclical to the twelve tribes, and information in Acts 15. In this chapter we will discuss Peter alongside Paul within a similar overall timeframe, 37–48.

Peter's is a fascinating and turbulent story. His eminence as the leading disciple of Jesus continued uninterrupted into earliest Christian history. For the first decade he was the unchallenged leader of the messianic movement, first in Jerusalem and then in the land of Israel following the cessation of Paul's persecutions. His flight from Jerusalem 42–4 allowed the leadership to pass to James, brother of the Lord, relegating Peter as the second 'pillar' in the church in the Holy City.

Although in *c.*47 he supported Paul against the 'false brothers' over the circumcision of Titus and agreed that Paul should 'go' to the uncircumcised with the circumcision-free gospel, that support may have further weakened his position in Jerusalem. His move to Antioch within a year may indicate a loss of influence in Jerusalem. In the Syrian capital his capitulation to the envoys from James brought him into sharp confrontation with Paul, and issued in a breach of fellowship between them. The information about Peter – between Jesus' call to him in Capernaum (in *c.*29) and the schism in Antioch (in *c.*48) – is extensive. After Antioch, however, we catch only a few fleeting glimpses of the disciple, called Peter by Jesus.

Peter in Jerusalem (AD 33–4)

Peter, witness of the resurrected Christ

Although the tradition Paul 'received' and 'handed over' only mentioned the risen Lord's appearance to Peter once, it is reasonable to assume that he saw the resurrected Jesus on multiple occasions, that is, when he also appeared to the twelve, to the 'more than 500 at one time', and to 'all the apostles' (1 Cor. 15:5–6). Peter was the first male witness of the resurrected Lord whom, however, he 'saw' on other occasions as well, in company with other disciples of Jesus. Peter's multiple engagements with the resurrected Messiah stamped him as the 'man of rock' and 'shepherd' that Jesus said he would become (Matt. 16:18; John 21:15–19).

Peter, the first herald of the gospel

Fortified by this multiplicity of resurrection appearances and empowered by the power from on high Peter repeatedly and fearlessly proclaimed the message of the now-resurrected Christ in the presence of the cult leaders in the Holy City (cf. Acts 4:1–3,5–22; 5:17–40). Acts 1 – 5 leaves us in no doubt that Peter was the founding leader of the Christian movement in Jerusalem in 33/4. Peter's voice is the only one Luke quotes. John is often with Peter, but only Peter speaks through the text.

Peter, shaper of the gospel tradition

It is evident from 1 Corinthians, written in early 55, that Paul had 'received' important 'traditions' that he had 'handed over' to the church five years earlier. He refers specifically to the 'Lord's Supper' tradition (1 Cor. 11:23–5) and the 'gospel' tradition (1 Cor. 15:3–7).

When and from whom did Paul 'receive' these pre-formatted 'traditions'? There are three possibilities. The latest is at Antioch in 46/47, which, however, is too late. Reports of Paul 'preaching the faith' in Syria–Cilicia had already been reaching the Jewish churches in Judea throughout the decade 37–47 (Gal. 1:23). The earliest possibility would have been at Damascus in c.34, but perhaps this is too early. Paul did preach Jesus as 'the Son of God', 'the Christ' who fulfilled the Scriptures (Acts 9:20,22; cf. Gal. 1:16) in the Damascene synagogues but this may have been dependent on the christophany outside the city and the teaching about the forgiveness of sins and the Holy Spirit he received at his baptism (Acts 9:17; 22:16; Rom. 6:3).

The most likely option would have been in Jerusalem in 36/7 from the mouth of Peter with whom he 'remained' for fifteen days (Gal. 1:18). This was Paul's first extended contact with the apostle who had been the leading disciple of Jesus, the authority guaranteeing the first written gospel, and the spokesman and leader of the messianic community in the Holy City during its first decade. (Nonetheless, if Paul had received the tradition in Damascus from Ananias and the fugitive Hellenists in 34 Peter would still have been the wellspring of that tradition.)

We reasonably conclude, therefore, that the Jerusalem community led by Peter had created the 'traditions' about the 'Lord's Supper' and the 'gospel' during the period between the first Easter in 33 and Paul's return visit to Jerusalem in 36/7.

It is consistent with the evidence that Peter 'handed over' these traditions to the former Pharisee at that time. Reports of Paul's preaching of 'the faith' during the next decade (37–46) were favourably received by the churches in Judea (Gal. 1:23) and when Paul revisited Jerusalem in *c*.47 the three 'pillars' acknowledged that (in his preaching) Paul 'was not running or had not run in vain' during the previous fourteen years and they 'added nothing' to the circumcision-free message he had preached to the Gentiles (Gal. 2:2,6).

The role of Peter in the formation of the biographical traditions

The 'gospel' format Paul repeated to the Corinthians centred on the death of Christ, his burial, his third-day resurrection and his manifold appearances (1 Cor. 15:3–7) whereas the 'Lord's Supper' tradition concentrates on the event of the Last Supper on the 'night he was betrayed' when he instituted the Remembrance Meal (1 Cor. 11:23–5).

Both these citations are from a narrow sequence of events in Jerusalem at the *end* of the Christ 'narrative', that is, the Last Supper, the betrayal, the crucifixion, the burial and the sequence of resurrection appearances. Paul cited both 'traditions' specifically to respond to serious pastoral problems in Corinth: gross selfishness at the Remembrance Meal (1 Cor. 11:11–22) and denial by 'some' of the resurrection of the body (1 Cor. 15:12). In other words, Paul rehearsed only those parts of an arguably greater tradition that were then applicable to the present crises in the Achaian capital.

A pointer to Peter as the source of Paul's 'gospel' tradition is to be seen in the similarity between the gospel Paul cited in 1 Corinthians 15:3–5 and the latter parts of Peter's message to Cornelius in Caesarea in the late thirties (Acts 10:40–41,43).

1 Corinthians 15:3–5	Acts 10:40–41,43
Christ <u>died for our sins according to the scriptures</u>.	To him <u>all the prophets</u> bear witness that every one who believes in him receives <u>forgiveness of sins through his name.</u>
He was raised [by God] on the <u>third day</u> (*tē hēmera tē tritē*)	God <u>raised</u> him on the <u>third day</u> (*tē tritē hēmera*)
He appeared to <u>Peter</u> . . . the <u>Twelve</u> . . . etc.	God gave him to be manifest . . . to <u>us</u> . . . witnesses

In these two passages we see identical ideas but also close verbal parallels. Both passages teach:

(i)   The vicarious death of '[the] Christ';
(ii) thereby fulfilling the prophetic scriptures;
(iii) God raised Christ 'on the third day';
(iv) he appeared alive to various witnesses.

So striking are these common ideas and words that some theory of dependence is to be inferred. The most likely explanation is that a prior Peter-tradition was the basis of the tradition underlying to Acts 40–41, 43 and that Paul 'delivered' to the churches of his mission, including in Corinth.

Because Paul's citation of the traditions in 1 Corinthians was to address specific pastoral issues we assume that had Paul needed to he could have cited previous elements – the 'Galilee' sequence

– of Peter's summarized verbal gospel-biography (Acts 10:36–9a).

The Acts of the Apostles gives several summary accounts of 'wide-angle' biographies of Jesus, one by Peter (in Caesarea) the other by Paul (in Antioch in Pisidia, a Roman colony, known as *Colonia Antiocheia*), each beginning with the preaching of John the Baptist and ending with Jesus' resurrection appearances in Jerusalem.

Peter (Acts 10)	Paul (Acts 13)
John preaching baptism	*John* preached a baptism of repentance
	Jesus, 'seed' of David
Jesus preached and healed in *Galilee* Peter a witness in galilee and Judea	
The Jews in *Jerusalem* put Jesus to *death*	Rulers in *Jerusalem* secure Jesus' *death at Pilate's hands*
	They buried Jesus in a tomb
God *raised* him on the third day	God *raised* him from the dead
God made him manifest to chosen *witnesses*	He appeared to those who came up from *Galilee* for many days
These he commanded to preach *to the people*	These are now *witnesses to the people*

The details and the emphases are not identical but a common storyline is clear. John the Baptist was the precursor to Jesus' ministry; that ministry began in Galilee and ended in Jerusalem with his death; God raised Jesus from the dead and he commanded the witnesses to proclaim him to the people. Peter would have been the source of Paul's Christ-biography.[1]

Following C.H. Dodd, many have noticed that the Gospel of Mark is an expanded form of this outline.[2] Mark's expansion is by means of various episodes narrating Jesus' miracles, his teaching and his debates with religious leaders. There is no good reason to doubt that both the outline (*kērygma*) and the amplifying stories had begun to be formulated between the first Easter in 33 and Paul's return to Jerusalem in 36/7. Peter would have refined and expanded the material as he preached and taught throughout decade in which he led the church in Jerusalem and then travelled throughout the three regions of the land of Israel (see below).

Peter and the apostolic college

Theological reflection within the Jerusalem community is implied by the words, 'They devoted themselves to the apostles' teaching and fellowship, to the breaking of bread and to prayers' (Acts 2:42). This reflection included:

(i)   finding proof texts and linked texts fulfilled in the now exalted *Kyrios* (e.g. Ps. 110:1 / Ps. 8:4,6; Deut. 21:22–3);
(ii) the early creation of the narrative of Jesus' final week in Jerusalem[3]; and
(iii) the Spirit-inspired memory of Jesus' words and actions as fulfilling prophecy (e.g. John 2:22 / Zech. 14:21 / Ps. 69:9; also John 7:37–9; 12:16).

As the leader of the apostles in Jerusalem we reasonably assume that Peter participated in formulating their reflections. Later texts tend to confirm Peter's involvement in the creation of this early apologetic material. The proof texts cited in (i) also appear many years later in 1 Peter (1 Pet. 3:22 / Ps. 110:1; 1 Pet. 2:24 / Deut. 21:22–3). Mark's narrative of Jesus' last days in Jerusalem (Mark 11 – 16) in (ii), combined with the earlier Galilee narrative (Mark 1 – 10), has strong historical associations with Peter. What, then, about the Spirit-inspired memory of Jesus' words noted by John 2:17,22; 7:39; 12:16; 14:26)? Here, too, Peter was probably involved; Peter and John were close associates. In other words, we have good reason to believe that Peter was a significant participant in the early theological formulations of the college of apostles in Jerusalem.

Summary

All the evidence points to the leadership of Peter in the first community of the Messiah in Jerusalem, as spokesman and as the first theologian of Christianity, though one whose theology is partially hidden in the shadows and has to be inferred.

The Authority of Peter Continued into Earliest Christianity

The unchallenged authority of Peter following the first Easter in 33 coincides exactly with the authority the first-written gospel ascribes to him in relationship with Jesus of Nazareth. Martin Hengel demonstrates that Mark signals Peter's pre-eminence by referring to him at the beginning and end of his gospel, thus creating his gospel as a Peter-*inclusio* (Mark 1:16; 16:7). Furthermore, Peter is the central character at the mid-point, at Caesarea Philippi and the transfiguration (Mark 8:27 – 9:8), as well as the dominant figure throughout the Gospel of Mark.[4]

Richard Bauckham points to historical literature of the period that exploits the practice of the 'first and final' reference to someone as a way of signifying the authority behind the text.[5] Bauckham specifically rebuts the claim of Joel Marcus that, 'were it not for Papias, one would never suspect that the Second Gospel were particularly Petrine'.[6] Both Hengel and Bauckham demonstrate that Matthew and Luke endorse the authority of Peter by means of the *inclusio* principle and the dominant role of Peter throughout their gospels.[7]

Thus we can say that the authority of Peter as the leading disciple of Jesus of Nazareth undergirding the Synoptic Gospels continued uninterrupted after the Easter event into the earliest period of Christian history. Accordingly, Peter in Jerusalem was a key figure in the formation of the foundational traditions of earliest Christianity.

Peter as Shepherd in the Land of Israel (AD 34–42)

Our sources are silent about the possibility of any engagement between Peter and Paul in the months immediately following the resurrection. Before a year passed, however, Peter would have become painfully aware of the presence of the young Pharisee. Through his violent attack Stephen was killed, many disciples were beaten in the synagogues and almost the whole membership of 'the church of God' in Jerusalem was forced to flee.[8]

Many (most?) of the Hellenists scattered from Jerusalem beyond the borders of the Holy Land, some to Damascus, others further afield to Phoenicia, Cyprus and Antioch (Acts 9:1; 11:19).

One exception was Philip who took the word of God to Samaria (Acts 8:5–13). The Hebrews (Aramaic-speaking Jews) 'scattered' seed-like from Jerusalem and 'took root' as churches throughout Judea, Samaria and Galilee (Acts 8:4; 9:31).

Once the wave of persecution had passed Peter (often with John) began to visit the congregations that had been established by the 'scattered' disciples from Jerusalem in Samaria, Judea and Galilee.[9]

Luke is aware of this critical milestone. Peter was no longer confined to Jerusalem but now began to apply his leadership throughout the whole Land of Israel. 'So the church throughout all *Judea* and *Galilee* and *Samaria* had peace and was being built up. And walking in the fear of the Lord and in the comfort of the Holy Spirit, it multiplied. Now as Peter went here and there *among them all*, he came down also to the saints who lived at Lydda' (Acts 9:31–2, our italics).

Peter now travelled throughout the constituent regions of the land of Israel – Galilee and Samaria. Luke's innocent verb *dierchomai* ('went here and there') may be a technical term for 'circuit preaching' for pastoral visitation from church to church. It serves to introduce Peter' journey to Lydda, Joppa, and Caesarea (Acts 9:32 – 10:48).

Paul's own brief report on Peter' mission to the circumcised confirms Luke's more expansive narrative, as noted above. 'On the contrary, when they [James, Peter and John] saw that I had been entrusted with the gospel to the uncircumcised, just as Peter had been entrusted with the gospel to the circumcised (for he who worked through Peter for his apostolic ministry to the circumcised worked also through me for mine to the Gentiles)' (Gal. 2:7–8).

Paul acknowledges a God-given equality with Peter. Just as God had entrusted to Peter the 'apostolic ministry (*apostolē*) to the circumcised' in the land of Israel and 'worked through' that ministry, so too had God entrusted a parallel 'apostolic ministry' to Paul in Damascus–Arabia and Syria–Cilicia and likewise 'worked through' that ministry. In short, God had called each man to his distinctive ethnic mission and worked through it, blessing it with fruitful response.

The combined impact of the Acts narratives and Paul's own words leaves with us a strong impression of Peter' engagement in ministry to the Jews in the Holy City and within the Holy Land throughout the years AD 33–42.

Peter as the Second 'Pillar' (AD 44–7)

Peter forced to flee c.42

About eight years after Paul's assault on the church of God the new king, Herod Agrippa I, launched a second major attack on the community in Jerusalem. Agrippa, the grandson of Herod the Great, had lived in Rome since infancy. Through the influence of Claudius Caesar in 41 Agrippa became king of a now reunited land of Israel. Because of his dubious past in Gentile Rome Agrippa sought to impress the Jews of his piety. '[Agrippa] enjoyed residing at Jerusalem and he did so constantly and he scrupulously observed the traditions of his people. He neglected no rite of purification, and no day passed for him without the prescribed sacrifice' (Josephus, *Jewish Antiquities* xix. 331).

Agrippa's assault on the church seems to have been part of his policy of impressing his Jewish subjects. The imprisonment of Peter in *c.*42 is a sure sign of Peter's leadership of the Nazarene movement in Jerusalem and in the land of Israel. Peter's escape and his flight to 'another place' spelled the end of Peter's leadership of the Christian movement in Jerusalem and Israel (Acts 12:17).

Second 'pillar' in the Jerusalem church (44–7)

Agrippa died suddenly in 44, which may have been the signal for Peter to return to Jerusalem. Our next glimpse of Peter, however, is not until *c.*47 when Paul made his second visit to Jerusalem (Gal. 2:1–10). By *c.*47, however, Peter was no longer the unchallenged leader of Christianity in the Holy Land. Paul's references to James, Peter and John as 'those who *seemed* to be influential . . . who *seemed* to be pillars' (Gal. 2:6,9, our italics) point to a reordered leadership with James and not Peter as the leader. Furthermore, it suggests that the 'false brothers'/'circumcision party' were now the truly influential people on Jerusalem Christianity, not the apostolic 'pillars'.

No reason is given for James' promotion and Peter' demotion. We may speculate that it was, first, because James was 'brother of the Lord' and, second, because he was more deeply embedded than Peter in the synagogue culture of Jerusalem. The death of Agrippa was followed by the reannexation of Judea as a Roman province, to which Galilee and Gaulanitis were now attached. The Romanizing era after Agrippa was met with sharp reaction by rising religious nationalism, reflected in the activities of insurgency and the 'sign' prophets like Theudas.[10] Peter's engagement with the Samaritans and his baptism of the God-fearer Cornelius would have marred his reputation in the Holy City and contributed to the elevation of James in his place (Acts 8:14–25; 10:48).

Furthermore, Peter's support for Paul in Jerusalem in c.47 would have further weakened his standing within the church that was entirely Jewish in a city that was entirely Jewish, the world capital of Jewry. Yet, in spite of this, Peter opposed the 'false brothers' who had insisted on the circumcision of Titus and he endorsed Paul's circumcision-free message to Gentiles and supported Paul's further planned missions to Gentiles (Gal. 2:1–10). It appears that Peter's actions in Jerusalem in c.47 spelled the end of his leadership in the city and within the land of Israel. From that time our few glimpses of Peter reveal an apostle who seems to be heading in a westward (Rome-wards) direction – Antioch, Jerusalem, (Anatolia?), Corinth, Rome.

Schism in Antioch (c.48)

James' envoys in Antioch and Peter's submission (c.48)

Following the meeting in Jerusalem c.47 (Gal. 2:1–10) the sequence of events seems to have been:

Paul and Barnabas return from Jerusalem to Antioch	Acts 12:25
Paul and Barnabas travel to Galatia and return to Antioch	Acts 13 – 14
Counter-mission travels from Jerusalem to Galatia	Galatians 1:8; 5:10
Peter arrives in Antioch; eats with Gentile believers	Galatians 2:11

James' envoys come from Jerusalem to Antioch	Galatians 2:12 / Acts 15:1
Peter withdraws from table fellowship with Gentiles	Galatians 2:12
Paul's confrontation with Peter	Galatians 2:14
Jewish believers separate from Gentile believers	Galatians 2:13

Galatians 2:11–14 portrays an exceptionally important event, perhaps the most important crisis in Christian history to that point.

Peter's action and Paul's reaction (Gal. 2:11–13)

2:11 But when Peter came to Antioch,
I opposed him to his face, because he stood condemned.
2:12 For before certain men came from James, he was eating with the Gentiles;
but when they came he drew back and separated himself,
fearing the circumcision party.
2:13 And the rest of the Jews acted hypocritically along with him,
so that even Barnabas was led astray by their hypocrisy.

It appears that Peter arrived in Antioch some time after Paul and Barnabas had returned from the missions in Cyprus and Galatia (Acts 13 – 14). At first Peter shared table-fellowship at the common meal with Gentile believers in the church in Antioch, including (presumably) the Remembrance Meal.

It is easy to understand why 'certain men . . . from James'[11] should make their target the man who had been the leading disciple of Jesus, the first witness to the resurrection, and the leader of the mission to Israel for the first decade afterwards. If Peter withdrew from table-fellowship with Gentiles in the common meal it would send the clear message to other Jews to follow him. James probably regarded Antioch as a daughter church of Jerusalem (founded by Barnabas) and subject to his authority.

Paul's verb tenses in his narrative (Gal. 2:11–13) are telling. Peter 'was drawing back' and 'was separating' (*hypostellen . . . aphōrizen*) himself from the Gentiles because he 'was fearing' (*phoboumenos*) the circumcision party, as if it didn't happen all at once but over a period of time. We have the impression of pressure being progressively applied to Peter, and Peter *progressively* succumbing to that pressure. Perhaps Peter 'was fearing' the 'circumcision party' because of their connections with the wider community of Jews in Antioch (where there was a large population of Jews).

The imperfective verb tenses that describe Peter 'drawing back' and 'was separating' are matched by the tenses in Paul's sober verdict. Paul observed that Peter was 'being condemned (*kategnōsmenos ēn*)' – by God – as he 'was separating' himself from his Gentile brothers (Gal. 2:11).

The reasons for Peter's capitulation in Antioch in *c.*48 in contrast to his firm resolution in Jerusalem a year earlier remain unclear. Perhaps fragile relationships between the Jews in Judea and the Roman occupiers had worsened in the meantime (see Chapter 6). James was sensitive to pressure from the 'false brothers' in Jerusalem and also perhaps because of the large Jewish community in Antioch.

Paul graphically describes the effects of Peter' ultimate withdrawal from Gentile table-fellowship: 'And the rest of the Jews acted hypocritically *along with him*' (Gal. 2:13, our italics).[12] In Paul's eyes their behaviour was 'hypocritical' because the Christian Jews of Antioch had merely *pretended* to welcome Gentiles in fellowship. When Peter withdrew they revealed that their real attitudes all along had been unwelcoming towards the Gentiles.

Most disturbing of all, Paul tells the Galatians '*even* Barnabas was led astray by their hypocrisy' (Gal. 2:13, our italics). Barnabas had presided over a racially mixed community of believers in Antioch, where their members were first called 'Christians' (Acts 11:26). Furthermore the Galatian Gentiles owed their spiritual freedom to Barnabas as much as to Paul. But now first Peter, then the Jewish believers and finally *even* Barnabas have fallen down under the impact of the 'men who came from James' to Antioch.

Paul's charge against Peter (Gal. 2:14)

> 2:14 But when I saw that their conduct was not in step with the truth
> of the gospel,
> I said to Peter before them all,
> 'If you, though a Jew,
> live like a Gentile and not like a Jew,
> how can you *force* the Gentiles to live like Jews?'

Paul said the Jewish believers were not 'in step' (*orthopodeō*, lit. 'not walking straight') 'with the truth of the gospel' and for this he directly blamed Peter. It was Peter's fault that these Jewish Christians had departed from the 'straight line' they had previously walked. They had shared equally in meals with Gentiles, but no more.

Paul uses here the key word, 'force' (*anangkazō*).[13] In Jerusalem in *c.*47, the false brothers had attempted to 'force' the circumcision of Titus (Gal. 2:23). In Galatia, following the mission of Paul and Barnabas, the 'troublers' sought to 'force' circumcision on Gentile males (Gal. 6:12). And now in Antioch, the effect of Peter's withdrawal was to 'force' Gentiles 'to live like Jews' (Gal. 2:14). Once the note of 'force' or 'compulsion' had been introduced, 'the truth of the gospel' was automatically destroyed (Gal. 2:5,14).[14]

Paul confronted Peter with the painful reality that since the time he entered the house of the Gentile Cornelius in Caesarea years ago he had 'lived like a Gentile', that is, eaten Gentile food in company with Gentiles (Acts 10:15,28–9). Indeed, this had been his practice recently in Antioch until the arrival of the 'men from James'. 'So', demanded Paul of Peter, 'How can you "force the Gentiles to live like Jews (*Ioudaizein*)"?'

Paul is critical of Peter's behaviour, of eating with Gentiles and then withdrawing from them. By his example as a noted church leader Peter has broken the previous united fellowship in the church in Antioch.

Summary

The motives of James in sending envoys to Antioch may have been good and Peter's motives in withdrawing from the common meal may have been equally good. The church in Jerusalem was embedded in the world-centre of Judaism. There was a large Jewish community in Antioch. Relationships with the Romans in Judea in the late forties were volatile. In such turbulent times peaceful relationships within worldwide Jewry and between Jews and Gentiles in the great cities would have been highly desirable, if not necessary.

That Peter, Barnabas and the whole Jewish cohort chose to follow James' envoys separating from the Gentile believers conveys something of the fraught situation.

For Paul, however, this behaviour introduced the notion of compulsion for Gentiles to 'Judaize', to live 'as if' Jews, to do 'works of the law' as a condition of fellowship. Ultimately, it implied the necessity to become Jewish proselytes. This meant nothing less than that 'Christ [had] died to no purpose' (Gal. 2:21). Furthermore, and closely connected, Peter's following James' initiative destroyed the ideal that those who belonged to Christ – Jew and Gentile – were 'one in Christ' (Gal. 3:28). By his action, Peter destroyed that unity in Antioch.

Conclusion

In the Synoptic Gospels Peter was the disciple above and beyond all other disciples. This incomparable prominence continued uninterrupted after the crucifixion when Peter witnessed the resurrected Christ not once but on numerous occasions. Peter was the undisputed leader in the earliest faith community and its spokesman both to the city at large and to its religious leaders. Peter seems to have presided over the scholarly reflection on scriptural texts seen as fulfilled in the Messiah Jesus, and in formulating didactic 'traditions' like those Paul 'received' and later 'delivered' to the Corinthians, the 'Lord's Supper' tradition and the 'gospel' tradition (1 Cor. 11:23–6; 15:3–7).

Following the cessation of Paul's persecutions (in *c*.34), when congregations had been established in Judea, Galilee and Samaria, we see Peter in the role as a travelling pastor and evangelist (Acts 9:31 – 10:48; Gal. 2:7–8; cf. 1 Thess. 2:14; Gal. 1:22). When the now-converted Paul made his first return visit to Jerusalem, it was with Peter that he 'remained' for no less than fifteen days (Gal. 1:18). It is reasonable to assume that Paul received extensive instruction from Peter about the 'words and works' of Jesus of Nazareth. The tone of Paul's words to the Galatians suggests that for his part Paul informed Peter of the content of his own preaching and received the stamp of approval from this leading apostle.

King Agrippa's assault on the Christians in *c*.42 forced Peter into hiding, perhaps in Galilee (Acts 12:17). This effectively ended Peter's primacy in the messianic movement in the land of Israel.

When we glimpse Peter next – in Jerusalem, in *c*.47 – he is now the second 'pillar', having lost the primacy to James. It is possible that Peter, who would have lost support in wider Jerusalem through his engagement with the Samaritans and the Gentile Cornelius (Acts 11:2), lost further support because of his backing of Paul and his circumcision-free ministry to the Gentiles. It appears that Peter's influence in Jerusalem had by then come to its end.

When Peter came to Antioch he entered into the table-fellowship that prevailed in the church. Whole congregations, Jews and Gentiles, shared the common meal. The arrival of emissaries from James applied pressure to Peter who eventually withdrew from that fellowship, accompanied by Barnabas and the rest of the Jews. A heated exchange with Paul followed, that led to a schism in the church along ethnic lines, and also a clear separation between Paul and the Gentile believers, on the one hand, and Peter and Barnabas and the Jews on the other.[15]

The division in Antioch effectively spelt the end of the relationships between James, Peter and Paul. Apart from his return to Jerusalem from the council meeting in *c*.49 Peter now moved westwards and did not return to Jerusalem.[16] Paul, too, moved west and established congregations in the provinces adjoining the Aegean and returned to the Holy City on only two later occasions. John, the fourth member of the meeting in Jerusalem, appears to have migrated to Roman Asia. The Incident in Antioch was far-reaching, but its consequences were not all bad. The four leaders – James, Peter, John and Paul – who went their separate ways drew gifted associates with them into mission partnerships and produced the mission literature that was later accorded canonical status as the New Testament.[17]

8

Paul, Christ and the Law (Gal. 2:15–21)

In Galatians 2:15–21 we find the key that unlocks the meaning of Galatians and therefore that opens the window to the mind of the post-Damascus Paul,[1] a mind that was formed to a significant degree in the decade in Syria and Cilicia that was immediately prior to the mission to Galatia and the writing of Galatians.

This is not to say that Galatians 2:15–21 easily yields its meaning for its exegesis in parts is difficult. Yet when the problematic parts are understood in terms of the whole paragraph a clear message emerges.

Paul's Reflections on the Incident in Antioch (Gal. 2:15–21)

Our first task, however, is to explain the relationship of verses 15–21 with its immediate predecessor, the Incident in Antioch (vv. 11–14). The pronouns are important.

| verses 5–17 | 'We' – i.e. Paul and Peter |
| verses 18–21 | 'I' – i.e. Paul |

Exchanges between Paul and Peter (vv. 15–17)

2:15 We ourselves are Jews by birth and not Gentile sinners;
2:16 yet we know that a person is not justified by works of the law but through faith in Jesus Christ, so we also have believed in Christ Jesus, in order to be justified by faith in Christ and not by works of the law, because by works of the law no one will be justified.

2:17 But if, in our endeavour to be justified in Christ, we too were found to be sinners, is Christ then a servant of sin? Certainly not!

In verses 15–16 Paul speaks for himself and Peter who 'know' that as Jews they have been 'justified by faith' and not by 'works of the law'. In verse 17 Paul attributes to Peter the contra sentiment that for Jews like them to be 'not just died but justified in Christ' would mean that Christ was 'a servant of sin' in lowering Jewish men like them to the same level as Gentiles.[3] Paul, however, vehemently rejects any suggestion that Christ was an agent or facilitator of sin who had reduced Jews to the same perception and practice of sinfulness as the sinning Gentiles.

Paul's own reflections (vv. 18–21)

2:18 For if I rebuild what I tore down, I prove myself to be a transgressor.
2:19 For through the law I died to the law, so that I might live to God.
2:20 I have been crucified with Christ. It is no longer I who live, but Christ who lives in me. And the life I now live in the flesh I live by faith in the Son of God, who loved me and gave himself for me.
2:21 I do not nullify the grace of God, for if righteousness were through the law, then Christ died for no purpose.

In v. 17 Paul emphatically rejects this jibe of Peter by exclaiming, 'Certainly not' (*mē genoito*). Christ is not a servant of sin and Paul is not a transgressor against Christ, which he would be if he 'pulled down' faith and began 'rebuilding' law.[4] It was Christ's death alone that made righteousness possible (v. 21) and Paul will not demolish that truth. Paul implied that it was not Paul but Peter who was the transgressor. His withdrawal from meals with Gentiles in Antioch had indirectly but effectively 'forced' Gentiles to 'Judaize' ('live like Jews'), ultimately to be circumcised as a condition of sharing fellowship with Jewish believers (Gal. 2:14).

In verses 19–21 Paul continued his personal reflection to Peter (introduced strongly by 'I' – *egō*) by going to the depths of his spiritual experience.

But first in verse 19a he explains the meaning of the previous verse, as signalled by the introductory, 'For' (*gar*): 'For through the law, I died to the law, so that I might live to God.'

In these paradoxical words we are hearing Paul's personal odyssey before, at and after Damascus. Before Damascus Paul had reached the conclusion, however dimly, that he could not 'live to God . . . through the law' (cf. Gal. 3:23 – 'Before faith came, we were held captive under law, imprisoned until the coming faith should be revealed').

Although he did not elaborate further he meant the Galatians to understand that he was incapable of fulfilling the demands of the law so as to find a way to 'live to God'. Later he explains, 'Cursed be everyone who does not abide by all things written in the Book of the Law, and do them' (Gal. 3:10). Paul felt himself to be under that 'curse'. At Damascus, whether on the road to the city or at his baptism,[5] he came to understand that it was 'in Christ crucified' where he found righteousness with God that made it possible to 'live to God' (Gal. 2:19).

Thus the purpose of Christ's 'death' was that he, Paul, might 'live to God' (v. 19). That statement, of course, is incomplete for he was not saying that merely abandoning law meant that he now automatically 'lived to God', as if by a simple psychological change of attitude. To the contrary, his exchange of death-to-law for life-to-God was entirely due to that new, 'by faith' union with Jesus Christ, whereby he declared that he had been 'crucified with Christ' (v. 20).

Second, in verses 19b–20a he amplified what he meant by 'live to God': 'I have been crucified with (*synestaurōmai*) Christ. It is no longer I who live, but Christ who lives in me.' At and since Damascus Paul had been attached to the cross with Christ,[6] spelling the end of his former law-directed life as the means of access to the Almighty. From that moment the risen Christ (through the Spirit[7]) lived within Paul.

These words, more than any other, explain the core meaning of his letter to the Galatians, and thereby explain the revolutionary paradigm shift at the centre of Paul's life. This was no later religious development in Paul, a progressive evolution from a law-centred to a Christ-centred life. It was a radical, life-changing experience for the young Pharisee that occurred at Damascus and was worked out in the years following, including in Syria and Cilicia.

Third, in verse 20b–c Paul clarified his previous statement by indicating that although 'Christ lives in' him he, too, '*now* lives in the flesh'. Paul himself lives, and Christ also lives – within him. This twofold reality prepares the way for his later exposition of 'the works of the flesh' and their antithesis, 'the fruit of the Spirit' (Gal. 5:16–25).

But the life he 'now lives in the flesh' is the life of faith (i.e. not of 'works of the law') that is directed toward the Son of God who – as Paul now knew – had 'loved' him and had 'given himself' in crucifixion 'for' (*hyper*) Paul, by becoming a curse 'for' (*hyper*) him (Gal. 3:13). This repeated preposition *hyper* indicates that in Paul's understanding the crucified Christ had 'stood in' for him, 'substituted' himself for him.[8] 'The life I now live in the flesh I live by faith in the Son of God who loved me and gave himself for (*hyper*) me.'

It was Christ's love for Paul demonstrated in his saving death for him that from Damascus became the driving force within this man throughout the remainder of his life (cf. 2 Cor. 5:14–15 – 'the love of Christ controls us, because we have concluded this: that one has died for all'). If we seek an explanation for the phenomenon of Paul we need to look no further. This statement explains all.

Fourth, Paul explained why he will not 'tear down' faith and 'rebuild' law as the way to know God (Gal. 2:21): 'I do not nullify the grace of God, for if justification (*dikaiosynē* – 'righteousness') were through the law, then Christ died for no purpose.' Here is Paul's final emphatic word to Peter who said that Paul should 'tear down' faith and 'rebuild' law. 'Justification' cannot be through law, for if it were then Christ had died for no purpose.

Analysis of the Critical Passage: Galatians 2:15–16

Galatians 2:15–16 is Paul's further response to Peter in verse 14: 'I said to Cephas . . . ."If you, though a Jew, live like a Gentile and not like a Jew, how can you force the Gentiles to live like Jews (*ioudaizien*)?"' In other words, Paul charged Peter the Jew with inconsistency regarding table-fellowship with Gentiles. Previously he had eaten with Gentiles but under pressure at Antioch he separated from his Gentile brothers and sisters. This had the effect of *compelling* Gentiles to 'live' like Jews, that is, compulsorily to follow

Jewish dietary practices, that is, 'works of the law'. Accordingly, Paul must remind Peter that as Jew he was 'justified by faith' and not by 'works of the law', implying that the same must apply to Gentiles.

> 2:15 We ourselves are Jews by birth and not Gentile sinners;
> 2:16 yet we know that a person is not justified by works of the law but through faith in Jesus Christ, so we also have believed in Christ Jesus, in order to be justified by faith in Christ and not by works of the law, because by works of the law no one will be justified.

Paul now reminded Peter of their *shared* theological conviction (*eidotes*, 'we know') that the need to be 'justified by faith' and not 'by works of the law' applied as much to them as Jews as it did to Gentiles. Evidently, Peter had said or implied that as Jews from birth, he and Paul were not 'Gentile sinners'. But that was not consistent with what Peter truly 'knew', that he had been 'justified by faith in Jesus Christ'. Paul must remind him of this.

How could one who had been the leading disciple of Jesus, who carried forward that leadership in the land of Israel after the first Easter, have failed to see this? The answer may be that Peter did not work things out with the consistent logic we associate with Paul, the educated rabbi who underwent the radical conversion at Damascus.

These two verses are exceptionally important because Paul now introduces into the letter his keywords: 'justified', 'faith', 'works of the law' and 'law'. Since Galatians is probably Paul's earliest surviving letter,[9] it means this was the first time historically we hear Paul actually using words he will repeat many times in his letters.

In verse 16a Paul says that 'a person' (*anthrōpos*) is 'not justified by works of the law' whereas in verse 16c, to strengthen the point even further, says 'no one' (literally, 'no flesh' – *pasa sarx*) 'by works of the law . . . will be justified' (cf. Ps. 143:2 LXX – 'before thee no one living will be justified'). Paul was saying, in effect, that 'a person' is 'flesh' (i.e. frail and fallen) and incapable of self- justification by 'works of the law'. So, three times in this one verse Paul rejects 'works of the law' as a way to be 'justified'.[10]

Verses 15–16 are connected by 'yet' to introduce a surprising item of 'knowledge'. It would not be surprising for Paul to say, 'We Jews know that law-less Gentile sinners are under God's judgement.' We are not shocked that he should say, 'We know that a person [a Gentile] is not justified by works of the law but through faith in Jesus Christ', but we are by his conclusion: 'so *we* [Jews] *also* have believed in Christ Jesus, in order to be justified by faith in Christ[11] and not by works of the law.'

Paul knew that Gentiles needed to be 'justified'. He lists typical 'Gentile' vices later in the letter, including 'sexual immorality, impurity, sensuality, idolatry, sorcery' (5:19–20). Because 'Gentiles' are without law (*anomos*) they are 'sinners', people unrestrained by God's law and therefore steeped in idolatry and fornication (Rom. 2:12–16; 1:18–32), needing to be 'justified by God'.

The big shock is that 'Jews by birth' – like Peter and Paul – who are not 'Gentile sinners', are not 'justified by works of the law'. They do 'the works of the law' (practise circumcision, observe Sabbaths and the calendar, follow dietary and purity rules), but are not thereby 'justified', that is, 'by God'.[12] Why? It is Paul's tacit acknowledgement that just as law-less Gentiles are 'sinners' who need to be 'justified' so too, do law-keeping Jewish 'sinners' need to be 'justified'. In Romans Paul will explain that both Jews and Gentiles belong to Adam's 'tribe', who therefore are equally subject to sin and death and who both 'fall short of the glory of God' (Rom. 5:12; 3:23).

But how is the Jew justified? Three times in Galatians 2:16 Paul uses the language of 'faith', the noun twice and the verb 'to have faith' (= 'to believe') once. By 'faith', however, Paul means faith *in* Jesus Christ. 'We (i.e. Peter and Paul) have *believed* in Jesus Christ in order to be justified by *faith* in Christ.' Peter and Paul, as Jewish Christian *believers*, no longer look to the 'works of the law' to be 'justified', but only to Christ cruci-fied and risen.

Paul could not be more specific about the basis of justification. The options for justification are clear and mutually exclusive. If it is 'through law' then 'Christ died for no purpose' (v. 21).[13] But there is no way to 'justification' (= 'life with God') that is possible 'through law' because – as he will point out – the law is unfulfillable (3:10–13). Law is a spiritual cul-de-sac; there is no way through to God. Faith in Christ crucified is the only way to be 'justified' and so 'live to God'.

Christ and the Spirit: the Significance of Galatians 2:15–21

This was not the first time Paul had articulated this doctrine. It lay at the heart of the gospel he had 'received' from God at Damascus a decade and a half earlier (1:12), the 'faith' that he had preached to Gentiles in Arabia and Syria and Cilicia for the previous fourteen years. The Jerusalem leaders Peter and James did not challenge this message when Paul returned to Jerusalem three years after his conversion (1:18–19), nor 'added to' it when he came there with the uncircumcised Titus a decade later (2:2, 6). They endorsed Paul 'going' to the Gentiles with that message (2:9). It was James and Peter who later had – for whatever reason – backed away from endorsing Paul's unchanging gospel message, 'the faith . . . he preached'.

Paul came to understand at Damascus that the Crucified One he had been persecuting had loved him and given himself in death for him. That coincided with his growing understanding that he did not 'know God' (Gal. 4:9), did not 'live to God' (2:19), and this because of his inability to fulfil the law of God, given to Moses. It was 'faith' in the Crucified One that 'justified' Paul and gave him access to the Almighty whom he now called, 'Abba, Father' (4:6).

This, however, was no mere psychological readjustment in his thinking. To the contrary, he cried out, 'I live, yet no longer I, but Christ lives in me' (Gal. 2:20; cf. Gal. 1:16 – 'God . . . was pleased to reveal his Son *in* me'; 2 Cor. 4:6 – 'God who said, "Let light shine out of darkness" has shone *in* our hearts'). This is the language of profound conversion.

Nor is Paul's forensic language as one 'justified' to be understood in grim and legalistic terms. The changed status whereby Paul was now 'justified by faith' had an accompanying subjective, other side, the inner blessing of Christ *in* him. This helps explain why Galatians combines both the forensic language of justification and, equally, the deeply personal and spiritual language about the indwelling Christ.

In this regard, F.F. Bruce comments:

The Letter to the Galatians can be thought of as so completely devoted
to the theme of justification by faith that its teaching on the Holy Spirit
may be overlooked. In fact, its teaching on the Holy Spirit is so inter-
woven with its teaching on justification by faith that the one cannot be
understood without the other, any more than in real life the justifying
grace of God can be experienced apart from the Spirit.[14]

When we move on into the next passage and confront the Galatians' experience of the Spirit (Gal. 3:1–5) we find a parallel with
Paul's own experience of the Spirit. In Galatians 2:19–21 Paul
teaches that his experience of the Spirit ('Christ . . . lives in me' –
v. 20) arose directly out of his access to God through faith in the
Crucified One without reliance on the works of the law (v. 16).
When we examine Galatians 3:1–5 we discover that the Galatians
received the blessing of the Spirit as they 'heard with faith' the
message of Jesus Christ crucified, independently of 'works of the
law'. What had been true of Paul had been true of the Galatians.

The immediacy of the Spirit as enjoyed by the Galatians occurred
as Paul preached Christ crucified to them. But this mirrored Paul's
own experience in Damascus a decade and a half earlier. In the
years since the message centred on the Crucified One and faith in
him had been central in the preaching of Paul to Jews and Gentiles
alike.

9

Christ Crucified, the Spirit and Scripture (Gal. 3:1–14)

Initially Paul addressed the Galatian churches directly (1:1–10) and then indirectly as a personal memoir from the time of his 'former life in Judaism' to his dispute with Peter in Antioch (1:11 – 2:21). Now, as from 3:1 he resumes his direct address to the Galatians.

Overlap between Galatians 3:1–14 and 2:15–21

At the same time, however, there is considerable overlap between the new, direct address (3:1–14) with its immediate predecessor, Paul's reflected dispute with Peter (2:15–21). Both passages focus on the blessings of the Spirit, within the life of Paul on the one hand (in particular 2:20), and within the recent experience of the Galatians, on the other (3:1–2).

Galatians 2:20	Galatians 3:1–2
I have been *crucified with Christ*. It is no longer I who live, but *Christ who lives in me*. And the life I now live in the flesh I live by *faith* in the Son of God, who loved me and *gave himself* for me	O foolish Galatians! Who has bewitched you? It was before your eyes that Jesus Christ was publicly portrayed as *crucified*. Let me ask you only this: Did you receive *the Spirit* by (*ek*) works of the law or by hearing with (*ek*) *faith*?

In both Galatians 2:15–21 and 3:1–14, it is 'faith in Christ [crucified]' and not 'works of the law' that is the instrument (*ek*) that initiates the heaven-sent Spirit (2:19b–20; 3:2,5). Indeed, *ek* understood as a human instrument dominates both passages occurring thirteen

times,[1] where *ek pisteōs* ('by faith')[2] is in antithetical contrast with
ex ergōn nomou ('by works of the law')[3] and *en nomo* ('by law').[4]

Another and related contact between Galatians 2:15–21 and
3:1–14 is the common 'righteousness'/'justification' language:

Galatians 2:15–21	Galatians 3:1–14
2:16 yet we know that a person is not *justified* (*dikaioutai*) by works of the law but through faith in Jesus Christ, so we also have believed in Christ Jesus, in order to be *justified* (*dikaiōthōmen*) by faith in Christ and not by works of the law, because by works of the law no one will be *justified* (*dikaiōthēsetai*)	3:6 just as Abraham 'believed God, and it was counted to him as *righteousness* (*dikaiosynē*)'
	3:8 And the Scripture, foreseeing that God would *justify* (*dikaioi*) the Gentiles by faith
2:17 if in our endeavour to be *justified* (*dikaiōthēnai*) in Christ we ourselves are found sinners	3:11 Now it is evident that no one is *justified* (*dikaioutai*) before God by the law, for 'The *righteous* (*dikaios*) shall live by faith'
2:21 if *justification* (*dikaiosynē* – 'righteousness') were through the law, then Christ died for no purpose	

Thus despite the different character of these adjoining passages
they have in common the critical cluster of elements – Christ crucified, faith not works of the law (or, law), the Holy Spirit and justi-
fication/righteousness. The critical thing to notice is that in the
first passage (2:15–21) Paul is referring to Jews (like himself and
Peter) whereas in the second (3:1–14) he is referring to Gentiles.
Despite significant differences between them they find righteousness with God and his Holy Spirit by identical means (*ek*), faith in
the Crucified One and not 'works of the law'.

Exegesis in Galatians 3:1–14

An inclusio

To reinforce further the correspondence between Galatians 2:15–21
and 3:1–14 Paul has written verses 1–14 as a kind of *inclusio* that

is 'framed' by reference to the 'Spirit' and 'faith' (vv. 2,14) that encloses references to the crucifixion (vv. 1,13).

2	Did you receive the *Spirit* by works of the law or by hearing with *faith*?
1	It was before your eyes that Jesus Christ was publicly portrayed as *crucified*.
13	Christ redeemed us from the curse of the law by becoming a curse for us – for it is written, 'Cursed is everyone who is *hanged upon a tree*' . . .
14	so that in Christ Jesus the blessing of Abraham might come to the Gentiles, so that we might receive the promised *Spirit* through *faith*.

Just as the cross of Christ, faith and the indwelling Spirit together (and not the law) were the engine that drove Paul (2:19–21), so also these (and not 'works of the law') had been the driving force for the Galatians, including the Gentiles among them, as witnessed by 'miracles' (*dynameis* – v. 5) and their cry as his children to 'Abba', Father (4:6).

The example of Abraham (vv. 6–9,14)

It is evident that other men had come to the Galatian churches after Paul seeking to correct his grace-based, circumcision-free gospel (2:21; 6:12).

1:7	there are some who trouble (*hoi tarassontes*) you
3:1	Who (*tis* – singular) has bewitched you?
5:10	the one who is troubling (*ho . . . tarassōn*) you
6:12	those who would compel (*anangkazō*) you to be circumcised

The singular references (*tis* – 3:1; *ho . . . tarassōn* – 5:10) are probably rhetorical, not literal.

Paul is referring to a group of Jewish-Christian counter-missionaries who are attempting to 'compel' Gentile believers in the Galatian churches to submit to (male) circumcision and other 'works of the law' (e.g. the Jewish Calendar – 4:9–11); in short to become Jewish proselytes. As noted earlier (Chapter 5), these men came from that section of the Jewish-Christian community in Jerusalem who were reacting against Paul's circumcision-free, law-free gospel for Gentiles.

Galatians is significant among other reasons because it outlines Paul's gospel message for both Jews and Gentiles and also provides his apologetic response to the counter-mission. Central to that apologetic, as we have seen, was Paul's witness to his own spiritual revolution through his faith in the Crucified One and the life-changing and empowering presence of the indwelling Christ (2:15–21). Equally, however, Paul was able to remind the Galatians of the impact on them of the presence of the Spirit as they heard with faith the message of Christ crucified (3:1–5).

Paul's opponents seem to have directed a two-pronged attack against Paul. First, they claimed that the leadership of the Jerusalem church (i.e. James) was authoritative, including over congregations in Syria–Cilicia and Galatia that owed their origin to Jerusalem. Paul will respond to that claim with the devastating allegory of Abraham's sons (4:21–31) that points to Jerusalem as under slavery and the instrument of slavery (see Chapter 10).

The opponents apparently informed the Galatians that Paul was self-appointed, wilfully claiming divine authority for his doctrines and mission. This explains why Paul must insist that his gospel came by divine revelation (1:10–12), not from his studies in Judaism (1:13–14), or from the apostles in Jerusalem (1:15–20), or from the churches in Judea (1:21–4). In fact, the Jerusalem leadership endorsed 'without addition' his circumcision-free message to Gentiles and agreed that he should 'go' to them (2:6–10).

Their second attack was scriptural and almost certainly began with reference to the circumcision of Abraham, as the basis for their demand for the circumcision of Gentiles. Had not God said to him, 'This is my covenant, which you shall keep . . . Every male among you shall be circumcised . . . Any uncircumcised male . . . shall be cut off from his people' (Gen. 17:10,14)? Circumcision was a non-negotiable condition for inclusion in the Lord's covenant with Abraham. Furthermore, they would have asserted that the obedience of 'works' was critical for that membership. Abraham 'obeyed' the voice of God's messenger to the point of willingness to sacrifice Isaac, upon whom rested the future hopes of the covenant line (Gen. 22:19). The counter-missionaries were, like Paul, biblical scholars who would have buttressed their demands to the Galatian Gentiles on these and similar texts.

It appears that the words following were Paul's response to the counter-missionaries' apologetic.

3:6 Just as[5] Abraham 'believed God, and it was counted to him as righteousness' [Gen. 15:6]

3:7 Know then, that it is those of faith (*ek pisteōs*) who are the sons of Abraham.

3:8 And the Scripture, foreseeing that God would justify the Gentiles by faith (*ek pisteōs*), preached the gospel beforehand to Abraham, saying, 'In you shall all the nations be blessed'. [Gen. 12:3]

3:9 So then, those who are of faith (*ek pisteōs*) are blessed along with Abraham, the man of faith.

The two texts to which Paul appealed – Genesis 15:6 and 12:3 – applied to Abraham *before* he was circumcised. Only later, when Abraham was ninety-nine, was he circumcised (Gen. 17:24–6). These great covenantal texts that relate to Abraham belong to his *pre*-circumcision days, making him especially important in Paul's arguments to *un*circumcised Gentiles among the Galatians.

In the first text God showed the childless Abram all the stars in the night sky and promised him, 'So shall your offspring be' whereupon 'Abraham believed God, and it was 'counted' to him as 'righteousness' (Gen. 15:6). 'Counted' or 'reckoned' (*logizomai*) is a bookkeeper's word, sometimes also translated 'imputed'.[6] On the basis of Genesis 15:6 Paul encourages the Galatians to 'know ... that it is *those of faith* (*ek pisteōs*)[7] who are the sons of Abraham'. Paul could not be clearer: Gentiles who *believe* in Christ are 'sons of Abraham', members of the divine covenant. Faith, not circumcision, made someone a 'son of Abraham'.

In Galatians 3:8, before Paul quotes his second text – 'In you shall all the nations be blessed' (Gen. 12:3) – he gives an explanation of it. Back then God was telling Abraham the good news that in the years to come all the nations would be blessed in him. This citation allows Paul to draw the critical conclusion to this all-important 'Abraham' passage (Gal. 3:9). This he introduces by *hōste*, '*so then* those of faith are *blessed* along with Abraham, the man of faith.' Let the Gentiles in the Galatian churches understand that as believers in Christ they are 'sons of Abraham' (v. 7), and 'blessed in' him and 'with him' (vv. 8,9).

Blessing and curse (vv. 9–13)

Paul's word 'blessed' in verse 9 serves not only to conclude the passage verses 6–9, but also introduces the next passage, verses 9–14, where the word 'blessing' occurs in verse 14. Thus verse 9 is a bridge between verses 6–9 and verses 9–14.

Sandwiched in between God's blessing of those with Abraham's faith (vv. 9,14) are references to God's curse (vv. 10,13). Thus verses 9–14 is a kind of *chiasma not* formed but framed by 'faith':

3:9	those who are *of faith* are blessed (*eulogountai*) with Abraham, the man of faith	
3:10	those who are *of works* of the law are under a curse (*kataran*) cursed by everyone who does not bide by . . . the law cursed	(Deut. 27:6)
3:11	in the law . . . it is clear that the righteous shall live by faith	(Hab. 2:4)
3:12	he who does them [the law] shall live by them	(Lev. 18:5)
3:13	Christ . . . becoming a curse for us	
3:14	*the blessing* (*eulogia*) of Abraham might come to the Gentiles, so that we might receive the promised Spirit by *faith*	

Thus Paul continues the contrast between those who are 'of faith' with those who are 'of works of the law', asserting that 'all those of works of the law (*hosoi . . . ex ergōn nomou*) are under a curse' (v. 10). That curse is for everyone who does not 'abide by' and 'do' everything written in the book of the law (LXX Deut. 27:26). This is a comprehensive statement referring to 'everyone' and 'all things' as well as 'abide by' and 'do'. In other words, God expects absolute compliance with his law.

It is possible, even probable, that the counter-missionaries in Galatia used this text to require the Gentile believers to submit to circumcision, to keep the requirements of the law of God. Paul, however, saw beyond the superficialities of 'works of the law' to the deeper intent of the law as the way to 'life' with God; a way, however, that was daunting and effectively impossible to fulfil.

Accordingly, in Galatians 3:11 Paul observes, 'It is evident (*delos*, 'clear') that no one is justified before God *by the law*', implying (but not saying outright) that 'no one' actually 'abides by' and 'does' all things written in the book of the law. Rather, he asserts that 'the righteous will live *by faith* (*ek pisteōs*)', quoting Habakkuk 2:4. It is possible that the *ek pisteōs* of Habakkuk 2:4 was the significant influence in Paul's repeated usage of these formulaic words in Galatians 2:16 – 3:9.

It is important to note that the words 'justified' and 'live' in Galatians 3:11 are in parallel so that to be 'justified' means 'to live', that is, live *eternally*. We recall that Paul wrote similarly about 'the *life* I now live' as one 'crucified with Christ' (2:20, our italics). To be 'justified by faith' is to have eternal 'life' with God.

In Galatians 3:12 Paul teaches, first, that the law is not 'of faith' because it does not arise out of faith and is incompatible with faith as a way of relationship with God. But, second, he asserts that the one who *does* them ('the *works* of the law') shall live by them. But that is exactly why there is the divine curse, because people don't actually *live* by the precepts of the law and so are unable to find 'life with God' through the law.[8]

We hear Paul's heartfelt words about Christ's death 'for' him in his words in verse 13. Through his failure to fulfil the law, and the works of the law, Paul had been under God's curse as one who knew but did not 'do' those 'works'.[9] But the gospel Paul 'received' from Christ (1:12) told him that he, Christ, had become 'a curse for us' (*hyper hēmōn katara*), that is, had borne that curse vicariously, in his place and for his sake. Previously, Paul had been a captive under the divine curse as a law-breaker but now, as he had been told by the Lord, he was free, liberated from that captivity.

It seems likely that from earliest times after the resurrection the disciples thought about the crucifying of Jesus as 'hanging' him 'on a tree'. Both Peter and Paul speak that way in sermons and in letters (Acts 10:39; 1 Pet. 2:24; Acts 13:29; Gal. 3:13).

Prior to his conversion, however, Paul the zealot and Pharisee would have automatically regarded the crucified ('hanged') Jesus as accursed, as a false-messiah (cf. Deut. 21:22–23). His duty to God would have been to destroy his followers, which he *zealously* attempted to do. Imagine, therefore his consternation when the Crucified One spoke to him out of the blazing heavenly light. God spoke to Moses out of the glory so Paul must conclude that the One who addressed him from the blinding brightness was the Lord. So what did it mean that Jesus had been 'hanged on a tree, accursed by God'? Just one thing: *vicariously* he bore the curse upon those who 'do not abide by all things written in the Book of the Law and do them'. He took their place on 'the tree', bearing their curse.

It is evident from verse 9 that the 'blessing of Abraham' (v. 13) was that God 'counted' his belief in God's promise as 'righteousness'. In other words, God 'justified' Abraham 'by faith'. Paul preached that the divine blessing had now come to the Gentiles among the Galatians who were 'of faith' and not of 'works of the law'. Along with God's favourable judgement *of* them in Christ (objectively, by status) was the gift of God's Spirit *in* them (subjectively, as in 3:2,3,5; 4:6).

Paul's close argument with substantiating texts (3:6–14) suggests years of debate in synagogues of Syria and Cilicia. The counter-missionaries' choice of texts points to men who were skilled exegetes of the Scriptures. It is evident that they have argued their case forcefully among the Galatians. The Galatians should have been grateful that the one who brought them the true gospel and who now defended it to them was such an accomplished scholar of those texts.

The passage could not be clearer. Those who rely on (are *ek* – 'of') works of the law are required to live by the law, otherwise they are under God's curse; but God redeems from that curse those who are 'in Christ', people 'of faith'.

Paul's Use of the Septuagint (Gal. 3:6–14)

It is well known that Paul often does not cite Old Testament texts exactly. Basically, there are two reasons for this. One is that he mostly depends on Septuagint and other Greek translations and not the Masoretic (Hebrew) text, and the other is that he adapts those Greek texts in line with his view of their fulfilment in Christ. Once this is recognized the next task is to see if there is a pattern or trend in the alterations he makes.

Accordingly we examine the six texts that Paul cites in Galatians 3:6–14.[10]

Galatians 3:6 – Genesis 15:6

	Septuagint	Paul
Gen. 12:3	And Abram believed God, and it was reckoned to him as righteous	Just as Abraham 'believed God, and it was counted to him as righteousness'

Paul's changes are minimal. He introduces the text with 'Just as' (*kathōs*) instead of 'And' and locates Abraham next in the sentence, ahead of the verb 'believed', perhaps for emphasis. Paul's debate with the 'agitators' centred on Abraham and their claim that his circumcision (Gen. 17:9–14) set the standard for covenant membership, including for the Gentiles of Galatia. Paul, however, points to Abraham's faith as the paradigm for the right covenantal response from the members of the Galatian churches, including the Gentile members.

Galatians 3:8 – Genesis 12:3; 18:18

	Septuagint	Paul
Gen. 12:3	and all the tribes of the earth will be blessed in you	'In you shall all the nations [Gentiles] be blessed'
Gen. 18:18	and all the nations of the earth will be blessed in him	

The 'blessing of Abraham' occurs no less than five times in Genesis but is variously stated (12:3; 18:18; 22:18; 26:4; 28:14). Galatians 3:8, however, combines Genesis 12:3 and 18:18:

(i)   Paul employs the same verb 'will be blessed' (*eneulogēthēsontai*) from both texts;
(ii) his 'in thee' (*en soi*) repeats Genesis 12:3; and
(iii) his 'all the Gentiles' (*panta ta ethnē*) repeats Genesis 18:18.

Furthermore, and significantly, the two Genesis texts Paul depends on relate to Abraham *before* he was circumcised. Paul's conflation, but abbreviation, of the two Genesis texts results in a terse, powerful statement to the Galatians. Retroactively the nations (= the Gentiles) were being blessed with their father Abraham back then.

Galatians 3:10 – Deuteronomy 27:26; 30:10

	Septuagint	Paul
Deut. 27:26	Cursed is every person, who will not abide by all the words of this law to do them	for it is written, 'Cursed be everyone who does not abide by all things written in the Book of the Law, and do them'
Deut. 30:10	the ones written in the book of this law	

In Galatians 3:10 Paul makes two main changes to Deuteronomy 27:26:

(i)   he substitutes 'everyone' (*pas*) for 'every man' (*pas anthrōpos*) and 'all things the things written' (*pasin tois gegrammenois*) for 'all the words' (*pasin tois logois*);

(ii) in place of 'of this law' in Deuteronomy 27:26 he imports 'in the Book of *the* Law' from Deuteronomy 30:10, a significant adaptation.

As it now stands Galatians 3:10 is an absolute statement. God pronounces his curse on 'everyone' who does not abide by 'everything' that is written in the 'Book of the Law', that is, the comprehensive statement of the law of God. In other words, Paul is raising the bar so high that there is no alternative but to turn to the One who became 'a curse for us'.[11]

Of supreme importance are Paul's own words which Deuteronomy 27:26/30:10 substantiate: 'For all who rely on works of the law are under a curse' (v. 10), in which 'rely on' translates '*of* works of the law' (*ex ergōn nomou*) where 'of' (*ek*) is instrumental and in antithetical contrast with 'of faith' (*ek pisteōs*), which had been repeatedly set alongside each other (Gal. 2:16; 3:2,5,7,8,9,10,12). God blesses 'faith' directed towards Christ crucified with his gifts of righteousness and the Spirit whereas reliance on 'works of the law' like circumcision is subject to the divine curse.

Galatians 3:11 – Habakkuk 2:4

	Septuagint	Paul
Hab. 2:4	but the righteous by (*ek*) my faith-fulness will live[12]	for 'The righteous shall live by (*ek*) faith'

In Galatians 2:16 Paul asserted that 'a person is not *justified* [righteous] by works of the law but through *faith* in Jesus Christ' which Paul restated positively but more briefly in Galatians 3:11 as 'for "The righteous shall live by (*ek*) faith"'. Both texts depend on Habakkuk 2:4.

Paul, however, has significantly adapted Habakkuk 2:4. By omitting '*my* faithfulness' he dramatically shifted the focus away from *God's* (or *Christ's*) faithfulness to the faith (or the faithfulness) of the righteous, i.e. Christian believers (specifically Gentile Galatians).

The cited text in Galatians 3:11 must, of course, be understood according to the words of Paul that it substantiates. Paul's words were negative, '*no one* is justified before God by law' whereas his citation of Habakkuk 2:4 is positive, 'for "the righteous by (*ek*) faith will live"'. In Paul's words, then, 'It is evident (*delos*, 'clear') that no one by law will be justified' because the 'righteous' ('those who are justified') enjoy that status on account of (*ek*) faith.

Galatians 3:12 – Leviticus 18:5

	Septuagint	Paul
Lev. 18:5	which (*ha*), having done, a person (*anthrōpos*) will live by them (*en autois*)	but 'the one who does them (*auta*) will live by them' (*en autois*)

Paul has omitted the initial 'which' (*ha*) and restated it as 'them' (*auta*), the antecedent of which appears to be 'all things written in the Book of the Law' (Gal. 3:10). The omission of 'person' (*anthrōpos*) seems to be stylistic (but see Gal. 2:16 – 'a person is not justified by works of the law').

Galatians 3:13 – Deuteronomy 21:23

	Septuagint	Paul
Deut. 21:23	for cursed (*kekatēramenos*) by God (*hypo theou*) is everyone being hung (*kremamenos*) on a tree (*xylou*)	for it is written, 'cursed (*epikataratos*) is everyone who is being hung[13] (*kremamenos*) on a tree (*xylou*)'

Paul makes two main changes to Deuteronomy 21:23. He omits 'by God' (*hypo theou*) and must therefore substitute an adjective *epikataratos* ('cursed') in place of the perfect participle *kekatēramenos* (also meaning 'cursed'). Some argue that Paul's omission of 'by God' means that the crucified Christ was not actually 'cursed *by God*'. However, the adjective may in fact point to the *absolute* nature of the curse. This would be consistent with Paul's introductory words, 'Christ . . . became a curse for us.' This prompts the question: how could Christ 'become a curse for us' unless it was by means of the curse of God upon him?

Summary

Paul's use of Old Testament (LXX) texts is none too subtle as he continues to argue that it is '*of* faith' and not '*of* works of the law' that people find the righteousness of God and the blessings of his Spirit. It is not possible to tell whether Paul is employing texts on this occasion that he had used during his synagogue debates in Syria–Cilicia, but in all likelihood his exposition of them to the Galatians was not novel, but had been developed as he 'preached the faith' in Syria and Cilicia.

Conclusion

In Galatians 3:1–14 Paul resumes his direct address to the Galatians. Yet as Paul had experienced the blessings of righteousness and the Spirit so too had the Galatians experienced those blessings, that is, by the instrumentality 'of faith' (*ek pisteōs*) not 'of works of the law' (*ek ergōn nomou*). His experience and theirs ran in parallel and depended on their faith-relationship with the Crucified One.

Following his questions to them about their reception of the Spirit Paul introduces and cites six LXX texts that he had adapted to demonstrate that God imputed righteousness (justification) to Abraham on account of his faith, that God had promised his blessing of the Gentiles to Abraham, but that on the contrary the curse of God falls on those who rely on works of the law as a basis of right standing with God, a curse that is unavoidable because God's expectation of compliance with the law is absolute. The way of faith in the One who became a curse is, therefore, the way of redemption from that slavery.

10

Freedom and Slavery: Two Jerusalems

The vocabulary of slavery and freedom is prominent in Galatians.[1] For Paul slavery and freedom were opposites. Slavery was evil and freedom was good. He writes expecting his Galatian readers to accept this antithesis without further explanation or debate. Paul's usage, however, was metaphorical. He was not referring to physical slavery and freedom, but to slavery and freedom understood spiritually.

What, then, according to Paul writing to the Galatians was the source of slavery, on the one hand, and freedom on the other?

To anticipate, we propose that redemption from slavery to law through faith in Christ crucified was the freedom that changed Paul at Damascus and became the driving force within him for the remainder of his life.

This 'freedom' from law was inextricably connected with that cluster of ideas that we have previously identified as the key to this letter and the window through which to see into the mind of the post-Damascus Paul (see Chapter 8). That is to say, at Damascus God gave Paul this 'freedom' as he grasped that the Crucified One had 'loved' him and given himself for him, so that he was now 'justified by faith', able at last to 'live to God', and empowered to do so, as he said, by the Christ who '[now] lives in me' (Gal. 2:19–20).

The Two Jerusalems (Gal. 4:21–31)

Slavery and freedom are critical in Paul's complex allegory[2] of the two sons of Abraham, which also contrasts two Jerusalems. This passage, despite its exegetical issues, is an entry point into the understanding of Galatians and Paul's struggles with 'Jerusalem' as the world centre of law observance.

'The present (*nun*) Jerusalem' (4:25), which is the 'Jerusalem that is *below*' (i.e. as implied by contrast with 'the Jerusalem that is *above*' – v. 26), is an unqualified evil. This 'Jerusalem' was born 'according to the flesh' (not 'through promise') to the union between Abraham and the 'slave woman' Hagar (v. 23). This 'slave woman' is 'from Mount Sinai in Arabia' (i.e. the law) who 'corresponds with the present Jerusalem for she is in *slavery* with her children'. Paul did not mean the bricks and mortar of the city but the law-centred worldview of her inhabitants that made them slaves.

Furthermore, 'just as at the time he who was born according to the flesh [Ishmael] persecuted him[3] who was born according to the Spirit [Isaac],[4] so also it is now' (v. 29). In other words, this enslaved 'Jerusalem' was a would-be slave master and persecutor of the free, that is, of Paul and of Paul's spiritual children in Syria–Cilicia and Galatia.

On the positive side of the allegory the child 'born through promise' to Abraham and Sarah corresponds to the 'Jerusalem above' who is 'free' (i.e. not under law). Paul concludes, 'So, brothers, we are not children of the slave but of the free woman. For freedom Christ has set us free; stand firm therefore, and do not submit again to a yoke of slavery' (4:31 – 5:1).

In sum, 'the present Jerusalem' is:

(i) in 'slavery' under law (cf. 4:3–5); and
(ii) is persecuting those who had been set free from law (those redeemed – liberated – in Christ, both Jews and Gentiles).

Freedom for Jews and Gentiles in Jeopardy (Gal. 3:15 – 4:10)

Paul writes at length about the freedom that Jews and Gentiles had enjoyed through welcoming the gospel message.

Freedom for Jews (3:15 – 4:7)

In his climax to the section beginning at verse 15 Paul declared to his *Jewish* readers that 'God sent forth his Son . . . to *redeem* those who were under law', adding, 'so you (singular) are *no longer a slave*, but a son, and if a son, then an heir through God' (4:4–5,7).

Paul reached this high point by three exegetical steps (3:15–25). First, in verses 15–18 Paul asserted that the law was given 430 years *after* God made his covenant with Abraham, a covenant that he would not annul because even human covenants are unchangeable. That covenant made a promise to Abraham's 'offspring' (*sperma*) in the singular sense, that is, to Christ (and those attached to Christ by faith, whom he was to 'inherit'). Paul excludes 'offspring' in the plural sense for that would mean Abraham's physical descendants, members of the Jerusalem-based nation Israel, who were under slavery. Rather, he is thinking of those who are 'in Christ', who have 'put on' Christ (3:26–9).

Second, in verses 19–20 Paul further diminished the status of law by implying that God made his covenant with Abraham *directly* whereas he gave the law at Mt Sinai indirectly 'through angels by an intermediary [Moses]'.

This prompts Paul to ask, 'Why then the law?' to which he replied, 'It was added because of transgressions', by which he most likely meant 'to *define*[5] transgressions'. This era of law was to be for a limited time 'until the offspring (Christ) should come to whom the promise had been made'. In other words, God gave the law for a negative purpose, to point up the need for the One promised to Abraham who was to set the people free from the slavery to law.[6]

Third, in verses 21–5 Paul points to the imprisoning effects of the epoch of law, which he signalled by a fivefold repetition of the preposition *hypo*, 'under', used negatively.

3:22	the Scripture imprisoned everything *under* sin
3:23	we were held captive *under* the law
3:25	we are no longer *under* a guardian
4:2	he is *under* guardians and managers (*epitropous . . . kai oikonomous*)
4:3	we were enslaved to (*hypo*, 'under') the elementary principles

To be 'under law' but unable and unwilling to 'abide by' and 'do' 'everything written in the Book of the Law' was, indeed, to be cursed – by God (3:10,13). But Christ redeemed Jews 'under law' (4:6) by 'becoming a curse' for us – i.e. us *Jews* (3:13; cf. 2:15–17).

Galatians 3:13–14	Galatians 4:4–6
Christ *redeemed* us from the curse of the law by becoming a curse for us . . . so that we might receive the promised *Spirit* through faith	God sent . . . his Son . . . born under the law, to *redeem* those who were under the law . . . God has sent the *Spirit* of his Son into our hearts

Because Israel was 'under law' its people were 'under sin' and accordingly under a *paidagōgos*, a harsh inference.[7] Thus the role of law was to deprive the covenant people of freedom,[8] to prepare them for the Son whom God was to send, whose mission was to set free those under the slavery of law.[9]

Paul's argument in Galatians 3:15 – 4:7 was that God had set his covenant people free from the curse of the law by sending them his Son and the Spirit of his Son. Those who 'belong to Christ' (*Christou*) are 'Abraham's offspring' (*sperma*), 'heirs according to promise' (3:29). His implied message to them was not to regard themselves any longer as 'captive under the law' (3:23).

It appears that those 'false brothers' who unsuccessfully demanded the circumcision of Titus subsequently reacted against Paul by reinforcing the Jerusalem believers in an ever-deepening expression of law-based Judaism. Paul's insistence on freedom for Gentiles appears to have caused a reaction towards a more intense engagement in law by the messianic community in the Holy City.

It was from that ever-more-conservative bastion among Jewish Christians in Jerusalem that various envoys went forth to impose the 'works of the law' on Paul's Gentile adherents in the Diaspora. In Galatia this meant submission to male circumcision (5:3,12; 6:12) and the observation of the Jewish Calendar (4:8–11; see below) whereas in Antioch it meant compliance with Jewish dietary requirements (2:11–14).

The argument in 3:15 – 4:7 is critically important. It demonstrated that Israel was now free through the Christ who had come, even if most Jews chose to remain in slavery. The reason Paul so carefully developed his exegetical argument related to *Israel* was to show his Gentile readers how foolish it would be to trade their new freedom for slavery.

Freedom for Gentiles (4:8–11)

(i) An exchanged slavery

In his initial visit Paul had been a messenger of freedom to the Galatian Gentiles among his readers. Previously they had been enslaved to 'those that by nature are not gods' (v. 8), most likely referring to their worship of the sun, moon and stars. On a spur of the Sultan Dagh range above Antioch of Pisidia was a major temple and cult for the Phrygian moon god, Mên. This lunar god was also connected with fertility, healing and punishment, and was characteristically depicted with the points of a crescent moon on his shoulders. Many people of the southern Galatian region were moon worshippers. But *God* created the heavenly bodies (as in Gen. 1:14–19). Accordingly they are not 'by nature' gods, in reality, 'not really gods at all' (Gal. 4:8, New Jerusalem Bible).

Paul, however, was not charging these Gentiles with returning to the slavery of their former gods. Rather, he was referring to them 'turning back'[10] to a new slavery, slavery to the law. Due to the powerful influence of the Jewish-Christian counter-mission they had begun to observe 'days and months and seasons and years', that is, 'the works of the law'. Paul is referring to their observances of the Jewish religious calendar, to Jewish days (Sabbaths), Jewish 'months' (e.g. the New Moon Festival – Num. 10:10), Jewish 'seasons' (Passover, Tabernacles, Pentecost), and Jewish 'years' (Jubilee and Sabbatical Years). In other words, they have exchanged the bondage to the former gods for the bondage of the Jewish Calendar.

Paul portrays these Jewish observances as 'the weak and worthless elementary principles of the world (*ta asthenē kai ptōcha stoicheia*)', words usually applied to the objects of pagan idolatry. Earlier (Gal. 4:3) he employed the words 'elementary principles of the world' to mean the first principles (like a, b, c in the alphabet), to point to the immaturity of the law-bound Jews who had not moved on to the maturity of 'freedom' in Christ. In verse 9 he seems to be combining the elements of both immaturity and idolatry.

So lacking in discernment are the Galatian believers that Paul fears he may have 'labored in vain' in coming to them (v. 11). Clearly they are in danger of coming under another slavery.

(ii) A new slavery

Paul narrated his allegory of Abraham's two sons in order to exhort the Galatian Gentiles not to submit to the imposition of circumcision by those who would 'force' this upon them (6:12). 'For freedom Christ has set us free . . . every man who accepts circumcision . . . is obligated (*opheitetēs*) to keep the whole law' (5:1,3). In Christ the Jews are free (4:4–5) so it follows that Gentiles are no less free, the sign of which is the inspiration of the Spirit enabling them to cry, 'Abba, Father' (3:1–5; 4:6). Having received the Spirit by 'hearing with faith' it would indeed be 'foolish' for Gentiles to turn to 'the works of law' (3:1,3).

Summary

Among Paul's Galatian readers were both Jews and Gentiles. Each had been subject to distinctive forms of spiritual slavery, Jews to the Mosaic law and Gentiles to the worship of the gods. In reaction to Paul, Christian Jews in Jerusalem were coming under renewed legalism and, through their counter-mission, Gentiles in the Diaspora were coming under slavery, whether the exchange of slavery from the worship of the gods to the observation of the calendar or the new slavery of circumcision. Jewish believers were intensifying their submission to law whereas Gentile believers were embracing 'works of the law' for the first time. Paul characterizes this submission to law – whether in Jerusalem or the Diaspora – as a mark of 'the present (*nun*) Jerusalem', that is, of slavery.

Who Does Paul Mean by this 'Present (*nun*) Jerusalem'?

The 'pillars' in Jerusalem?

Paul's 'allegory' of the 'two sons' is, in effect, his damning critique of 'the present Jerusalem'. But of whom is he speaking? It does not appear to have been the 'pillars' James, Peter and John. These leaders supported Paul against the 'false brothers' in Jerusalem in resisting the demand for Titus' circumcision, who 'added nothing' to Paul's circumcision-free message to the Gentiles which he had been preaching for many years, and who endorsed his circumcision-free mission to 'go' to the Gentiles (Gal. 2:3–6,9). Based on Paul's account of his visit to Jerusalem in *c.*47, it does not appear that Paul regarded the three 'pillars' as 'the present Jerusalem' since they had been so supportive at that time.

But what are we to make of the events only a year or so later, when *James* sent envoys to Antioch to put pressure on *Peter* and the Jewish members who withdrew from table-fellowship with the Gentiles (Gal. 2:11–12)? These men who had supported Paul in Jerusalem now opposed him.

The most reasonable explanation is that geopolitical circumstances in Judea in the late forties had changed,[11] that had the effect of shifting the balance of power in Jerusalem from James and Peter to the circumcision activists. In any case, Peter would have been long regarded with suspicion in Jerusalem because of his engagement with the Samaritans (Acts 8:14–25) and with the gentile Cornelius (Acts 11:2 – 'when Peter went up to Jerusalem the circumcision party criticized him, saying, "You went to uncircumcised men and ate with them"').[12]

Jerusalem's circumcision activists

Galatians bears witness to profound opposition to Paul by a group within the messianic community in Jerusalem. We encounter them first as 'false brothers' in Jerusalem in *c.*47 who attempted to impose circumcision on Titus, the Greek (2:3–5). Next we meet them as those who had travelled from Jerusalem to 'agitate' the Galatians by requiring the circumcision of the Gentile believers (1:7; 5:2; 6:12). Next, chronologically speaking, we meet them as 'the circumcision party' who had come from Jerusalem[13] to Antioch demanding that Jewish believers not eat with their Gentile brothers and sisters thus demanding that Gentile believers 'Judaize', 'live as Jews' (2:11–12). Finally, we see them 'troubling' Paul's Gentile churches in Syria and Cilicia (Acts 15:23,41).

The 'false brothers' in Jerusalem and the 'agitators' (from Jerusalem) in Galatia were quite direct in their demands to Gentile believers: 'we require you to be circumcised'. Their counterparts in Antioch, however, sought to achieve the same outcome indirectly by insisting that Gentiles fulfil 'works of the law' by dietary compliance.[14] The circumcision party from Jerusalem might not have directly insisted on the circumcision of Gentile believers in the Syrian capital but that seems to have been their long-term objective.

Some scholars think that these are different groups representing differing viewpoints. Why else would Paul refer to them in three different ways? The answer may be that Paul did not wish to inflate their mission in the minds of the Galatians by giving it a uniform title. In any case, that mission might not have been tightly coordinated, but might have represented a loose association within the faith community in Jerusalem.

Objectives of 'the present Jerusalem'

The three references to activist groups give us some idea of their concerns. The 'false brothers' attempted to have the 'Greek' Titus circumcised (Gal. 2:3–4). The Jerusalem 'agitators' in Galatia sought to impose circumcision on Gentiles (Gal. 5:2; 6:12) and the observation of the Jewish Calendar (Gal. 4:10) regarding 'days' (Sabbaths), 'months' (e.g. the New Moon Festival – Num. 10:10), 'seasons' (Passover, Tabernacles, Pentecost), and 'years' (Jubilee and Sabbatical Years). 'The circumcision party' from Jerusalem in Antioch demanded dietary compliance from Gentiles (Gal. 2:12; cf. Acts 15:1) and, it appears, circumcision in wider Syria and Cilicia (cf. Acts 15:23,41).

When the objectives of these three groups are considered together a picture emerges of Jewish Christians in Jerusalem who were strongly committed to the 'traditions' of their fathers and who insisted that inclusion in the covenant required, in effect, that Gentile believers 'live like Jews' (i.e. 'to Judaize' – cf. Gal. 2:14), ultimately to become Jewish proselytes.

This understanding is consistent with Luke's account of the Incident in Antioch and the subsequent council in Jerusalem. The 'believers' who declared that it was 'necessary (*dei*) to circumcise [the Gentiles] and to order them to keep the law of Moses' belonged to 'the party (*haeresis*) of the *Pharisees*' (Acts 15:5). These 'believers' who were 'Pharisees' had visited Antioch and then reiterated their strong viewpoint shortly afterwards in Jerusalem (Acts 15:1,5).[15]

Later references confirm this general picture. In *c.*57 when Paul made his final visit to Jerusalem he was told of 'many thousands ... among the Jews of those who have believed. They are all *zealous for the law,* and they have been told about you that you teach all the Jews who are among the Gentiles to forsake Moses, telling them not to circumcise their children or walk according to our customs' (Acts 21:20–21, our italics). Even allowing for some exaggeration this is evidence for a large group of Jewish believers in Jerusalem who were zealous for the law, and who believed that Paul urged Jews in the Diaspora to abandon Moses (i.e. law) and taught them not to circumcise their children or follow Jewish practices.

This description points to a substantial church in Jerusalem that was 'Pharisaic' in outlook. While their complaint was about Paul and his influence with Jews, and not Gentiles, it is reasonable to regard Jewish Christianity in Jerusalem in the late fifties as a conservative intensification of the situation a decade earlier where the believers who belonged to 'the party of the Pharisees' were powerfully influential, even if they did not carry the day at the Jerusalem Council. By *c.*57, however, conservative influences had become dominant.

Finally, in AD 62, following Annas' unlawful execution of James in Jerusalem, those who successfully protested to the incoming procurator (Albinus) were the 'inhabitants of the city who were considered the most fair-minded and who were *strict in observance of the law*'.[16] These influential and effective protestors appear to have been Pharisees, and among them would have been friends and supporters of James, that is to say, *believers who were Pharisees.* Josephus' comment about the conservative supporters of James is consistent with Luke's snapshot of the Jerusalem church five years earlier.

Paul's narrative in Galatians 2:1–10 gives the impression that the 'pillars' were all-powerful in *c.*47, securing victory for Paul against the attempt of the 'false brothers' to circumcise Titus. However, Paul's words that the 'pillars' '*seemed* to be influential' (2:2,6, our italics) may not have been sarcastic, but may have represented the truth that the 'false brothers' were actually very powerful in Jerusalem. Was Paul actually saying that the 'false brothers' were truly 'influential' ones in the Jerusalem church, even though on this occasion Paul got the better of them?

On that occasion, Paul and the 'pillars' did prevail, but it was the last time they did – at least in Jerusalem. The worsening relations between the Jews and their Roman occupiers in the fifties and sixties were accompanied by the rise of violent factions like the *Sicarii*[17] and apocalyptic 'sign prophets', for example, the 'Egyptian prophet'.[18] In these circumstances the wider population of the Holy City – which was entirely Jewish – inevitably became more conservative, that is, 'Pharisaic', and therefore increasingly hostile to Paul and his circumcision-free mission among Gentiles.

Paul's Biblical Apologetic (Gal. 3:6–25)

In Galatians 3:6–25 Paul expounded his scriptural apologetic which served both as his defence of his gospel and as his attack against the counter-mission.

When did Paul develop this way of interpreting Israel's history? It would not have been his understanding pre-Damascus. Furthermore, it is unlikely that he worked it out only when he came to write to the Galatians. It is more likely that he had developed this narrative during the decade or so he spent in Syria and Cilicia (AD 37–47), if not beforehand in Damascus and Arabia (AD 34–6). Therefore, these texts would have been thoroughly worked out and settled in Paul's mind when he travelled to Galatia and preached 'the faith' to Jews and Gentiles. In Galatians 3:6–25 Paul was reminding the Galatians of what they already had been told.

Accordingly, the opinion that Paul was *responding* to the texts of the counter-mission is less likely than that this apologetic was already well formed beforehand, including in 'the regions of Syria and Cilicia'.

The counter-mission's awareness of Paul's scriptural apologetic

Likewise, it is unlikely that the Jerusalem circumcision activists in Galatia were hearing Paul's gospel and scriptural apologetic for

the first time. According to Galatians 1:23 the churches in Judea
– including the church in Jerusalem – were hearing reports from
'the regions of Syria and Cilicia' throughout Paul's ten years there
that he was 'preaching the faith he had once tried to destroy'.
Since Paul was preaching that faith to Gentiles as well as to Jews it
is reasonable to assume that the churches in Judea were aware of
Paul's view of the Old Testament texts that emphasized Abraham
and de-emphasized Moses. Paul's faith-centred but circumcision-free gospel demanded Paul's concentrated 'faith' focus in
Galatians 5:6 ('in Christ Jesus neither circumcision nor uncircumcision counts for anything, but only faith working through love').

Moreover, it is likely that Paul employed these texts when
he brought Titus the uncircumcised Greek to Jerusalem in *c*.47
(Gal. 2:3–4). Paul may well have applied these texts to secure the
support of the 'pillars' and to resist pressure of the 'false brothers'
for the circumcision of Titus.

Furthermore, we note that James' letter also cited Genesis 15:6
but to argue against 'faith' without 'works' (Jas 2:23,14–20) and to
assert that 'a person is justified by works and not by faith alone'
(Jas 2:24). The verbal parallels with Paul's preaching (as reflected in
Gal. 2:16) are too close to be accidental.[19] This cluster of keywords
when considered alongside James' citation of Genesis 15:6 suggest
that Paul's scriptural apologetic – or, probably a distorted version
of it – was known in Jerusalem well before Paul's departure for
Galatia. We conclude that the circumcision activists in the Holy
City knew Paul's scriptural arguments before they set out to
correct his teachings.

'Jerusalem' in Galatians and Romans

How are we to reconcile Paul's negative references to 'Jerusalem'
in Galatians 4:25 (and by inference, Gal. 4:26) with his positive reference in Romans 15:19? Galatians 4:21–31 portrays 'the
present Jerusalem' as enslaved by the law and, by implication, a
persecutor of those free from law – believers among the Galatian
Jews and Gentiles – children who had been born according to the
divine promise.

By contrast, in Romans 15:19 Paul declared that Jerusalem was
the pivot from which his gospel has been 'fulfilled' among the

Gentiles 'in a circle' around as far as Illyricum. Paul did not say, as many translations do, that he had 'fully *preached*' the gospel in that arc, but that he had 'fulfilled the gospel of Christ' (*peplērōkenai to euangelion tou Christou*). The context indicates that by his gospel activities (which were more comprehensive than preaching alone)[20] Paul was being used by Christ in bringing the promises of God to the patriarchs into reality among the Gentiles (Rom. 15:8,18).

Furthermore, Paul was in the process of bringing back to Jerusalem the material gifts of the Gentiles, to acknowledge their spiritual debt to the believers in that city from which the gospel had originally come forth (Rom. 15:27).

How are we to explain Paul's radically different references to Jerusalem? The answer is that the apostle did not write his letters to become raw materials for 'theologies of Paul'. To the contrary, each letter Paul wrote was for a distinct and living situation. Accordingly, his letters are to be read on a case-by-case basis, aware of Paul's passionate way of writing. It is doubtful that Paul would find any inconsistency between Galatians and Romans in their respective references to Jerusalem. At their respective times of writing both perspectives were true. This provides a caution against a 'flat' systematizing of Paul's theology, independent of the respective contexts of the letters.

In passing, the radically different understandings of 'Jerusalem' in Galatians and Romans suggest that Paul had not written these letters in close sequence. It is often assumed that Paul wrote Galatians at about the same time as Romans, on account of their similar interests in 'faith' and 'justification'. According to the argument in Appendix 1, Galatians was Paul's earliest (extant) letter, written in *c*.48. His radically different understanding of 'Jerusalem' supports a lapse of time before Paul wrote Romans, which most scholars think was written in *c*.57.

Spiritual Freedom

Paul emerges from his letter to the Galatians as a 'free' man and as a staunch defender of 'freedom' against those who were attempting to deprive Jewish and Gentile believers of their freedom.

In the course of the letter Paul reviewed his life story from the time he 'persecuted the church' (1:13) until the Incident in Antioch (2:11–14), a period of about fifteen years (34–48). An important question is: when, within this period, did Paul regard his 'freedom' to have begun?

Possible options include:

(i)   from the Damascus event in *c.*34;
(ii) from the first return visit to Jerusalem in *c.*36 when he 'visited' Peter and 'saw' James;
(iii) during his Syria–Cilicia years, *c.*37–46;
(iv) during his sojourn in Antioch, *c.*46–7; or
(v)   at the time of his second visit to Jerusalem in *c.*47.

Based on the following observations in Galatians we conclude that Paul became 'free' from the time of the Damascus event in *c.*34. First, 'the gospel' Paul preached to the Galatians in *c.*47 'came to' him in *c.*34 'by revelation' (1:11–12), when God was 'pleased to reveal his Son to [in]' him for him to proclaim him 'among the Gentiles' (1:16).

Second, Paul did not then confer (*prosanethemēn*) with 'flesh and blood' – including the Jerusalem apostles – about the gospel he 'received' at Damascus (1:16–17). Paul visited the leading apostles Peter and James in Jerusalem in *c.*36 but strongly implies that they were not the source of the divine commission to proclaim the Son of God.

Third, when Paul returned to Jerusalem in *c.*47 he stated explicitly that James, Peter and John 'added nothing' (*ouden prosanethento*) to the circumcision-free gospel he had been preaching among the Gentiles. Rather, they supported Paul against the false brothers' attempt to circumcise Titus and endorsed his plan to 'go' to the Gentiles with the circumcision-free message (2:3–6,9).

In short, Paul's insistence on the law-free message throughout Galatians, whether directly to the Galatians (2:21), or indirectly to Peter, Barnabas and the Jewish believers in Antioch (2:11–14), is consistent with the 'gospel' that 'came to' him 'by revelation', when 'it pleased God to reveal his Son to [in]' him in Damascus.

An important point to make is that Paul did not separate God's *commission* to proclaim a message among the Gentiles with the actual content of the message he was to proclaim. Commission and message are inseparable. So it was not that the message *evolved* over the years after the commission in Damascus. The gospel he preached among the Galatians in *c*.47 was the gospel he 'received' in Damascus in *c*.34. God revealed his Son to (and in) Paul for Paul to proclaim him 'among the Gentiles' (*en tois ethnesin*).

How is it, then, that Paul came to insist that the 'truth of the gospel' was its freedom from the *necessity* to be circumcised (2:5; cf. 2:14; 6:12)? Had there been a shift from a message centred on the Son of God to a message about freedom from 'works of the law', circumcision in particular? Was Paul's gospel message actually constant throughout the years between Damascus and writing to the Galatians?

The answer is found in his words, 'through the law I died to the law, so that I might live to God' (2:19). Paul acknowledged that as one who lived 'through the law', and who 'was advancing in Judaism' (1:14), he 'did not live to God'. It was only when he 'died to the law' that he 'lived to God'. He defines that *moment* by the words, 'it is *no longer* (*ouketi*) I who live, but Christ who lives in me' and 'the life I *now* (*nun*) live in the flesh I live by faith in the Son of God, who loved me and gave himself for me' (2:20, our italics). The eschatological moment signalled by 'no longer'/'now' points to the time when 'faith came' (3:23), which for Paul meant understanding that 'the Son of God . . . loved me and gave himself for me'. That was the moment when Paul 'died to the law' and began 'to live to God'.

Paul's proclamation of the Son of God was no abstract, merely doctrinal message. Paul underwent a profound and permanent change in his heart of hearts. It is inferred from his words that – however dimly beforehand – he knew that law provided no access through to the Almighty. At Damascus God 'revealed' his crucified and risen Son as the means of that access into the presence of the One he now called 'Abba, Father' (4:6).

But this Christ-centred access meant that there was no other access because Paul now knew that God required absolute compliance with the law (3:10), the law that exposed human sin and was therefore unfulfillable. In a word, Paul came to understand that as a man 'in Christ' he was blessed with the heaven-sent Spirit but that on the contrary, as a man 'in' and 'under' law, he was subject to the divine curse. The Damascus revelation, which opened Paul to the Son of God *crucified*, at the same moment closed Paul to law, and 'works of the law' as a means to 'live to God'. Thus 'faith in Christ' and 'works of the law' could not be complementary, as the circumcision agitators claimed, but were irreconcilably antithetical.

This 'revelation' from God about his crucified Son established the fact of universal sinfulness, a fact that was as true for law-keeping Jews as for law-less Gentiles. Thus Paul must forcibly insist to Peter that 'we [Jews] have believed in Christ Jesus, in order to be justified by faith in Christ and not by works of the law, because by works of the law no one [lit. no flesh] will be justified' (2:16). Because of sin law was not a route to righteousness for Jews, any more that it was for Gentiles.

Paul's paradigm shift was by no means merely theoretical. Rather, Paul's radical and sustained change in direction cannot be explained apart from the divine presence that was now 'in' him. He testified that God was pleased to 'reveal his Son in (*en*) me' (see 1:16) and that 'Christ . . . lives in me' (2:20). He wrote that 'God has sent the Spirit of his Son into our hearts, crying, "Abba! Father!"' (4:6) and that 'through the Spirit, by faith, we ourselves eagerly wait for the hope of righteousness' (5:5). Paul's moral compass was now the Spirit, not the law (although the law informed the directions of that compass). 'The fruit of the Spirit is love, joy, peace, patience, kindness, goodness, faithfulness, gentleness, self-control' (5:22–3) – the character traits of the Son of God whom Paul preached – against which, he added ironically 'there is no law'.

The Galatians received the Spirit as they 'heard with faith' the message of the Crucified One, not by doing the 'works of the law' (3:1–3). Their recent spiritual revolution had been Paul's story a decade and a half earlier and throughout the years since. His story and theirs coincided.

This was the spiritual freedom of those who belong to the 'Jerusalem that is above' which the members of the 'present Jerusalem', the 'Jerusalem' that is 'below', were seeking to take away, replacing it with slavery under law. The freedom that Paul had come to know at and from Damascus, and for which he had contended in Jerusalem, Galatia and Antioch, was the liberty of 'the heart set free'. Paul now knew that the law was beyond fulfilment and that under law he was under a curse but that, more importantly still, the Son of God had borne that curse for him to bring him freedom, in the power of the Spirit and in the ready access he enjoyed to his 'Abba, Father'.

Conclusion

In Paul's allegory of the two sons of Abraham he identified 'the present Jerusalem' as both enslaved and the instrument of slavery and persecution. She is enslaved because she does not claim the freedom that is hers in Christ but retains her commitment to law (3:6 – 4:7). She is an instrument of slavery because her emissaries go forth and seek to enforce that slavery upon Gentiles, in Galatia (5:1,3; 6:12; 4:8–11), Antioch (2:11–14) and Syria and Cilicia (Acts 15:23,41).

Who, then, does Paul identify as 'the present Jerusalem'? While Paul gives due prominence to the 'pillars', James, Peter and John, it is evident that he does not regard them as the slave master, 'the Jerusalem that is below'. Rather, he directs the Galatian readers' attention to those he does not name, but variously describes as 'false brothers' (2:4), 'agitators' (1:7; cf. 5:10,12; 6:12), and 'the circumcision party' (2:12). Based on hints in the book of Acts it seems that these activists for 'works of the law' were connected with the Pharisees (Acts 15:1,5; cf. 21:20). It seems that the more liberal attitudes of James and Peter diminished in Jerusalem in the face of more conservative forces that were reacting against Paul's teaching on freedom from law.

Paul, however, was a champion for 'freedom' against those who sought to impose the slavery of 'works of the law'. Paul's own sense of freedom was profound. Confronted at Damascus by the crucified but glorified Christ Paul comprehended that the Son of God had loved him and had given himself for him. Through that understanding Paul 'died to the law', now grasping that it did not provide a route to knowing God. Rather, his new faith in the Crucified One was accompanied by an outpouring of the Spirit, providing a radically new inner dynamic and new moral direction.

Accordingly, Paul implies that he was a true son of Abraham, a man of faith, to whom righteousness was imputed (3:7), no longer a slave but set free by faith in the death of the Promised One and blessed by the inner presence of the Spirit of God's Son (4:6,7).

Paul's witness was directed to Jews and Gentiles among the Galatians. Galatian Jews could not have been unaffected by Paul's biblical arguments about the priority of God's dealings with Abraham, the man of faith, and the enslaving nature of law, and Paul's own discovery of freedom in the Son of God who had loved him and given himself for him. The Gentiles among his readers would have heard strong arguments not to submit to circumcision and other 'works of the law'. No doubt Paul wrote his allegory of the free son and the slave son to give very strong direction to Jews and Gentiles to choose the path of freedom and not be diverted from it.

11

Syria and Cilicia as the Background to Galatians

It is striking that there are so few references to Paul's activities in Syria and Cilicia even though he spent about ten years there and, moreover, at a very early period in Christian history (AD 37–47). There are a relatively small number of studies of Paul's activities in Syrian and Cilicia, corresponding with the paucity of biblical texts – Galatians 1:21–3; 2:2,7–9 and Acts 15:23,41.

Nonetheless, if Galatians is to be dated soon after the mission work in Galatia it would follow that Paul's activities in Syria and Cilicia form the immediate background for both the Galatian mission and the Galatian letter (see Appendix 1 for argument favouring an early dating of Galatians). Yet even if Galatians was written later – whether from Corinth AD 50–52 or Ephesus AD 52–5 – it would remain true that the epistle reflected Paul's thought as worked out in ministry in Syria and Cilicia, including his distinctive exegesis of Old Testament passages that elevated Abraham and diminished Moses.

A major question is: to whom did Paul preach during his decade in Syria and Cilicia? Some scholars argue that Paul did not begin preaching to Gentiles during the 'unknown years', including the decade in the 'regions of Syria and Cilicia'. They point to Acts 13:46 that states Paul only 'turned' to the Gentiles in Antioch in Pisidia, that is in c.47. Against that, however, Acts 15:23,41 and Galatians 2:2,8 (cf. Gal. 1:21–4) make it clear that Paul did preach to Gentiles/the uncircumcised in the years between his 'call' at Damascus and his second return visit to Jerusalem (Gal. 2:1).

Paul in Syria and Cilicia (AD 37–47)

The five synagogue beatings (2 Cor. 11:24) seem to have happened
during the 'unknown years', in particular in Syria and Cilicia in
37–47; Luke's extensive narrative of Paul's later missions, including
his sufferings, has no reference to synagogue beatings in Acts 13 –
28. This would imply that Paul preached in the synagogues during
the 'unknown years'. A good case can be made that the beatings
occurred because Paul informed God-fearers that Christ crucified
and not circumcision was the divinely appointed means of finding
'life' with God. It is likely that Paul gathered believing God-fearers
into the Gentile churches referred to in Acts 15:23,41.

Paul's preaching of 'the faith' in 'the regions of Syria and Cilicia'
repeatedly came to the attention of the churches in Judea (Gal.
1:21–3), no doubt including the church in Jerusalem, during that
decade. Paul had become well known as the former persecutor
who had become an active herald of the faith he had previously
attempted to destroy.

Paul's 'rapture' to paradise 'fourteen years ago', as referred to
in 2 Corinthians 12:2, would have occurred during Paul's years
in Syria and Cilicia, and with it the onset of the 'thorn' for 'the
flesh' (2 Cor. 12:7) that continued with Paul throughout the intervening years. Paul's words are crafted apologetically in answer
to the claims of the 'super-apostles' in Corinth. The Corinthians
would have known what Paul meant but unfortunately from this
distance we don't.

Paul's years in Syria and Cilicia would have provided him with
opportunity to develop his skills as a preacher of the faith. It is
a priori likely that his letters reflected his pastoral preaching in
the Gentile congregations he established within that province (cf.
Acts 15:23,41). Was Paul's letter to the Galatians shaped by Hellenistic speech rhetoric, as urged by H.D. Betz? That seems unlikely,
not least since we have no extant examples of such rhetoric that
might have provided a model for Paul to use. It does seem likely,
however, that elements in the epistle reflected his pastoral teaching
in the churches, for example, the telling of his own story (as in Gal.
1:11–2:14), his distinctive exegesis of Old Testament passages (as
in Gal. 3:6–14; 4:21–31), and his Spirit-based paraenesis (as in Gal.
5:16 – 6:10).

Some scholars have been fascinated by Paul's sojourn in Antioch, capital of the province, despite the probability that Paul spent less than two years there prior to setting out for the mission in Cyprus, Pisidia and Lycaonia (Acts 11:25–6). They believe that Paul's distinctive theology of Jesus as the *Kyrios* and *Huios Theou* were developed in Antioch, as influenced by the Graeco-Oriental cults of the city. However, the possibility of a former Pharisee being captured by such syncretistic influence is slight and, in any case, our knowledge of Antioch's religious world comes from later centuries.

It appears that Paul worked out his basic Christology from the time of the divine intervention at Damascus that was refined during his years of synagogue and church teaching in Syria and Cilicia. The evidence that Antioch influenced Paul's Christology is lacking. It does appear, however, that Paul's decision to travel more intentionally with the circumcision-free message happened during his period in the Syrian capital. It is possible that the period of civic peace under Claudius together with Paul's sense that God had brought 'hardening' to Israel (Rom. 10:16,18–21; 11:7–10,25–32) to open the door to the Gentiles, for the ultimate salvation of Israel, had influenced Paul's missionary decisions while in Antioch.

Paul forced the issue of the circumcision-free gospel in Jerusalem in *c.*47 when he brought the uncircumcised Titus to Jerusalem. Titus was not forced to be circumcised but enjoyed fellowship with the apostolic leadership, who were all Jews.

Paul in Jerusalem and the Counter-Mission to the Uncircumcised (Gal. 2:1–10)

Paul's letter to the Galatians makes it clear that he did not receive his 'call' to proclaim the Son of God among the Gentiles from the apostles in Jerusalem. Paul was not an apostle of the apostles, but of the Lord, Christ. God was the unmediated source of Paul's apostolic commission and authority. Nevertheless, Paul sought the endorsement of Jerusalem for his proposed mission to the uncircumcised.

As Paul 'set before them . . . the gospel [he] proclaimed to the Gentiles' their reaction was to 'add nothing' (Gal. 2:6) to his message and to agree that he 'had not run in vain' throughout the previous fourteen years, including the ten years in Syria and Cilicia (Gal. 2:1–2). The 'pillar' apostles recognized Paul's ministry and message to the Gentiles just as they recognized Peter's ministry and message to the circumcised (Gal. 2:7–8). They supported Paul against the demands of the 'false brothers' for the circumcision of Titus (Gal. 2:3) and gave to Paul the right hand of fellowship for him to 'go' to the Gentiles with the circumcision-free gospel message (Gal. 2:9).

Thus encouraged, Paul accompanied Barnabas on the mission to Cyprus and the borders of Southern Galatia. The outcome of this mission was the formation of the Galatian churches, whose membership now included uncircumcised Gentiles.

Paul's victory in Jerusalem and his subsequent missionary success provoked significant reaction among the pro-circumcision faction within the messianic community in the Holy City, a faction that seems to have been influenced by believers who were Pharisees. The circumcision activists launched three counter-missions attempting to overturn Paul's circumcision-free ministry. One group travelled to Galatia and sought to impose circumcision on Gentile believers. Another group travelled later to Antioch and applied pressure on the Jewish members to withdraw table-fellowship from their Gentile brothers and sisters, a likely first step to requiring them to 'Judaize', that is, to become Jewish proselytes which for males meant circumcision. Yet another group (or perhaps the same group) travelled among Paul's Gentile churches in Syria and Cilicia and, it appears, attempted to impose circumcision and other 'works of the law' upon them (Acts 15:28–9). These incidents following the unsuccessful attempt to force circumcision on Titus were the significant counteractions of the pro-circumcision party in Jerusalem.

Paul's letter to the Galatians was his response to the circumcision mission among the Galatians and the attempt to impose dietary rules on the Gentiles in Antioch. It is reasonable to conclude that Paul wrote Galatians soon after the Incident in Antioch, that is, before the Jerusalem Council in *c*.49 which met to address the issues arising from the Incident in Antioch and the foray of the circumcision party into Paul's churches in Syria and Cilicia.

James and Paul

Like Paul, James had not been a disciple of the historical Jesus. In fact, both men became believers soon after the lifespan of Jesus, James through witnessing the Risen One and Paul through the Damascus christophany. It appears that at first James and his brothers met apart from the mainstream Peter group in Jerusalem (Acts 12:27). This book has argued that various 'sayings' of Jesus that were subsequently incorporated in the Letter of James were collected in Jerusalem by James and his companions.

When in *c*.42 Peter was forced to flee from King Herod Agrippa I, the leadership of the Jerusalem Christian community naturally fell to James, brother of the Lord. When Agrippa died in 44 it was possible for Peter to reappear in Judea, but by then James was firmly in charge as the first of the three 'pillars' of the Jerusalem church. By the time of the Jerusalem Council in *c*.49 James was clearly the sole leader of the Jerusalem church, a position he would hold until his martyrdom in *c*.62.

On Paul's return to Antioch in *c*.48 following the mission to Galatia he was confronted with the crisis known as the Incident in Antioch. Circumcision activists came from James to Antioch and applied pressure on Peter to separate from Gentile believers at the common meal. Peter succumbed to this pressure, followed by Barnabas and the entire Jewish cohort. Although the presenting issue was dietary the ultimate question was whether Jewish believers could have fellowship with the uncircumcised. This represented pressure on Gentiles in Antioch to become fully-fledged proselytes. Paul vehemently but unsuccessfully opposed this.

James' volte-face remains a mystery. After having endorsed Paul's proposed circumcision-free mission in Jerusalem we can only guess James' motive for acting as he did so soon afterwards. The geopolitical situation in Jerusalem under Tiberius Alexander may have plunged the Jews of Jerusalem into ever-deeper religious nationalism. Perhaps that situation contributed to James' change of heart.

Whatever the reason, it appears that this incident spelled the end of Paul's direct relationships with James. Even Paul's final visit to Jerusalem in *c*.57 was marked by cool exchanges.

Peter and Paul

Despite Luke's overall focus on Paul in the book of Acts, Peter was the dominant figure in the first decade and a half in early Christianity. Peter was the first (male) witness of the resurrected Christ, who saw him more than once. Peter's unchallenged leadership of the twelve disciples of Jesus continued after the first Easter as the head of the new movement in Jerusalem and the land of Israel. This leadership was made clear by the narrative of Acts 1 – 11 and by Paul's references to Peter in Galatians. It was to Peter that Paul came to 'visit' during his first return visit to Jerusalem (Gal. 1:18) and by reference to his mission to the circumcised throughout the intervening years AD 33–47 (Gal. 2:7–9).

It seems, though, that Peter's leadership in Judea became progressively problematic. His visit to the Samaritans, with whom Jews would not fraternize, followed by his baptism of the Gentile, Cornelius, must have cast a shadow over Peter in the wider Jewish community of the Holy City, as well as among the believers. Agrippa's opportunistic capture of Peter with the intention of execution is a clear indication of his unpopularity and vulnerability in Jerusalem. Peter's support for fellowship with the uncircumcised Titus would have confirmed the worst fears that many felt about Peter within the narrower community of the believers, to say nothing of the outrage felt within Jewish Jerusalem.

Peter's migration to Antioch must be understood in terms of his increasingly precarious position in Jerusalem. Inevitably, though, news came back to Jerusalem about Peter's now established unreliability in upholding Jewish values. Peter was eating with Gentiles in a common meal in Antioch. This invited a rebuke from James that was sent to Antioch via envoys whom Paul calls 'the circumcision party' (Gal. 2:12).

It is not clear why James had retreated from his support of Paul's circumcision-free gospel in Jerusalem a year or so earlier. As suggested above, James' stance may have been influenced by unexpected political developments that made even more tenuous the already difficult situation of Christian Jews in Jerusalem. Furthermore, Antioch had a large and volatile Jewish community whose negative reaction to Peter may have sent a backwash south to Jerusalem.

In the ensuing public showdown in Antioch, Peter followed by Barnabas and the entire membership of Jewish believers resisted the arguments of Paul and held their line against the Gentile Christians. This resulted in the schism in the church in Antioch. The Jews, with Peter and Barnabas, went one way while Paul and the Gentiles went another.

The schism in Antioch in *c*.48 seems not to have ended the cooperation between Peter and Paul. Evidently Peter visited Corinth AD 52–4 during Paul's absence in Ephesus. Paul's several references to Peter in 1 Corinthians are generally positive however (1 Cor. 1:12; 3:21; 9:6; 15:5). It is possible, however, that Paul later blamed Peter for providing an open door for the Jewish 'super-apostles' to visit the Achaian capital and pursue ministry with the Jews, including Jewish Christians, in that city (cf. 2 Cor. 10:13–16). Paul's decision not to settle in Rome, but merely to pass through en route to Spain, was due to his scruple not to build on 'another man's foundation', a likely reference to Peter who appears to have come to Rome by the time Paul wrote Romans (in AD 57).

In fact, the incident in Antioch coincidentally marked the end of Peter's historical visibility. After the schism in Antioch in *c*.48 Peter becomes an almost invisible man. We know that he was still around, but we are unsure where he was or what he was doing.

Window into the Mind of Paul: Galatians 2:15–21

In a soliloquy-like passage Paul reflects further on the Incident in Antioch and speaks, as it were, for himself and Peter. His point is that, even as lifelong Jews he and Peter could not be justified by 'works of the law' but only 'by faith in Jesus Christ' (2:15–16). Paul, resists Peter's counter-argument that such an understanding would lower law-keeping Jews like them to the same low standard as Gentile sinners (2:17).

Furthermore – and now speaking just for himself – Paul rejects absolutely the possibility that he will restore the law as a means to finding 'life' with God (2:18; cf. 2:19). To the contrary, his previous attempts to reach God through law failed so completely that he will say, 'through the law I died to the law' (2:19a). Although a tantalizingly brief statement it does imply that during his pre-Damascus

years Paul had become aware of his failure to observe the law of
God. Presumably, this means a failure to observe the law *from the
heart* since elsewhere he was 'confident' that he was 'blameless' in
regards to the rites of the law considered from an external viewpoint (Phil. 3:4–6). Inwardly, however, Paul faced another reality
– the ineradicable sin he found within him in relation to the law, as
explored later in Romans 7:7–25.

In Paul's next few sentences (Gal. 2:19b–20) he takes us into his
mind, as from the Damascus event when God revealed his Son *in*
Paul (Gal. 1:16; cf. 2 Cor. 4:6 – 'God shone in our hearts'). From
that moment Paul had been 'crucified with Christ', attached to his
cross, spelling his death to law and his resurrected life to God, his
'Abba', Father. From that moment the risen Christ (through the
Spirit[1]) lived within Paul.

This was the life change for Paul that explains the radical new
direction he took, that changed his understanding of the meaning
of the sacred Scriptures, as in his exegesis of texts in Galatians
3:6–14; 4:21–31.

Although Paul continued to live 'in the flesh' Christ also (by the
Spirit) lived in him, a twofold reality that prepared the way for
his later exposition of 'the works of the flesh' and their antithesis,
'the fruit of the Spirit' (Gal. 5:16–25). But the life he 'now lives in
the flesh' was the life of faith (i.e. not of 'works of the law') that
was directed toward the Son of God who – as Paul now knew –
had 'loved' him and had 'given himself' in crucifixion 'for' (*hyper*)
Paul, by becoming a curse 'for' (*hyper*) him (Gal. 3:13).

This explains why Paul would be a 'transgressor' if he were to
reinstate law as a way of reaching God. Accordingly, he concludes
his argument, 'I do not nullify the grace of God, for if justification (*dikaiosynē* – 'righteousness') were through the law, then
Christ died for no purpose' (2:21). These are Paul's last words in
response to Peter's admonition to Paul that Gentile believers in
Antioch should 'Judaize', 'live like Jews' and practise 'works of
the law' like dietary compliance.

Paul concluded his extensive memoir with his verbalized reflection on the confrontation with Peter in Antioch. When we move on
into the next passage and hear of the Galatians' experience of the
Spirit (Gal. 3:1–5) we find a parallel with Paul's own experience
of the Spirit. In Galatians 2:19–21 Paul wrote that his experience

of the Spirit ('Christ . . . lives in me' – v. 20) arose directly out of his access to God through faith in and attachment to the Crucified One without reliance on the works of the law (v. 16). The Galatians received the blessing of the Spirit as they 'heard with faith' the message of Jesus Christ crucified, independently of 'works of the law'. What had been true of Paul had been true of the Galatians.

The immediacy of the Spirit the Galatians enjoyed occurred as Paul preached Christ crucified to them, corresponding with Paul's own experience in Damascus a decade and a half earlier. The message centred on the Crucified One and faith in him had been central in the preaching of Paul to Jews and Gentiles alike throughout the subsequent fourteen years.

Scriptural Exegesis in Galatians 3:1–14

Galatians 3:1–14 is a semi-*inclusio* that is framed by references to the Spirit and 'faith' that encloses references to *Christ crucified*.

2	Did you receive the *Spirit* by works of the law or by hearing with *faith*?
1	It was before your eyes that Jesus Christ was publicly portrayed as *crucified*.
13	Christ redeemed us from the curse of the law by becoming a curse for us – for it is written, 'Cursed is everyone who is *hanged upon a tree*' . . .
14	so that in Christ Jesus the blessing of Abraham might come to the Gentiles, so that we might receive the promised *Spirit* through *faith*

Paul had established the relationship between Christ crucified, faith and the Spirit in the immediately prior passage (2:17–21), a relationship he correspondingly applied to the Galatians based on his preaching to them. There is a clear congruence between Paul's cross-centred *experience* at Damascus and his cross-centred preaching in the following years.

Since the Damascus experience brought to an end Paul's dependence on law as the means to access with God it is not surprising that he magnified the faith of Abraham for righteousness and eliminated the role of Moses/law for righteousness. Paul had preached the cross message for the response of faith whereas the 'agitators' had proclaimed the necessity of 'works of the law' for righteousness. The texts Paul appealed to were consistent with his viewpoint (Gen. 15:6; 12:3; Deut. 27:26; Hab. 2:4; Lev. 18:5; Deut. 21:23).

Paul's adapted use of these Old Testament (LXX) texts is none too subtle as he continues to argue that it is 'of faith' and not 'of works of the law' that people find the righteousness of God and the blessings of his Spirit. It is not possible to tell for certain that Paul was employing texts that he had used during his synagogue debates in Syria–Cilicia, but in all likelihood this was indeed where Paul developed this apologetic.

The Two Jerusalems

Slavery is a prominent theme in Galatians occurring as many as twenty times and is specifically connected with 'the present Jerusalem', which is (by inference) 'the Jerusalem that is below' (Gal. 4:25,26). Pointedly the 'slavery' in this 'Jerusalem' is identified with Mt Sinai (=Moses/law), which in the setting of Galatians is the demand that Gentiles submit to works of the law, including circumcision. The antithetical 'freedom' in Paul's 'allegory' is the redemption from the curse of the law through faith in Christ crucified and the accompanying presence of Christ within, by the power of the Spirit (Gal. 3:13–14; 4:4–6).

The revolutionary element in this paradigm is that both Jews and Gentiles are enslaved. Gentiles are in bondage to gods 'that are by nature not gods' (Gal. 4:8) and – radically speaking – the historic covenant people are also enslaved. They are enslaved 'under law' (Gal. 3:23,25; 4:4). Paul was concerned for the Gentiles in Galatia lest they exchange slavery to the gods for slavery to 'works of the law', specifically male circimcision and the observation of 'days, months, seasons, years' under the Jewish Calendar (Gal. 4:10).

Paul's exceedingly negative portrayal of 'Jerusalem' in Gal. 4:21–31 prompts the question about its identity. Is Jerusalem the wider community of Jews, the circumcision activists or the group associated with the 'pillar' apostles? The general argument of the letter passes a disappointing verdict about James and Peter (Gal. 2:11–14), though it is doubtful that Paul regards them in such a negative term as slave masters. At the same time, it is doubtful that Paul was referring to the wider Jewish community in Jerusalem. Paul makes no reference to them as such in this letter. Thus it appears that Paul had in mind the circumcision activists whom he variously described as 'false brothers', 'agitators' and the 'circumcision party'. These are the people that would impose the 'yoke of slavery' on the Gentile believers in the Galatian churches (Gal. 5:1, 13).

Appendix 1

Dating Galatians

The Galatians

Galatia and Galatians

Augustus Caesar created the province of Galatia in 25 BC. It was so named because of the predominance of Celtic (Gallic) peoples who had migrated into central Anatolia in previous centuries. Several references in the New Testament attest the existence of the province of Galatia (Gal. 1:2 and 1 Cor. 16:1 – 'the churches of *Galatia*'; 2 Tim. 4:10 – 'Crescens has gone to *Galatia*'; 1 Pet. 1:1 – 'to the exiles of the dispersion in Pontus, *Galatia*, Cappadocia, Asia and Bithynia', our italics). Clearly there was a province of Galatia.

It might be thought, therefore, that the term 'Galatian' (as in Gal. 3:1) referred simply to those Gallic people who lived within the province of Galatia. In fact, however, 'Galatian' was used in two distinct ways. It was applied

(i)   to the descendants of *ethnic* Celtic peoples who lived mainly in the northern parts of the province; but also
(ii) to the inhabitants of various races of the *province* of greater 'Galatia' that extended from Pontus in the north to Pamphylia and Cilicia in the south.[1]

Does Paul address his readers as 'Galatians' (Gal. 3:1) in the ethnological sense or in the provincial sense?

If Paul's Galatians were in the central and northerly parts of the province the ethnological meaning is possible, even likely. If, however, these 'Galatians' were located nearer to the southern parts of Galatia they would be less likely to be *Celtic* Galatians since they were not noticeably present there. In short, the prior question is: were the churches to whom Paul writes in northern or southern Galatia?

The 'northern' and 'southern' theories

Scholars are divided over this question. The division is between those who hold that Paul's Galatian readers were ethnic 'Galatians' in the northern part of the province and those who believe Paul wrote to the peoples in the regions of Pisidia and Lycaonia in and beyond the southern fringes of the province.[2]

The 'northern' hypothesis depends mainly on the nature of the information in the book of Acts. The 'northern' champions point out Luke does not employ the words 'Galatia' or 'Galatians' for the regions and peoples of Pisidia and Lycaonia that Paul visited during his first missionary journey, narrated in Acts 13 – 14. Furthermore, when he does refer to 'Galatia' (*Galatikos*) it is in Paul's *second* and *third* journeys, both of which he connects with the 'region' (*chōra*) called 'Phrygia' (Acts 16:6 and 18:23).

Journey	Date	
II	AD 52	And they went through the region of *Phrygia* and *Galatia* (*tēn Phrygian kai Galatēn chōran*), having been forbidden by the Holy Spirit to speak the word in Asia. (Acts 16:6)
III	AD 52	After spending some time there, he departed and went from one place to the next through the region of *Galatia* and *Phrygia* (*tēn Galatēn chōran kai Phrygian*), strengthening all the disciples. (Acts 18:23)

Accordingly, 'northern' Galatian supporters argue that the silence regarding 'Galatia' in Acts 13 – 14, on one hand, and its mention later connected with the 'region' of 'Phrygia', on the other, points to a later mission, directed to more northerly parts of the province.[3]

Against this reconstruction and in favour of the 'southern' hypothesis the following may be said. First, the 'region' called 'Phrygia' in Acts 16:6 and 18:23 does not point to a location in central and northern Galatia. The 'region' of 'Phrygia' straddled the *lower* parts of the province of Galatia in the east extending into the province of Asia in the west. According to F.F. Bruce, 'the region of *Phrygia* and *Galatia* means the territory through which Paul and his friends passed after leaving Lystra in which Iconium and Pisidian Antioch were located'.[4]

More precisely, according to Stephen Mitchell, the 'region' described in Acts 16:6 ('Galatian Phrygia') was 'the country of Phrygia Paroreius which lay on either side of the Sultan Dagh, the mountain range that divided Pisidian Antioch from Iconium, an area that was ethnically Phrygian, but was divided between the Roman province of Asia and Galatia'.[5] Mitchell notes that both routes implied by Acts 16:6 and 18:6 (between the Galactic country and Phrygia) 'can only have intersected . . . the region of Phrygia Paroreius, not conceivably in N. Galatia, which would have involved a huge detour'.[6]

Understanding Acts 16:6 and 18:23

(a) Acts 16:6 ('through the region of *Phrygia* and *Galatia*') should be understood as Paul travelling 'through the Phrygian and Galactic region' where Luke uses the noun 'Galatia' as an adjective – as Galatic (or eastern) Phrygia.[7] In other words, Luke is describing Paul's east-to-west travels in the band of territory in the regions of Lycaonia and Pisidia, revisiting the churches in Derbe, Lystra, Iconium and Antioch he had established in the first journey.

(b) Acts 18:23 ('through the region of *Galatia* and *Phrygia*'), however, should be understood as Paul's route from *Galatian* Phrygia (the territory of Lycaonia and Pisidia) into *Asian* Phrygia. Here Luke is describing Paul's journey out of the province of Galatia into the province of Asia toward Ephesus. Probably he is referring to Paul's route through the Lycus Valley region. The 'disciples' Luke refers to may have been members of congregations in Colossae, Laodicea and Hierapolis established by Epaphras (Col. 1:7; 4:12–13).[8]

Accordingly, the second missionary journey began in Syrian Antioch and passed through Derbe, north-west to Lystra – and presumably proceeded northwards to Iconium, and then west-wards to Antioch in Pisidia[9] – then diverting north-west towards Mysia (Acts 15:41 – 16:2,7). The third journey followed a similar route through Galatic Phrygia except that it terminated in Ephesus (Acts 18:22; 19:1).

Second, the book of Acts is silent about any mission of Paul in the arid steppe lands of central and northern Galatia that was (and remains) sparsely settled. The Celts in this region retained their traditional culture and Celtic dialect. It is by no means easy to associate the sophisticated Greek-speaking readers presup-posed by Paul's letter with these Celtic 'Galatians'. Paul's brief and busy Ephesus-based ministry would not have afforded the apostle the opportunity to establish churches in northern Galatia, as this theory necessitates.

Third, in response to the claim that the cities of Pisidia and Lycaonia did not belong to the province of Galatia there is epigraphic evidence that districts to both the north and south of the province proper were deemed to be 'Galatian'. For example, there is a Latin inscription by a Roman governor of 'Galatia, of Pisidia, of Phrygia, of Lycaonia, of Phrygia, of Isauria, of Pontus Galacticus, of Pontus Polemoniacus, of Armenia'.[10] This inscrip-tion allows cities of Pisidia and Lycaonia that Paul visited (Acts 13:14,51; 14:6) to be regarded as 'Galatian'.

Another inscription from the era makes it clear that 'Galatia' was not narrowly applied to the confines of the political province. The city of Pednelissus is on the southern edge of Pisidia, yet it was called 'a city of Galatia'.[11] It is clear that a city south of the formal border of the province could be called 'of Galatia'.

These arguments overturn the necessity of 'north' Galatian theory while demonstrating the possibility, even probability of the 'south' Galatian theory. While the 'northern' theory is supported by numbers of biblical scholars there are eminent classicists who contend for the 'southern' hypothesis, notably Sir William Ramsay.[12] Stephen Mitchell, who is equally eminent as a scholar of ancient Anatolia, noted that 'the most authoritative champion of the Southern Galatian Theory was the great explorer of Asia Minor, W.M. Ramsay, and although the North Galatian Theory finds many supporters, his work long ago should have put the matter beyond dispute'.[13]

The 'southern' hypothesis is substantially settled, however, by references within the New Testament.

> Now concerning the collection for the saints: as I directed the churches of *Galatia*, so you also are to do. (1 Cor. 16:1)

> Sopater of Berea, the son of Pyrrhus from Berea, accompanied [Paul]; and of the Thessalonians, Aristarchus and Secundus; and Gaius of *Derbe*, and Timothy; and the Asians, Tychicus and Trophimus. (Acts 20:4)

Paul raised money for Judea from Christians in the provinces of Achaia, Asia, Macedonia and Galatia. Acts 20:4 names the delegates accompanying the collection from three provinces, Macedonia, Galatia and Asia.[14] The significance of Acts 20:4 when read alongside 1 Cor. 16:1 is that since Gaius was from Derbe we conclude that city to have been of *Galatia*. Lystra, Timothy's home (Acts 16:1), is probably also identified as 'of Galatia'. Accordingly we conclude that the 'churches of Galatia' (1 Cor. 16:1) were in the southerly part of the province, and indeed, beyond its borders.

It is reasonable to conclude, therefore, that the 'northern' hypothesis is not correct but that the 'southern' alternative is correct.[15]

Dating Galatians[16]

According to the book of Acts[17] Paul visited these 'Galatian' regions on three known occasions:

Galatians visits		Acts
I	The initial visit	13:4 – 14:23
II	First return visit	16:1–6
III	Second return visit	18:23

So did Paul write to the Galatians after Visit I, after Visit II, or after Visit III? He sends greetings to the Galatians from 'the brothers who are with me' (Gal. 1:2). Was that greeting sent from Antioch in Syria in 48 (after Visit I), from Corinth in 50–51(after Visit II), or from Ephesus in 52–5 (after Visit III)?

The most likely answer is that Paul wrote to the Galatians from Antioch in Syria after Visit I in 48, making Galatians Paul's earliest extant letter and arguably the earliest written text of Christianity (or the Letter of James).[18]

Also relevant to the dating question are Paul's visits to *Jerusalem* as mentioned in Galatians[19] and in the Acts of the Apostles. The most likely reconstruction is:

Jerusalem Visits		Galatians		Acts
I	36/7	1:18–20	Paul meets Peter and James	9:26–30
II	47	2:1–10	Barnabas and Paul meet 'pillars'	11:29–30
III	49		Jerusalem Council	15:4
IV	52		Third return visit	18:22
V	57		Final visit	21:15

It is striking that Galatians mentions only *two* visits to Jerusalem and in particular makes no reference to Visit III for the occasion of the meeting of the Jerusalem Council.[20] This supports the reconstruction that Paul wrote Galatians after Visit I to Galatia, which was after Visit II to Jerusalem (to meet the 'pillars') and before Visit III (for the council meeting in AD 49). Accordingly, the sequence is as follows:

Visit II to Jerusalem	c.47
Visit I to Galatia	47/48
Paul's letter to the Galatians	48
Visit III to Jerusalem: Jerusalem Council	c.49

Following are some reasons to support this opinion. First, the Galatian churches in Pisidia and Lycaonia were a natural geographical extension of the church in the great Syrian metropolis, Antioch.[21] Problems in these daughter churches would come more naturally

and easily to the attention of the mother church in Syria and therefore to the attention of Paul. By contrast, the Galatian churches
did not have any natural geographical affinity with either Corinth
or Ephesus. It is not hard to imagine the news of 'trouble' in the
Galatian churches finding its way to Antioch in Syria but rather
more so in reaching Paul in more distant Corinth or Ephesus.

There appears to have been conflict between Jerusalem and
Antioch regarding their respective spheres of influence. The
mother church in the Holy City regarded Antioch as a daughter
church, subject to her direction, as witnessed by the dispatch
first of Barnabas and later of 'men from James' (Acts 11:22; Gal.
2:12/Acts 15:1).[22] Since the churches of Pisidia and Lycaonia were
geographically and politically congruent with Antioch, the 'false
brothers' in the Holy City may have regarded these churches also
to be part of Jerusalem's jurisdiction. This did not prove to be the
attitude of the Jerusalem Council who sent no message to the Galatian churches, but only to the Gentiles in the churches in Antioch
and Syria and Cilicia (Acts 15:23,41). By contrast the circumcision
party in Jerusalem had earlier dispatched preachers to the Galatian churches to correct or complete Paul's circumcision doctrines,
men Paul calls 'agitators' (Gal. 1:7; 5:10).

Second, Paul's review of his life story in Galatians begins as a
persecutor in Jerusalem (1:13) but ends in the dramatic schism in
Antioch (2:11–21). Paul's autobiography stops in Antioch in Syria.
Paul is silent about the decision of the Jerusalem Council about
circumcision for the very good reason that it had not yet taken
place. Furthermore, he reports no incidents relating to subsequent
mission journeys in Macedonia, Achaia or Asia. Paul's narration
of his life story is fundamental to his argument, but that story
stops at the Incident in Antioch. The most natural conclusion
is that Paul wrote the letter relatively soon after the Incident in
Antioch (also recorded in Acts 15:1–2).[23]

Third, the prominence Paul gives Barnabas in the letter makes
best sense if the Galatians knew him (2:1–14). Paul and Barnabas
evangelized the Galatians in 47/8 but Barnabas did not accompany
Paul on subsequent visits (Acts 16:6; 18:23). Had Galatians been
written after Visits II or III there would be no need to make any reference to Barnabas, but that was not the case. Barnabas is negatively
prominent in Galatians ('even Barnabas was led astray' – Gal 2:13,

our italics), which suggests the agitators were pointing to Barnabas for support against Paul.

The agitators visited Galatia after Paul's first visit, but when? As suggested earlier,[24] the counter-mission probably set out from Jerusalem to Galatia shortly after Paul's return to Antioch. Lack of detail leaves us to speculate about the circumstances. Had Paul told the 'pillars' in Jerusalem of the plan to visit Galatia? Did John Mark report on this on his return to Jerusalem? Were Jews in Galatia the source of the report?

One way or another we can envisage the news reaching the Holy City inspiring the 'false brothers' to send a delegation to Galatia to correct Paul's teachings. This would mean the following sequence:

	Galatians	Acts
Visit II to Jerusalem	2:1–10	11:29–30
Visit I to Cyprus and Galatia	3:1; 4:13–14	13:4 – 14:26
Agitators in Galatia	1:8–9; 3:1; 4:17; 5:12; 6:12	
Incident in Antioch	2:11–14	15:1
News from Galatia about the agitators, Paul writes Galatians	1:1–2; 6:11	
Visit III to Jerusalem		15:2–29
Visit II to Galatia		15:41 – 16:6

The passion and urgency that are the marks of Galatians is consistent with Paul's reaction to the 'hypocritical' action of Peter followed by the weakness of Barnabas and the Jewish believers in Antioch, on the one hand, and to the news that the agitators had attempted to capture his Galatian churches, on the other.

In fact, the situation in Antioch was more serious than our two main sources indicate (Gal. 2:11–14; Acts 15:1–2). Those texts imply that the problem was confined to the Syrian capital whereas a later source tells us that the 'circumcision party' did not confine its mission to Antioch but pursued it throughout the province. The encyclical from the Jerusalem conference was directed to Gentiles in 'Antioch *and* the churches in *Syria and Cilicia*' (Acts 15:23,41).

This letter, borne by 'official' envoys from Jerusalem, Judas Bars-abbas and Silas, relieved these Gentiles of the 'burden' imposed by the group who had visited them earlier. The letter, as quoted by Luke, does not identify the 'burden' but in view of the earlier reference to circumcision in Antioch this was clearly intended (Acts 15:1, our italics – But some men came down from Judea and were teaching the brothers, 'Unless you are *circumcised* according to the custom of Moses, you cannot be saved').

Fourth, had Visit III to Jerusalem for the meeting of the 'apostles and elders' (Acts 15:6) preceded the Galatians crisis we would have expected Paul to have appealed to its resolution 'not to trouble' the Gentiles over the circumcision matter (Acts 15:19,24; cf. 15:1,10–11). Paul, however, argues against the necessity for the circumcision of Gentiles based on his victory with the 'pillars' against the demand of the 'false brothers' for the circumcision of Titus (Gal. 2.1–6).

In sum, there are cogent reasons for adopting an early dating for the Letter to the Galatians.[25]

There are, however, several arguments in favour of a later dating.[26]

Paul's exclamation, 'I am astonished that you are so quickly deserting him who called you in the grace of Christ and are turning to a different gospel' (1:6) could refer to the Galatians' grave lapse after visits I, II or III.

Likewise, Paul's complaint that they had 'so quickly' fallen away could refer either to a brief time since he had been with them or to a brief time since the false teachers had arrived. Nonetheless, the passion and immediacy of these words fits well a situation *soon after* their conversion (cf. 3:1 – O foolish Galatians! Who has bewitched you?).

Supporters of a later dating also refer to Paul's comment 'You know it was because of a bodily ailment that I preached the gospel to you at *first*' (*to proteron* – 4:13) where 'at first' meant the *earlier* of several visits.[27] But the expression could simply refer to Paul's preaching when he 'first' arrived. Paul journeyed directly from Perga near the coast of Pamphylia up to Antioch in Pisidia without preaching anywhere along the way (Acts 13:13–14), suggesting he was hurrying to arrive in the high plateau region of *Colonia Anti-ocheia*. By contrast, on his return route Paul did preach in Perga before sailing from nearby Attalia back to Syria (Acts 14:24–5). His apparent urgency travelling from Perga to Antioch in Pisidia is consistent with the reference to illness in Galatians 4:13. In short, Galatians 4:13 is consistent with the travel narrative of Acts 13:13–14.

The major argument against the AD 48 dating of Galatians is associated with J.B. Lightfoot.[28] He claimed that the many similarities between Galatians and Romans (written in AD 57) made it likely that the two letters were written more or less at the same time. It is agreed that the two letters most closely resembling one another are Romans and Galatians. Consider, for example, their common interest in faith, justification and grace as opposed to 'works of the law', circumcision notably.

Against that view, however, is the fact that Paul's letters were *occasional*. Paul's Thessalonian letters do not address law-related concerns but local apocalyptic concerns. His letter to the Galatians does not address apocalyptic concerns but law-related issues. Paul's letters were so pastorally focused that it is difficult to draw conclusions as to the sequence of their composition.

Furthermore, similarity of argument does not necessarily demand proximity of dating. For example, not much more than a year separates 1 Corinthians and 2 Corinthians, yet these letters are quite different in content and tone.

Other factors need to be considered in regard to Galatians. First, Paul had been actively involved in preaching the circumcision-free gospel to Gentiles for a decade and half – in Damascus, Arabia, Judea, Syria–Cilicia and Galatia 1:21–24; 2:1–3,6) by AD 48 when he wrote to the Galatians (Gal. 2:1–3,6). During those years Paul had vigorously engaged with Jews as well as Gentiles. His five synagogue beatings probably occurred in this early period (2 Cor. 11:24), due apparently to Paul's major disputes with rabbis throughout those years. Paul's arguments were well formed by the time he travelled to Jerusalem to force a no-circumcision verdict from the 'pillars' regarding Titus followed immediately by his circumcision-free mission journey to southern Galatia. The issues Paul faced among the Galatian churches when he wrote Galatians would not have been new to him. Similar situations prompted Paul to present similar arguments, including his well-rounded scriptural arguments in Galatians 3:6 – 4:7.

Second, Paul may have kept copies of his letters allowing him access to an earlier letter like Galatians for reusing arguments and expressions in writing to the Romans.[29] Paul did not usually write his letters alone, but was joined by trusted associates and experienced secretaries like Tertius for the writing of Romans (Rom. 16:22). We know Paul used an amanuensis in writing Galatians (see Gal. 6:11). The possibility that Paul retained copies of letters and that the drafting of letters was done by groups of helpers may explain the similarities between Galatians and Romans. A common time of origin is not the only explanation for textual similarity.

Conclusion

The 'north' Galatian theory demands a later date for the writing of the letter since Paul's founding of congregations there could only have occurred during his time in Roman Asia (i.e. 52–5). The book of Acts makes no reference to such a mission, but implies that Paul remained in Ephesus throughout that mission (Acts 19:10).

Stronger arguments support the 'south' Galatian hypothesis, especially the detailed narrative of Acts 13 – 14. Good reasons support the proposition that the churches of Antioch, Iconium, Lystra and Derbe should be considered 'Galatian', as noted above.

The 'south' Galatian resolution does not demand a verdict for an earlier or later date. Once the 'south' Galatian option is settled, however, the case for the early date becomes more feasible.[30] That case depends mainly on the likely proximity of the Incident in Antioch and the crisis in Galatia. Because Paul ended his memoir at Antioch (Gal. 2:11–21) and immediately asked the Galatians, 'Who has bewitched you?' (Gal. 3:1) we conclude that the Galatian crisis came to Paul's attention soon after the schism in Antioch. It was then, most probably, that Paul wrote to the Galatians. The early dating of the letter makes the best sense of its message.

Appendix 2

Luke's Acts as a Historical Source for Paul

The Acts of the Apostles is critical to historians for establishing:

(a) the connection between Jesus and earliest Christianity; and
(b) a chronology of the life of Paul and its relationship with his letters.

In this brief appendix we will direct our attention to (b).

During the twentieth century, however, four criticisms were directed against the usefulness to historians of the book of Acts for providing a historical and chronological basis for the life and ministry of Paul.[1]

Four Criticisms of the Acts of the Apostles

(i) As compared to Paul's own references the Acts is not to be regarded as a 'primary reference' but as a 'secondary reference'.[2] For some authorities Acts as a 'secondary reference' means that it is of little or no use to the historian, whereas for others it means that it is of use where it can be shown to agree with Paul.[3]

(ii) Closely connected is the viewpoint that discovers historical divergences in Acts making it an unreliable secondary source from Paul as the reliable primary source.[4] These include the omission by Acts of Paul's sojourn in Arabia (Gal. 1:17) and its conflicting accounts of Paul's first and second return visits to Jerusalem (Gal. 1:18–21 / Acts 9:26–7; Gal. 2:1–10 / Acts 11:27–30).

(iii) Passages in the Acts of the Apostles are historically inaccurate and significantly diminish the value of its text. A prime example is Gamaliel's speech to the Sanhedrin where he locates the revolutionary prophet Theudas *before* the insurrectionist Judas, contrary to the witness of Josephus (Acts 5:33–9).[5]

(iv) There is such theological disparity between the Acts of the Apostles and Paul's letters that the two authors must have been unknown to each other. It is claimed, for example, that the two authors do not share the same attitude to the *law*, and therefore to the centrality of the *cross* of Christ and the role of *faith* for divine *justification*.

Responses to These Criticisms

It is possible to make reasonable responses to these criticisms.

Criticism (i)

Two responses may be offered to the distinction between Paul as the 'primary source' and Luke's Acts as the 'secondary source'. By 'secondary source' critics of Acts do not mean that Acts is directly derived from or dependent on the Pauline literary corpus (as Luke's Gospel was directly derived from Mark's Gospel). In their view, to the contrary, Luke's Acts depends on extraneous, late and unknown sources.

This brings me to response (a) to this criticism. It is that the 'we' and 'us' passages (Acts 16:10–16; 20:5 – 21:18; 27:1 – 28:16) are most sensibly understood as indicating the author's presence alongside or near Paul during the five years those passages narrate.[6] Significantly, these chapters are intensely more detailed than the preceding chapters of Luke–Acts[7] prompting J.A. Fitzmyer to refer to a 'a diary-like record': 'they [details in Acts] are drawn from a diary-like record that the author of Acts once kept and give evidence that he was for a time a companion of Paul.'[8]

Understanding in this way means that the 'we' and 'us' chapters should be read alongside Paul's letters (insofar as the narratives overlap) as an equal primary source. Paul's letter to the

Romans spells out his intention *to come to Rome* and his letter to the Philippians (most probably) written *from Rome* indicates that he did in fact reach Rome. Acts 27 – 28 authentically narrates why and how Paul travelled *from* Corinth via Judea *to* Rome.

Luke's companionship with Paul AD 57–62 would have provided opportunity for the author of Acts to know about Paul's life beforehand. Through conversation and perhaps written memoirs Luke would come to know of Paul's birth in Tarsus, his resettlement in Jerusalem, his conversion, his 'unknown years' between Damascus and Antioch, and his subsequent westward missionary journeys prior to their years of companionship.

Response (b) is to point out that 'primary source' material isn't necessarily free from bias and that 'secondary source' material isn't necessarily inferior or inaccurate. Who is to say, for example, that Paul did not underplay certain details in his memoir to the Galatians in the first two chapters of that letter? This is not to say that he did, only that the possibility is there. On the other hand, based on the hypothesis that Paul told Luke about his earlier life, is there any good reason to argue that he falsified the details at hand? It is not doubted that he shaped his raw material, but that is not the same as arguing against his integrity overall or in matters of detail.

Criticism (ii)

That Luke's details vary from Paul's at some points does not necessarily indicate that the author of Acts was ignorant of Paul's missionary movements. Such a hypothesis would suggest that Luke's source for Acts 13 – 28 (as well as details of Paul's life to that point) was remote from Paul, not dependent on him.

In fact, both the Acts (explicitly) and the Pauline corpus (implicitly) refer to the same theological-geographical 'narrative' for Paul. Both writers interpret the promises of the Old Testament as confirmed in Christ and envisage the gospel message proceeding from Jerusalem to the Gentile world. More specifically, both Paul and Luke trace the spread of the gospel from Jerusalem in a westerly, Rome-ward direction. That sense of direction emerges clearly from Paul's Romans (15 – 16) and from the entire narrative of the book of Acts.

Luke was constrained by the capacity of his scroll and was forced to abbreviate and omit detail to fulfil his Jerusalem-to-Rome narrative.[9] This might explain why, for example, he passes over Paul's story from Damascus to Antioch, a period of about fifteen years, in a few sentences and omits Paul's journey to Arabia altogether.

The major problem identified by scholars is the disparity between Paul's second return visit to Jerusalem narrated on the one hand by Paul (Gal. 2:1–10), and on the other by Luke (Acts 11:27–30). According to Paul the purpose of the visit was to secure the 'pillar' apostles' recognition of Paul's proposed circumcision-free mission to the Gentiles, whereas Luke states that it was to deliver famine relief from Antioch.[10]

It is right to ask, however, why Luke's account should be treated as incorrect. It is quite possible that Paul focused on the divisive issue of circumcision while passing over the delivery of famine relief (as in Luke's narrative). It is well known that Luke generally tends to play down divisions within the apostolic community whereas Paul was prepared to highlight them, which he does implicitly in Jerusalem and explicitly in the 'Incident in Antioch' (Gal. 2:1–10,11–14) – especially when defending his doctrines to the Galatians, as he does throughout this letter.

Furthermore, Luke's account of the beginnings of the westward missions from Antioch occurred immediately after Paul's return from Jerusalem (Acts 13:1–3). This is entirely consistent with Paul's note that the Jerusalem 'pillars' agreed that Paul and Barnabas should 'go' to the Gentiles (Gal: 2:9). Their condition was that Barnabas and Paul were to 'remember the poor', which, Paul adds, was the 'very thing I have taken pains also to do' (Gal. 2:10[11]). Paul's retrospective defensive remark confirms Luke's account that the journey from Antioch to Jerusalem was to bring famine relief (Acts 11:27–30).

Many scholars, however, seek to eliminate Acts 11:27–30 as narrating a genuine visit to Jerusalem and prefer to equate Galatains 2:1–10 with Acts 15:4–29 (otherwise known as the Jerusalem Council) as Visit II.

There are substantial problems with this reconstruction. One is that Visit II according to Galatians was specifically held 'privately' between Barnabas and Paul and James, Peter and John (Gal. 2:2) whereas the Acts 15 meeting involved 'the apostles and elders with the whole church' (Acts 15:6,22,23). Furthermore, the *private* meeting in Jerusalem (Visit II) *preceded* the missions to the Gentiles (Gal. 2:9) and the *plenary* meeting in Jerusalem (Visit III) *succeeded* the mission to the Gentiles, and was held to address the issues raised by the missions of Barnabas and Paul 'among the Gentiles' (Acts 15:12). The Jerusalem Council wrote to the Gentiles in the churches in Antioch, Syria and Cilicia (Acts 15:23,41).[12] Subsequently Paul and Silas delivered the decisions of the apostles and elders to the Galatian churches (Acts 16:4).

Galatians does not mention a Visit III to Jerusalem for the simple reason that it had not yet happened when Paul wrote the letter. Paul wrote to the Galatians following the Incident in Antioch (Gal. 2:11–14), which occurred after his return to the Syrian capital after his missions in Galatia. It was only then that Barnabas and Paul travelled to Jerusalem for Visit III, the Jerusalem Council.

Table A2.1 sets out Paul's visits to Jerusalem.[13]

Table A2.1 Paul's visits to Jerusalem				
Jerusalem Visits		**Galatians**		**Acts**
I	36/7	1:18–20	Paul meets Peter and James	9:26–30
II	47	2:1–10	Barnabas and Paul meet 'pillars'	11:29–30
III	49		Jerusalem Council	15:4
IV	52		Fourth visit	18:22
V	57		Final visit	21:15

Criticism (iii)

What, then, can be said regarding passages in Acts that are regarded as historically inaccurate, in particular Gamaliel's speech to the Sanhedrin where he locates the revolutionary prophet Theudas *before* the insurrectionist Judas?

It is possible that Gamaliel is referring to an otherwise unknown Theudas who preceded Judas. Theudas is an abbreviation of

Theodotus ('gift of God') that in turn is the Greek version of the Hebrew name, 'Jonathan'. Was Gamaliel referring to an insurrectionist named Theudas who arose during the time of Archelaus (3 BC to AD 6) or, before him, in the time of Herod (40–4 BC)? While this is theoretically possible it is unlikely because Gamaliel's quoted words about Theudas and Judas closely match Josephus' references to men of that name. It appears, then, that Luke has reversed the true sequence of Judas and Theudas and placed words anachronistically in the mouth of Gamaliel.

In defence of Luke it is possible that the fault lay with the source or sources that Luke used. Our thesis is that Paul was a good source for Luke, based on their extensive companionship. But for other events like the Gamaliel incident Luke depended on hearsay or written fragmentary chronicles. It is not reasonable to fault Luke for matters about which he would have been dependent on hearsay or upon an earlier written account of that incident.

In any case, the reference to Gamaliel is but one problematic reference among many references to people cross-referenced in world history that are regarded as historically reliable. These include the named members of the Annas dynasty (Acts 4:6), the famine that occurred in the days of Claudius (11:28), Herod the king (12:1), Sergius Paulus, proconsul of Cyprus (13:7), the 'politarchs' of Thessalonica (17:8), the exile of Jews from Italy (18:2), the arrival of the proconsul Gallio in Achaia (Acts 18:12), and the 'Asiarchs' of Ephesus (19:31).

Thus while candour requires acknowledgment of problems in the Gamaliel incident, this needs to be recognized in the broader context of many other unproblematic references.

Criticism (iv)

It does not come as a surprise that there is theological disparity between the Acts of the Apostles and Paul's letters. Luke was probably a Gentile and a God-fearer whereas Paul was a Jew, in fact a strict and educated Pharisee.

The pre-Christian Paul may have outwardly seemed 'under law blameless' (Phil. 3:6), but within his conscience he was aware – however dimly – that he was 'a captive under law, a prisoner' (Gal. 3:23–5), a Jew like other Jews 'under a curse' as a law-breaker

(Gal. 3:10), in desperate need of divine redemption (Gal. 3:13; 4:4). Given this circumstance it is understandable that Paul should write so passionately about the cross of Christ as God's instrument of freedom, and of the role of faith not 'works of the law' (Gal. 2:21; 5:11; 6:14–15).

Nonetheless, there are echoes of Paul's 'righteousness' language in Luke–Acts (Luke 18:9,14; Acts 13:38–9). Luke was already a disciple (from Antioch?) by *c.*50 when he joined Paul in Troas and travelled to Philippi where he remained for the next seven years (Acts 16:10; 20:6). By the time he rejoined Paul in AD 57 he had doubtless formed his own theological views so that there is no reason to expect these to have been identical with Paul's very distinctive theology.

Thus it is quite unreasonable to demand similarity of viewpoints between Paul and Luke and to argue that Luke could not have known Paul because these were not identical.

Summary

Our argument has been that the case against the historical value of Acts based on historical and theological divergences from Paul is significant but not ultimately sustainable. The 'primary' versus 'secondary' viewpoint fails because a 'primary' source may be tendentious or forgetful and a 'secondary' source may be based accurately on the witness of the 'primary source'.

Moreover, it is fallacious to require a 'secondary' source slavishly to follow the narrative of the 'primary source'. Both Paul and Luke follow a Jerusalem-to-Rome missionary thrust, but for his part Luke omits and compresses his narrative according to his overall literary-theological design. While the Gamaliel incident raises significant questions for Luke's accuracy this issue must be seen within the broader context where his historical competence is demonstrable, especially in the 'we' and 'us' passages.

Furthermore, the demand that Luke's theology must cohere tightly with Paul's is unreasonable. Paul was an intensely religious Jew and Luke was apparently a Gentile so that to expect an identical theological framework is unfair to both men.

Unimaginable Details in Acts 13 – 20

The data about Paul in the book of Acts is extensive, especially for the span of years between his persecutions and his final journey to Jerusalem, where the principal 'we' and 'us' passage begins. Within that quarter of a century Luke narrates Paul's movements and mission in considerable detail, especially the westward mission decade AD 47–57.

That extensive detail includes the names of people and places and the passage of time and these are too numerous to repeat.[14] Did Luke invent these details, as some suggest, so that these narratives should be regarded as fictional? One has only to compare the Acts accounts with various later apocryphal works to see how unlikely this suggestion is.

For the moment let us consider a few unimaginable details, but details that have been confirmed through modern study. One such example is the travel information related to the journey of Paul and Barnabas through Pamphylia, Pisidia and Lycaonia, the so-called 'first missionary journey' (Acts 13 – 14). Paul and Barnabas passed through Perga and travelled directly to Antioch in Pisidia and from there to Iconium, Lystra and Derbe, whereupon the missionaries retraced their steps to Perga but departed for Antioch from Attalia.

What is not clear from these references is the nature of the cities and network of roads between them. From modern scholarship including archaeology we have information about these cities and roads that most likely would not have been available to a writer who was inventing this narrative. How could a fictional writer located elsewhere know that the relatives of Sergius Paulus, proconsul of Cyprus, were significant in Pisidia, as demonstrated by the discovery of the Paulli inscription[15] in Antioch? This would explain why Paul was so keen to travel directly from Cyprus to Antioch, without preaching in the major city of Perga. Could someone who invented these narratives know that Antioch, Iconium and Lystra were Roman colonies and thus relatively safe for Paul the Roman citizen to visit, and explain why he bypassed other major cities in that region? Would a novelistic writer know that Antioch, Iconium and Lystra were connected by a network of well-made *Roman* roads, including the *Via Sebaste*, providing further reason why the missionaries preached in *those* cities? Could pure invention explain why they travelled on a non-Roman road to obscure Derbe, except to escape the immediate danger from Lystra and Iconium?

Similar questions could be posed about Paul's numerous other travel details, which modern scholars understand through easy access to research information but which would not have been apparent to an anonymous chronicler in antiquity who would have lacked access to maps and encyclopaedias to inject verisimilitude into contrived narratives.

It is more realistic in every way to attribute the travel and other information in Acts 13 – 20 to Paul himself who, in turn, passed it on to Luke, whether orally or by writing or both.

But this brings us again to the significance of the 'we' and 'us' passages in the Acts of the Apostles.

The Plausibility of the 'We' and 'Us' Hypothesis

Our argument is that the unimaginable and otherwise inexplicable details in Acts 13 – 20 are best understood as originating directly from Paul to Luke, who then wove them into his global narrative in Luke–Acts.

The significance of the 'we' and 'us' narratives, especially in Acts 21 – 28, is that they directly connect Luke as Paul's companion and for no less than five years. The overwhelming probability is that Luke became acquainted with Paul's earlier life, including his missionary travels, through those years of companionship. Although many scholars dispute the 'we' and 'us' passages as pointing to this, Martin Hengel is clearly positive: 'the remarks in the first person plural refer to the author himself. They do not go back to an earlier independent source, nor are they merely a literary convention, giving the impression that the author was an eyewitness . . . "We" therefore appears in the travel narratives because Luke simply wanted to indicate that he was there.'[16] Such a conclusion is straightforward and sensible. If indeed true it undergirds the historical integrity of the greater part of the book of Acts. Without that integrity, as indicated earlier, it would not be possible to identify the connection between Jesus of Nazareth and earliest Christianity, or to provide any kind of framework for the missionary career of Paul and the dispatch of his letters to the churches of his mission.

Although written many years ago, the verdict of Alfred Plummer continues to be applicable: 'It is perhaps no exaggeration to say that nothing in biblical criticism is more important than this statement' – 'The Author of Acts was a companion of S. Paul.'[17]

Conclusion

Although the various criticisms of Acts appear to damage the credibility of that text for commentary on Paul, those criticisms diminish when carefully evaluated. The 'we' and 'us' passages in Acts 27 – 28 are most cogently understood as depending on of a companion of Paul throughout the five years, AD 57–62. Such a companionship would equip one who was to write about Paul's earlier years, especially the decade of westward mission, AD 47–57. The alternative is that such narratives were essentially invented and therefore novelistic. However, the numerous details of Paul's journeys narrated in Acts, which are corroborated through modern research, would have been unimaginable to the writer of a contrived chronicle.

Appendix 3

Barnabas, Peter and James after the Incident in Antioch

Barnabas

Despite their strong earlier relationships in Antioch (Acts 11:23–6), Jerusalem (Gal. 2:1,9) and mission journeys to Cyprus and southern Galatia (Acts 13 – 14), it does not appear that Paul and Barnabas worked in close association after the schism in Antioch in c.48. There was already tension over Barnabas' nephew, John Mark (Acts 13:13; 15:36–9). Barnabas was pointedly not a co-sender with Paul in the letter to the Galatian churches. Nonetheless, while the one subsequent reference Paul makes to Barnabas is not negative (1 Cor. 9:6) the schism in Antioch effectively appears to have spelled the end of their partnership.

Peter's 'Dark' Period (48–65)[1]

There are relatively few references to Peter after the Incident in Antioch. In c.49 he played an important but secondary role at the Jerusalem Council (Acts 15:7–11). The addressees of 1 Peter – exiles in Pontus, Galatia, Cappadocia and Bithynia – may suggest that Peter travelled to these regions. But reference to 'those who preached the good news to you' (1 Pet. 1:12) indicates that Peter was not the primary evangelist. Be that as it may, it is clear enough that Peter accompanied by his wife visited Corinth between Paul's first and second visits, that is, between 52 and 55 (1 Cor. 1:12; 3:22; 9:5). As 'apostle to the circumcised' he probably preached to Jews in Corinth, although his sympathy for Paul's message to the uncircumcised and his years of 'living as a Gentile' make it likely that he included Gentiles within his sphere of ministry. From Corinth he seems to have travelled to Rome, as indicated by 1 Peter written from 'Babylon', in association with Mark and Silvanus (1 Pet. 5:12–14). Paul's letter to the Romans makes no direct mention of Peter, though he may be the unnamed 'foundation' layer whose presence precluded Paul conducting a sustained ministry in Rome (Rom. 15:20). According to Hengel, Paul was thereby 'distancing himself from a competitive mission movement . . . which was almost surely the Petrine mission'.[2] Even so, Paul's implied respect for the 'someone' who 'laid the foundation' in Rome should be noted.

James

The period between the Jerusalem Council in *c*.49 and Paul's final visit to Jerusalem in *c*.57 is cloaked in darkness so far as James is concerned. These years were noted by ever-worsening relationships between the Jews and their Roman occupiers. Groups like the *Sicarii* faction and the apocalyptic 'sign' prophets[3] flourished in these circumstances. The ever-deepening religious nationalism among the Jews could not have failed to leave its mark on the Christian Jews in the Holy City. It is reasonable to assume that the messianic movement became more intensely conservative during those years.

Significantly Paul did not stay with James in 57 when he finally arrived in Jerusalem (Acts 21:15–26). Rather, disciples from Caesarea escorted Paul and Luke to the house of Mnason, 'an early disciple' (Acts 21:16). Despite Luke's best efforts to portray a warm reunion between Paul and James the text conveys a rather icy meeting (Acts 21:19–21). There is no mention of the Jerusalem church welcoming and receiving the collection. Rather, the emphasis, on the one hand, is that the 'thousands' of Jewish Christians in Jerusalem were 'all zealous for the law', whereas, by contrast, Paul had failed to reinforce Jewish practices out in the Diaspora and to uphold the letter from the Jerusalem Council to the Gentiles a decade earlier (Acts 21:21).

Our final glimpse of James is through the sympathetic eyes of Flavius Josephus. In AD 62, in the interregnum following the death of the procurator Festus, the high priest Ananus (Annas) II convened the Sanhedrin and arraigned James, who was subsequently stoned. Such was the outcry of 'those of the inhabitants of the city who were considered the most fair-minded and who were strict in observance of the law' that, following representations to Herod Agrippa II, Albinus the incoming procurator deposed Ananus, even though he had held the office for only three months.[4]

Luke reveals that James was head of a large faith community of Christian Jews in Jerusalem who were 'all zealous for the law' (Acts 21:20). Josephus, for his part, indicates that James was deeply respected by conservative (Pharisaic) Jews in Jerusalem. A significant overlap between unbelieving Jews of Judea (as Paul calls them – Rom. 15:31) and James' Christian Jews in Jerusalem is to be inferred.

Mission Groups and Mission Literature

James' embassy to Antioch in *c*.48 led to a schism between Peter and Paul, but also between Peter, Paul and James. The unity in Jerusalem in *c*.47 (Gal. 2:1–10) was not rediscovered. Furthermore, John Zebedee disappears from view in the narrative of the New Testament.

These four leaders – James, Peter, John and Paul – effectively went in their own directions. James remained in Jerusalem as head of a large community of Christians who were conservatively Jewish, embedded in the ultra Judaism of the Holy City in the fifties and sixties. Peter seems to have established his own mission, which now appeared to include Gentiles (God-fearers?) as well as the circumcised. John migrated to western Asia, perhaps in the mid-to-late fifties (the date is uncertain), although he remained there into old age, becoming the *Hagios Theologos* (Holy Theologian) in the eastern tradition. Paul recruited new associates like Timothy, Titus and Luke and established a network of congregations in Asia Minor and Greece, in addition to those already formed in Syria–Cilicia.

In the decades after the Incident in Antioch in *c*.48, these four leaders and their associates created the mission literature that would become the New Testament.[5]

The relationship between James and Matthew is not easy to establish. Both writers seek to present the teaching of Jesus and appear to have been dependent in part on the Q and M sources and, in the case of Matthew, upon the Gospel of Mark as well. Furthermore, the direction of Matthew's Gospel from beginning to end is away from Israel towards the nations (Matt. 2:1–12; 10:5–6; 25:32; 28:19).

In Peter's case the situation is more straightforward. His protégé Mark wrote his gospel under Peter's authority and his colleague Silvanus wrote 1 Peter under Peter's authority. The origin of 2 Peter is not known.

Likewise straightforward is Paul's mission literature. His companion Luke wrote Luke–Acts and Paul himself wrote the corpus of letters that bear his name, often with the assistance of co-senders and amanuenses.

John may have written an early draft of his gospel in Palestine but 'published' it later in Ephesus.[6] John wrote his three letters and his letter-book, the Revelation to John, in the latter years of the first century.

Mission leader	Mission literature
Peter	Gospel of Mark
	1, 2 Peter, Jude
John	Gospel of John
	1, 2, 3 John, Revelation
Paul	Luke–Acts
	Paul's letters[7]
James	Gospel of Matthew
	Letter of James

Thus the Incident in Antioch had far-reaching consequences, but by no means were they all negative. The rich diversity of the literature of the New Testament was the indirect result of the historic confrontation between Peter and Paul at Antioch in *c*.48.

Appendix 4

James' Encyclical to the 'Twelve Tribes of the Diaspora'

Of the five men in the New Testament named James the most likely author of James' encyclical to the 'twelve tribes of the Diaspora' is either James Zebedee or James, brother of the Lord.[1] James Zebedee is eliminated due to the earliness of his death (by execution) in the early forties (Acts 12:2). But there are positive reasons to identify the author as James, brother of the Lord.[2]

The unadorned opening of the encyclical epistle from 'James the servant of the Lord Jesus Christ' addressed to 'the twelve tribes in the Dispersion' implies a sender of the considerable authority that James enjoyed (Gal. 2:9,12; Acts 15:19–21).[3]

Dating of James' Encyclical

When did James write the encyclical? The timeframe of the epistle is defined by James' rise to power in c.42 and his martyrdom in 62.[4] Did James write at the beginning of this two-decade period, at the middle or at the end?

Much depends on one's attitude to James' use of the words 'faith', 'saved', 'justified' and 'imputed' (Jas 2:14–26). It is too much of a coincidence that Paul also uses this vocabulary (Gal. 2:16; 3:6; Rom. 4:1–6). This prompts the question, who was responding to whom? The more polemical tone in James 2:14–16 suggests that James was responding to Paul, not vice versa.

Was James responding to Romans (as in Rom. 4:1–6), a response that would date James after Romans[5] that Paul wrote in AD 56/7? Or, was James responding to Paul in Galatians (as in Gal. 2:16), thus dating James' letter after *c*.48, the probable year Paul wrote Galatians? Both these alternatives imply James was responding to what Paul had *written*. In any case, however, how confident could we be that James had read Galatians or Romans?

There is another possibility, namely that James was responding not to a letter but to *verbal* reports about Paul's keywords, a possibility that could make James' letter quite early, as early as the mid-to-late forties. The following circumstantial details suggest an early dating of the James' encyclical.

First, James in Jerusalem had the opportunity to know about Paul's preaching in Syria–Cilicia. Reports of his preaching 'the faith' in Syria–Cilicia *c*.37–46 came to the attention of 'the churches of Judea that are in Christ', inevitably also to James' attention in Jerusalem (Gal. 1:21–4).[6] As argued earlier,[7] Paul's 'preaching of the faith' must have included a ministry to Gentiles. James' *other* letter, which issued from the Jerusalem Council in *c*.49 (Acts 15:22), was addressed to *Gentile* churches in Antioch, Syria and Cilicia (Acts 15:23,41). Who else could have founded these Gentile churches during the previous years except Paul? By the early-to-mid forties James would have been aware of Paul's 'preaching of the faith' to the Gentiles.

Second, the early dating of the fivefold floggings Paul received in the synagogues (2 Cor. 11:24) seems to have overlapped with Paul's years in Syria–Cilicia when he was establishing Gentile congregations. Many scholars believe that these scourgings occurred before Paul began his westward missions in *c*.47.[8] That would mean it was during Paul's years in Syria–Cilicia AD 37–46 that the synagogue authorities arraigned Paul and subjected him to this sequence of violent punishments.[9]

These beatings indicate that Paul continued to attend the synagogues and to engage in activities that offended the Jewish leadership. One probable scenario was that Paul sought to influence the God-fearers who were within the orbit of the synagogues. Based on his arguments in Galatians Paul would have asserted that faith-union with Christ crucified and not the Torah was the way to 'life' (Gal. 3:11).[10]

The Mishnah tractate *Makkot* ('Stripes') reflected rules and procedures applicable to the 'forty lashes less one' and the tractate *Kerithoth* ('Extirpation', i.e. excommunication) identified the relevant offending sins as *blasphemy* and breaches of *the law of circumcision* (*Ker.* 1.1). The offender faced excommunication but could choose instead to undergo the synagogue beating.[11] Paul chose the beating. His *blasphemy* was to deny the saving power of the law, and his breach of the law of *circumcision* was to deny its necessity to Gentile proselytes. It is likely that Paul developed the controversial language 'justified' and 'faith' with its key text, Genesis 15:6, in the context of these synagogue controversies, explaining how the vocabulary came to James' attention in Jerusalem.[12]

Third, the evidence of an early mission to the circumcised allows for an early encyclical to the circumcised. Such evidence is found in:

(i)   Peter's mission to the Jews in the land of Israel AD 33–47 (Gal. 2:9; Acts 9:31–2);

(ii) in the agreement in Jerusalem in *c*.47 for a *continuing mission to the circumcised* by the 'pillars' of that church (Gal. 2:9); and

(iii) in Paul's passing reference to 'the brothers of the Lord and Cephas' in Corinth (1 Cor. 9:5) implying a mission to the circumcised that had reached as far as the Achaian capital by *c*.53 (a mission that the 'super-apostles' later probably looked to as justification for their ministry there – cf. 2 Cor. 10:15).

Were there Jewish churches in the Diaspora? It is clear that from as early as the mid-to-late thirties there were exclusively Jewish congregations in Damascus and Antioch where the disciples were probably still also embedded within the orbit of the synagogues.

Fourth, consistent with the existence of a Jewish mission outside Israel with exclusively Jewish membership, James sent envoys to Antioch in *c*.48 to *segregate* Jewish from Gentile members of the church, an objective in which he was successful (Gal. 2:11–13). It appears that James' vision was for a continuing Jewish mission that sought to establish a network of exclusively Jewish congregations. By contrast, Paul was committed to 'mixed' churches of Jews and Gentiles (see Gal. 3:28 – 'There is neither Jew nor Greek ... you are all one in Christ Jesus').

Fifth, James' encyclical to 'the twelve tribes' is consistent with the existence of an early mission to the circumcised. The epistle is entirely and exclusively Jewish in tone. It is addressed to 'the twelve tribes of the Diaspora' (cf. 'our twelve tribes – Acts 26:7). The local meeting of the 'brothers' is called a 'synogogue' (Jas 2:2; but cf. 'church' in 5:14). There is strong reference to the *Shema*' (God is 'one' – Deut. 6:4), to 'the law' (i.e. the commandments) of God (Jas 2:9–11), to 'Abraham our father' (2:21), and to 'the Lord of hosts' (5:4).

Furthermore, the 'testing' that the poorer readers were facing does not seem to have come from Gentiles, but from wealthy fellow-Jews who 'oppress you . . . drag you into court . . . blaspheme the honourable name by which you were called' (2:6–7). In fact, the provenance of the letter is Palestinian,[13] with its reference to 'early and late rains' (5:7), an Old Testament allusion (Deut. 11:4; Jer. 5:24; Joel 2:23; Zech. 10:1) that points to climate of Palestine and southern Syria. The allusion to wealthy landowners withholding wages of the labourers reflects the pre-66–70 Palestine, a situation that changed after the war when the social fabric of the land of Israel was destroyed.

James' encyclical does not mention 'Gentiles' or their sins of idolatry and fornication. The letter confronts the readers with *Jewish* abuses and temptations, for example, hypocrisy and economic discrimination. There is no hint of the division Paul's circumcision-free gospel to Gentiles created or any reference to Jewish circumcision practices, or dietary rules. In James' encyclical it was as if the Gentile world and Gentile believers did not exist.

These and other matters point in the direction of James' encyclical as an early[14] epistle.

The Synoptic Sources Underlying James' Encyclical

One striking feature of the Letter of James is its many allusions to the Jesus tradition in the synoptic tradition. These belong to two categories. First, there are a number of 'content links' between individual words in Matthew and James, for example 'perfect' (Jas 1:4; Matt. 5:48; 19:21), 'righteousness' (Jas 1:20; 3:18; Matt. 3:15; 5:6,10,20; 6:1,33), 'church' (Jas 5:14; Matt. 16:18; 18:17), 'parousia' (Jam. 5:7; Matt. 24:3,27,37,39), 'oaths' (Jas 5:12; Matt. 5:33–7).[15]

Second, there are textual allusions involving several words, though it is difficult to identify these precisely. According to P. Davids there are up to thirty-five such echoes, mostly from the Matthew/Luke material underlying the Sermon on the Mount/Plain.[16] J. Painter has combined the lists of R.P. Martin and P.J. Hartin, making thirty-three in all.[17] Rather more conservatively, I have identified twenty-one likely textual links.

James	Matthew	Luke
1:2 Count it all *joy* . . . when you meet various trials 1:12 *Blessed* is the man who remains steadfast under trial	5:10,12 *Blessed* are those who are persecuted . . . Rejoice and be *glad* [Sermon on the Mount]	
1:5 If any of you lacks wisdom, let him *ask* God, who gives generously to all 1:17 Every *good gift* . . . coming down the Father	7:7 *Ask*, and it will be given to you [Sermon on the Mount] 7:11 how much more will your Father . . . give *good things* to those who ask him [Sermon of the Mount]	11:9 *Ask*, and it will be given to you [Q source] 11:13 how much more will the heavenly Father give the Holy Spirit to those who ask [Q source]
1:20 the *anger* of man does not produce the righteousness that God requires	5:22 everyone who is *angry* with his brother will be liable to judgement [Sermon on the Mount]	
1:22 be *doers* of the word, and not hearers only	7:24 Everyone . . . who hears these words . . . and *does* them [Sermon on the Mount]	
2:5 has not God chosen those who are *poor* . . . to be . . . *heirs of the kingdom* . . . ?	5:3 Blessed are the *poor* in spirit, for theirs is the kingdom of heaven [Sermon on the Mount]	6:20 Blessed are you *poor*, for yours is the *kingdom* of God [Q source]
2:8 the royal law . . . 'You shall love your neighbour as yourself'	Mark 12:31 'The second is this: 'You shall love your neighbour as yourself' = Matthew 22:39	10:27–8 You shall love . . . your neighbour as yourself [Q source]

2:10 whoever keeps the whole law but fails in one point has become accountable for all of it	5:19 whoever relaxes one of the least of these commandments . . . will be . . . least in the kingdom . . . but whoever does them . . . will be called great in the kingdom [Sermon on the Mount]	
2:13 For judgement is without *mercy* to one who has shown no mercy. *Mercy* triumphs over judgement	5:7 Blessed are the *merciful*, for they shall obtain *mercy* [Sermon on the Mount]	6:37 forgive, and you will be forgiven [Q source]
2:14 What good is . . . if someone says he has faith, but does not have works?	7:21 Not everyone who says to me, 'Lord, Lord', will enter the kingdom of heaven, but the one who does the will of my Father [Sermon on the Mount]	6:46 Why do you call me 'Lord, Lord', and not do what I tell you? [Q source]
3:12 Can a *fig* tree . . . bear olives, or a grape-vine produce figs?	7:16 Are *grapes* gathered from thorn-bushes, or *figs* from thorn bushes? [Sermon on the Mount]	6:44 figs are not gathered from thorn bushes, nor are grapes picked from a bramble bush [Q source]
3:13 Who is wise and understanding among you? By his good conduct let him show his works in the *meekness* of wisdom	5:5 Blessed are the *meek* [Sermon on the Mount]	
4:4 Do you not know that friendship with the world is enmity with God? Therefore whoever wishes to be a friend of the world makes himself an enemy of God	6:24 No one can serve two masters; for either he will hate the one and love the other or he will be devoted to the one and despise the other. You cannot serve God and money [Sermon on the Mount]	16:13 No servant can serve two masters; for either he will hate the one and love the other, or he will be devoted to the one and despise the other. You cannot serve God and money [Q source]

4:8 Cleanse your hands, you sinners, and *purify your hearts*, you double-minded	5:8 Blessed are the *pure in heart*, for they shall see God [Sermon on the Mount]	
4:9 Be wretched and mourn and weep. Let your laughter be turned to mourning and your joy to gloom		6:25 Woe to you that laugh now, for you shall mourn and weep
4:10 *Humble* yourselves before the Lord, and he will exalt you	23:12 Whoever *exalts* himself will be humbled, and whoever *humbles* himself will be exalted	14:11 Everyone who exalts himself will be humbled, and he who humbles himself will be exalted [Q source]
4:11 Do not speak evil against one another, brothers. The one who speaks against a brother or judges his brother, speaks evil against the law and judges the law	5:22 everyone who is angry with his brother shall be liable to judgement [Sermon on the Mount] 7:1 Judge not, that you be not judged [Sermon on the Mount]	
5:1 Come now, you *rich*, weep and howl for the miseries that are coming upon you	19:23 only with difficulty will a *rich* person enter the kingdom of heaven	6:24–5 woe to you who are rich, for you have received your consolation. Woe to you who are full now, for you shall be hungry [Q source]
5:2 Your *riches* have rotted and your garments are *moth-eaten*	6:20 lay up for yourselves *treasures* in heaven, where neither *moth* nor rust consumes [Sermon on the Mount]	
5:12 *do not swear*, either by *heaven or by earth* or by any other oath, but let your 'yes' be yes and your 'no' be no, that you may not fall under condemnation	5:34–5 *Do not take an oath* at all, either *by heaven*, for it is the throne of God, *or by the earth*, for it is his footstool [Sermon on the Mount]	

5:19–20 My brothers, if anyone among you wanders from the truth and someone brings him back, let him know that whoever brings back a sinner from his wandering will save his soul from death and will cover a multitude of sins	18:15 If your brother sins against you, go tell him his fault, between you and him alone. If he listens to you, you have gained your brother	

Even in this conservative list there are no exact or clear-cut quotations by James from the synoptic traditions. There are fifteen texts that have words common to the synoptic traditions (Jas 1:2,12,5,17,20,22; 2:5,13; 3:12,13; 4:8,10; 5:1,2,12), of which all but one are from Matthew's Sermon on the Mount (4:10). There are six others texts from James where the similarity is in the congruence of ideas (2:8,10,14; 4:11; 5:19–20). Nonetheless even these weaker echoes are sufficiently strong to conclude that James had access to synoptic traditions.

Of the fifteen texts from James that have verbal connection to the Sermon on the Mount it appears that five were from the Q source (1:5,17; 2:5; 4:10; 5:1). This suggests that when James echoes (a version of) the Sermon on the Mount it was an *entity* that had already combined the underlying sources 'M' (special to Matthew) and the 'Q'.

What Was the 'Word' that James' Readers Needed to 'Hear' and to 'Do'?

What is the relationship between the pre-synoptic tradition evident in James' encyclical and what he calls 'the word' (Jas 1:18,21,22,23)? While it was that 'word' that had *regenerated* James' readers (1:18) it is clear that it was a 'word' whose outworking was ethical, a 'word' that was to be 'heard' and 'done'. Since there are no echoes of the death and resurrection of Jesus but numerous references to the Lord's ethical teachings (as above), we reasonably conclude that James thought of the 'word' as the *teaching* of

Jesus (from the Sermon on the Mount in particular), as we find it in this letter.

The Encyclical of James and the Cross of Christ

How is it that Paul's emphasis on the atoning death of Christ is met with silence in James' encyclical letter when James himself appears earlier not to have disagreed with that doctrine?

According to Paul in Galatians 2:1–10 James did not disagree with Paul's gospel at the meeting in Jerusalem in *c*.47. First, James, Peter and John 'added nothing' to Paul, confirming that he 'was not running in vain and had not run in vain' in respect of his gospel message to the Gentiles (Gal. 2:6,2). Second, James, Peter and John supported Paul against the 'false brothers' who attempted to 'force' the circumcision of Titus as basis for covenant fellowship (Gal. 2:3). Third, James and the other 'pillars', having recognized that God had already 'worked through' Paul's mission to the Gentiles, gave to Barnabas and Paul 'the right hand of fellowship' for them to 'go' to the Gentiles with a message that did not require circumcision of Gentile males (Gal. 2:8–9).

Furthermore, in Paul's first letter to the Corinthians he states that the risen Christ 'appeared to Cephas, then to the twelve . . . all the apostles, and James'. Paul insists that he and they – including James – proclaim the same message, including 'that Christ died for our sins in accordance with the Scriptures' (1 Cor. 15:3–5).

These passages from Galatians and 1 Corinthians indicate that, to say the least, James did not disagree with Paul's 'cross-centred' preaching and that he, too, preached that 'Christ died for our sins'. The problem we face is that James' encyclical letter, one that implies a *comprehensive* statement of Christian belief, makes no reference to the death of Christ for sins and does not even declare that Christ had died.

Possible reasons for James' silence about the cross

How, then, can we account for the curious absence from James' encyclical of cross-based atonement theology such as we find in

the writings of mission leaders Paul, Peter, John and by the writer
to the Hebrews?

First, James was not initially a disciple of the Lord, but a convert
following his resurrection. Unlike Peter, John and the other disciples, James would not have heard Jesus' own cross-based teachings
on the journey between Caesarea Philippi and Jerusalem. James
was not present at the Last Supper when the Lord commanded, 'Do
this in memory of me', that is, of Jesus' death and the reason for it.

Immediately after the resurrection the disciples led by Peter
(including the Hellenists?) began to formulate key teachings about
the death and resurrection (as in 1 Cor. 15:3–7) and the words
of the Lord's Supper liturgy (as in 1 Cor. 11:23–5). These were
the 'traditions' that Paul subsequently 'received' (in Damascus
or Jerusalem) and in turn 'handed over' to the churches of the
Gentile mission. The traditions that James incorporates, however,
give 'the impression of an almost pre-crucifixion discipleship'.[18]

Second, 'James and the brothers' appeared to have met sepa-
rately from Peter's group in Jerusalem (Acts 12:17). Given James'
preoccupation with the teachings of Jesus in his encyclical, especially in the Sermon on the Mount (see earlier), it seems likely that
he and his brothers (i.e. his siblings) were particularly engaged in
gathering and arranging those teachings as the basis of the 'word'
they taught in the Jewish mission.

Third, James seems to have remained firmly within the synagogue culture of Jerusalem. James was so respected within the
wider community in Jewish Jerusalem that, at his execution in
62, 'those who were considered the most fair minded and who
were strict in observance of the law' petitioned both Agrippa II
and Albinus, the incoming procurator, over his illegal execution.[19]
Subsequently Agrippa deposed Ananus II for his execution of
James.

The integration of Jewish disciples within the synagogue
communities was not confined to Jerusalem. It appears that
the synagogues in Rome had Christian members from the early
thirties until Claudius' expulsion of the Jews from Rome in AD
49.[20]

Accordingly, James' encyclical to the 'twelve tribes of the
Dispersion' appears to have been written to Jewish disciples who
were still embedded in the synagogues, still part of the ethos and

practices of Judaism. There is no way of knowing how many such situations there were, but they may have been numerous.

One important factor here was the continuing membership of Jewish Christians in Jewish synagogues. Whereas Paul's Jewish mission-converts withdrew from the synagogues (except in Berea – Acts 17:10–12) to form mixed churches, in James' mission (cf. 1 Cor. 9:5) Jewish disciples appeared to have remained as members of synagogues. This was true in earliest times in Jerusalem (Acts 26:11) and Damascus (Acts 9:2). The church in Antioch was initially of exclusively Jewish membership (Acts 11:19).

As discussed earlier, James calculated polemical use of distinctly anti-Pauline language in James 2:14–26 ('faith', 'works', 'save', 'justified', 'counted' and 'righteousness') may have arisen from Jewish disciples embedded in the synagogues of Syria–Cilicia whose complaints against Paul had filtered through to James in Jerusalem (as noted above). This integration within synagogues by disciples continued for many years and only began to terminate after the Council of Jamnia in the eighties.[21]

James doubtless assented to the message of the cross, but his late conversion and his continuing engagement with the culture of the synagogue may explain his silence on the issue of the atonement.

James' High Christology

Although James' epistle is 'cross-free' it does not imply that it is merely a collection of ethical teachings. In fact, the letter is permeated with the teaching of Jesus in the context of a 'high' Christology.

We constantly hear echoes of the teachings of 'Jesus Christ, the Lord of glory' echoed in James' encyclical, for example: the Father's generous gifts to his children (1:17; cf. Matt. 7:11); the need not merely to hear but to do the word (1:22–5; cf. Matt. 7:24); the unity of the law (2:10–11; cf. Matt. 5:19); the plight of the hungry and ill-clad (2:15 cf. Matt. 25:3); the effects of evil speech (3:6; cf. Matt. 12:36; 15:11); the wrongness of judging a brother (4:11–12; cf. Matt. 7:1); the ban on oaths (5:12; cf. Matt. 5:34–7); the nearness of the Lord to the doors (5:8–9; cf. Matt. 24:33); and the importance of saving a sinner (5:19–20; cf. Matt. 18:11).

Who, then, did James think Jesus was? He is the giver of the royal law (2:8), that is, the law of the King, the law that liberates. It comes as no surprise that James writes of 'the wisdom from above' (3:17) in a manner suggestive of Jesus as the incarnation of 'wisdom'. James implies that *Jesus* was the 'righteous person' who did not resist his oppressors (5:6). Explicitly, he refers to Jesus as 'Christ' (1:1; 2:1) whose return as 'judge' was near (5:8–9). Furthermore, James often uses the word 'save' in an eschatological sense (1:21; 2:14; 4:12; 5:20). Above all, James employs the same word of Jesus as he does of God, namely 'Lord' (1:1 cf. 1:8; 5:7,8,15). This 'glorious Lord' (2:1) will 'raise up' the sick and, by implication, raise the dead at the end (5:15).

James' silence about the death of Christ does not mean that he was opposed to this teaching. To the contrary, his high Christology and references to 'save' and 'salvation' are consistent with a cross-centred soteriology. Whereas such soteriology was explicit in Paul it seems to have been implicit in James.

Conclusion

In this appendix we have attempted to establish the following:

(i)   James, brother of the Lord, was the author of the encyclical to 'the twelve tribes of the Diaspora'.

(ii)   It was an early letter, as early as the mid-to-late forties.

(iii)   The Letter of James has numerous links to the Jesus tradition in the synoptic tradition, especially from the Sermon on the Mount, which depends on the 'Q' and 'M' sources.

(iv)   James and his siblings may have had a particular role in assembling and shaping these teachings.

(v)   The 'word' that James asserts regenerated his readers, and which has to be 'done' as well as 'heard', was the teaching of Jesus chiefly derived from an early version of the Sermon on the Mount.

(vi)   As to the painful question about James' silence about the atoning death of Christ, the most likely answer is that James had not personally been exposed to that teaching in the way Peter and the other disciples had been. Moreover, James

remained embedded within the synagogue culture of Jerusalem where Paul's preaching of the *crucified* Messiah would
have been unacceptable (cf. 1 Cor. 1:23).

(vii) The complaints about Paul's language of 'faith', 'works',
'save', 'justified', 'counted' and 'righteousness' (Jas. 2:14–26)
may have arisen from Jewish disciples embedded in the
synagogues of Syria–Cilicia whose complaints against Paul
had filtered through to James in Jerusalem.

(viii) Although James' epistle is 'cross-free' it nonetheless has
many expressions of a 'high' Christology (e.g. 'Jesus Christ,
the Lord of glory' – Jas. 2:1) and a strong view of the immi-
nence of his return (Jas 5:8–9).

Appendix 5

The 'New Perspective on Paul' According to James Dunn

Professor Dunn is a distinguished scholar and a prolific writer, including on the writings of Paul the apostle. Dunn coined the phrase 'a new perspective on Paul' and he has written about this in, for example, *The Theology of Paul the Apostle*, and in his commentary on Galatians, *The Epistle to the Galatians*.[1]

A Theology of Paul

Let me begin by referring to his *Theology of Paul*.

Dunn and Sanders

Dunn's starting point is to agree with E.P. Sanders' 'New Perspective on Judaism'.[2] Sanders wrote that Judaism was a religion based on grace where the law was the means of maintaining the covenant that God had initiated by grace. Sanders called this arrangement 'covenantal nomism', a *covenant* based on *nomos* (law).[3]

Comment: Echoes of legalistic, merit-based thinking among Second Temple Jews undermine Sanders' position that Judaism was a grace-based religion in the era of Paul.

> The beginning of wisdom is the most sincere desire for instruction, and concern for instruction is love of her, and love of her is the keeping of her laws, and giving heed to her laws is *assurance of immortality*, and immortality brings one near to God; so the desire for wisdom leads to a kingdom.(*Wisdom of Solomon* 6:17–18, our italics)

Whoever honours his father *atones for his sins*,
And whoever glorifies his mother is like one who lays up treasure . . .
For kindness to a father *will not be forgotten*,
And *against your sins it will be credited*. (*Sirach* 3:3–4,14, our italics)

The *Mishnah* is a collection of Jewish teachings from about AD 200 but many of those teachings were current in the time of Paul.

Great is the law, for it gives life to them that practise it both in this world and in the world to come. (*Aboth* 6:7, our italics)

The Holy One, blessed is he, was minded to grant merit to Israel; therefore hath he multiplied for them the law and commandments, as it is written, *It pleased the Lord for his righteousness' sake to magnify the law and make it honourable'*. (*Makkot* 3.16, our italics)

'Life' (i.e. *eternal* life) and 'merit' flow from the good works. Clearly this is contrary to Sanders' assertion that at heart covenantal nomism was *grace*-based.

Dunn's separation from sinners

Dunn develops the idea of Israel's necessary separation from the nations. The covenant people were to do this defining separation by means of 'works of the law' – circumcision, dietary regulations, Sabbath-keeping, religious festivals.[4] In support he quotes various texts from Second Temple Judaism.

In his wisdom the legislator [Moses] . . . surrounded us with unbroken palisades and iron walls to prevent our mixing with any of the other peoples in any matter . . . To prevent our being perverted by contact with others or by mixing with bad influences, he hedged us in on all sides with strict observances connected with meat and drink . . . after the manner of the Law. (*Epistle of Aristeas* 139, 142)

Separate yourself from the nations, and eat not with them . . . .
for their works are unclean, and all their ways are a pollution and an abomination and an uncleanness. (*Jubilees* 22:16)

Comment: First, it is noted that 'works of the law' is not terminology found in the Old Testament and, second, the defining items noted in the *Epistle of Aristeas* are social expressions and no comment is made about their usage affecting one's relationship with God.

There is a possible allusion to 'works of the law' in the Qumran literature but it is too brief and ambiguous to cast light on this issue.

> Now, we have written to you some of *the works of the law*, those which we determined would be beneficial for you and your people . . . Understand all these things and beseech Him to set your counsel straight and so keep you away from evil thoughts and the counsel of Belial. Then you will rejoice at the end time when you will find the essence of our words to be true. And it will be *reckoned to you as righteousness*, in that you have done what is right and good before Him, to your own benefit and to that of Israel. (4QMMT,[5] our italics)

So far from supporting Dunn's 'new perspective' this text points in the opposite direction:

(i)   'the works of the law' are not items that separate Israel from the nations but relate directly to *God*; and

(ii) in the *doing* of the 'works of the law' it will be 'reckoned to you as righteousness' (the opposite to Paul's teaching, e.g. in Gal. 2:15–16).

Paul's 'zeal'

According to Dunn the pre-Christian Paul was noted for his 'zeal' in his 'former life Judaism', 'zeal' he expressed violently as a persecutor of the *Hellenist* (Greek-speaking Jewish) Christians.[6] This was because in bringing the gospel to Gentiles they 'failed to require of . . . Gentile converts circumcision and the practice of covenantal distinctives'.[7]

Comment: There is no evidence that the Hellenists were making converts among Gentiles when Paul began his persecutions. Stephen was criticizing the temple and Moses (Acts 6:11, 13) and the view that the temple-city was the epicentre of God's end-time purposes (Acts 7:44–50). This teaching may have *implied* evangelism of Gentiles and indeed issued in such evangelism, first by Philip and then by Paul. But this was not happening to our knowledge when Paul began his persecutions.

Furthermore, Dunn is incorrect in suggesting that Paul confined his persecution to the Hellenists. Paul 'attempted to destroy the church of God' (Gal. 1:13), that is, the Jerusalem church, whose members – Hebrews and Hellenists – later scattered throughout the land of Israel (Acts 8:2; 9:31–2). The members of 'the churches of Judea' (i.e. composed of *Jewish* Christians) later referred to Paul as having persecuted 'us' (Gal. 1:23).

A psychological explanation

Dunn offers a psychological explanation about Paul's 'conversion experience' which he said is 'easily recognisable and cannot easily be discounted'.[8] The pre-converted Paul was a man of extreme 'zeal' dedicated to a separateness from both mainstream Judaism, not to mention Gentiles.[9]

Comment: The capacity of a biblical scholar to offer a psychological explanation of someone in a different culture two thousand years ago is to be doubted.

According to Dunn, Paul was an atypical Jew who converted from radical extremism to a more reasonable, Gentile-inclusive version of Judaism. Paul, however, was a disciple of the great teacher, Gamaliel (son or grandson of the famous Hillel) who was renowned for his moderation and who urged a 'wait and see' policy towards the disciples of Jesus (Acts 5:33–9).

Dunn seems to be saying that the Christian Paul had become a 'moderate' Jew who welcomed the Gentiles into the covenant on the basis of faith in Christ. This enables him to retain the 'law' as the basis for the covenant with the Jews, that is, 'covenantal nomism'.

Inclusion of Gentiles

The now-converted Paul saw a way to 'include' Gentiles in the divine covenant. Dunn writes:

> We also begin to see more clearly that the law did become a concern for Paul, but primarily in its boundary defining role, that is, as separating

Jew from Gentile. Moreover, it now becomes more apparent how it was that justification through faith emerged in Paul's theology, precisely as Paul's attempt to explain why and how Gentiles are accepted by God and consequently should be accepted by their Jewish fellow believers.[10]

Comment: It is doubtful that Paul saw law as '*primarily* in its boundary defining role', as if 'law' and 'works of the law' were chiefly 'horizontal', related to ethnic differentiation. True, Paul acknowledged that law was the 'dividing wall of hostility' (*to mesotoichon tou phragmou*) between Jews and Gentiles (Eph. 2:14). But it was no less true that due to sin the 'law' and 'works of the law' were barriers to 'peace with God', a barrier removed only by the 'blood of Christ', the instrument of reconciliation (Rom. 5:1,9–10).

Table A5.1 of references to 'law' and 'works of the law' in Galatians indicates that the two entities are integrally related.

Table A5.1 References to 'law' and 'works of the law' in Galatians

Law	Works of the Law
	2:16 (x 3)
2:19,21	
	3:2,5,10
3:11–13	
3:18 – 4:5	
4:21 – 5:4	
5:14	
5:18	
5:23	
6:13	

In Galatians there are alternating references to 'works of the law' and 'law' where 'works of the law' (2:16 [x 3] and 3:2,5,10) are followed respectively by 'law' (2:19,21 and 3:11–13). The proximity of these alternating references indicates that Paul regarded the 'works of the law' as *expressions* of the 'law'. Luther put it like this: 'for Paul "works of the law" means the works of the entire law. Therefore one should not make a distinction between the Decalogue and ceremonial laws.'[11]

Paul's use of the word 'works' is 'loaded' and negative, whether 'works of the flesh' (5:19) or 'works of the law' (2:16; 3:2,5,10).[12] 'Flesh' is invisible but 'works of the flesh' are the flesh's evil activities that make 'flesh' visible. Likewise, 'law' is invisible and 'works of the law' are law's activities that are physical and visible expressions of the law. Law is hidden to our sight but is made manifest in 'works', including rituals like circumcision, food laws and Sabbaths. Paul rejects both the 'law' and its 'works' as a basis of justification with God (see Gal. 2:16).

Second, Dunn's argument is difficult to follow. On the one hand, he states that 'justification through faith emerged in Paul's theology, precisely as Paul's attempt to explain why and how Gentiles are accepted by God' (quoted above). On the other hand, however, in Galatians 2:15–16 Paul reminds his *fellow-Jew* Peter that even law-keeping Jews like them are not justified by works of the law but only by / through faith. Paul teaches that Jews are justified only by faith and not by works, yet Dunn's position depends on the belief that Jews are *already* members of the covenant *based on law*, implying that they do not need to be justified in Christ.

His reconstructions imply that Jews are saved through their continuing engagement with law and that Gentiles are justified by faith in Christ. This suggests two different routes to divine acceptance, one for Jews (law) the other for Gentiles (Christ). This is theologically impossible and contrary to Paul's explicit teaching elsewhere (e.g. Rom. 3:28–30). All people, Jews and Gentiles, are the seed of the rebel, Adam (Rom. 5:12) and all continually 'fall short of the glory of God' (Rom. 3:23). Only in Christ is the Jew saved and only in Christ is the Gentile saved.

Keeping the law

One of the planks of the 'new perspectives' is that it was *possible* to keep the law of God. According to Dunn:

> More contentious is Gal 3:10 (For all who rely on works of the law are under a curse; for it is written, 'Cursed be everyone who does not abide by all things written in the Book of the Law, and do them'). This

verse has caused more confusion than almost any other on this issue because of what Paul does *not* say, what he takes for granted. Most assume that the hidden premise runs like this: the law requires perfect obedience ('all that has been written in the book of the Law' – Deut 27:26) but since that is impossible, all are under sin's curse. There is no evidence that the law was understood to require 'perfection' in that sense . . . Obedience was considered practicable.[13]

Comment: Here Dunn reveals an optimistic belief about human capacity to please God via the law, a view that does not emerge from Galatians. So far from being easy-to-keep injunctions to mark Israel off from the nations, Paul teaches that the law was given to reveal 'transgressions' until the promised 'offspring' of Abraham (Christ) should come (Gal. 3:19). This was because the law was incapable of making people 'alive', that is, to be the source of *eternal* life (3:21). Rather, law was a prison, a harsh jail-keeper 'until Christ came' (3:23–4). In other words, contrary to Dunn's assertion about law, people under the old covenant were not able – because they were not willing – to fulfil the law. According to Timothy George, 'What was seen as a prophylactic fence of protection around the people of Israel becomes a barbed wire prison wall shutting up all of rebellious humanity . . . under its dominion and condemnation.'[14]

At heart, then, the 'new perspective' is 'semi-pelagian', that is, it holds to the belief that people in cooperation with God and by his grace can be saved. People must help God! Perhaps this is the underlying problem with the 'new perspective', the source of other difficulties.

The death of Christ

Because the 'new perspective' on Paul, as expounded by Dunn, diminished the depth and immoveable character of sin it tends also to diminish the sin-bearing work of the crucified Christ. The critical text in Galatians is: 'Christ redeemed us from the curse of the law by becoming a curse for us – for it is written, "Cursed is everyone who is hanged on a tree"' (3:13). The curse – God's curse – is on those who 'rely on' but who do not 'abide by all things written in the Book of the Law' (3:10). By coming under that curse the crucified Christ liberated law-breakers from the divine curse. This speaks of substitution by Christ for sinners but according to Dunn, 'In his death [Christ] identified with the sinning Jew and Gentile alike.'[15]

Comment: To *identify* with sinning people is by no means the same as 'bearing their curse in their place'. Furthermore, Dunn implies that this identification is confined to 'sinning' Jews and Gentiles, that is, in regard to specific sinning action, not to their settled, rebellious *natures* as sinners.

Dunn betrays his true position when he observes, 'That was why the gospel could be good news to Gentiles, as also to Jews who did not cling to covenant prerogatives.'[16] Presumably this means that the Jew who did cling to such prerogatives by observing the law – which Dunn said he was capable of doing – had no need for Christ to die under the divine curse for him.

Dunn's semi-pelagianism and a diminished atonement theology are different sides of the same coin.

Justification

Consistently with the drift of his argument Dunn is ambivalent about the nature of justification. He refers to 'the essentially relational character of Paul's understanding of justification'.[17]

Comment: Whatever else 'justification' might be, and be the basis of (e.g. reconciliation with God), it is first and foremost the *forensic* declaration 'acquitted' pronounced over the guilty so that they are now 'righteous before God' (cf. Rom. 2:13; 1 Cor. 4:3).

Dunn adds, 'The debate on whether "the righteousness of God" was subjective or objective genitive, an "activity of God" or "a gift bestowed by God" can too easily become another piece of either-or exegesis.' But then Dunn says, 'God's righteousness was to be understood as God's activity in drawing individuals into and sustaining them within the relationship, as "the power of God for salvation". The other dispute . . . was whether the verb *dikaioō* means "make righteous" or "reckon as righteous" . . . the answer is not one or the other and but both.'

Comment: Dunn's 'the answer is not one or the other and but both' tends to diminish one or the other, in this case the option, 'reckon as righteous'. Paul's use of the verb 'reckon' or 'count' (*logizomai*) from Genesis 15:6 LXX (Abraham 'believed the LORD, and he *counted* it to him as righteousness') really clinches the matter and settles the question that Dunn leaves open. That is to say, God imputes righteousness to those who are united by faith to Christ crucified and risen, as Paul says repeatedly throughout Romans 4, but also in Galatians 3:6 and 2 Corinthians 5:19.

Commentary on Galatians 2:16a–b

Ambiguity

| v. 16a | we know that a person is not justified by works of the law but (*ean mē*) through faith in Jesus Christ |
| v. 16b | so we also have believed in Christ Jesus, in order to be justified by faith in Christ and not by works of the law, because by works of the law no one will be justified. |

Dunn's comments on Galatians 2:16a are not easy to follow. He classifies *ean mē* as an 'exceptive' ('but only'), not as a direct 'adversative' ('but'). Accordingly he suggests that ' "faith in Jesus Christ" [is] the one *exception* to the rule that "no one is justified by works of the law" '. Thus people can be justified by works of the law as long as they have faith, a statement Paul reverses in the latter part of the verse. Dunn concludes that ' "works of the law" and "faith in Jesus Christ" are not necessarily being posed here as mutually exclusive antitheses'.[18] In short, he thinks Paul has introduced 'ambiguity' into his argument that he must then clarify.[19]

The problem, however, is that while *ean mē* ('but only') is formally an exceptive in reality in verse 16a it is effectively an adversative, 'but', and is so translated by RSV, NRSV, NIV and ESV. How else could the sentence be translated? The 'exceptive' option is empty of meaning. In other words, Dunn has found 'ambiguity' in verse 16a that is not there. Paul's intention in his 'not . . . but' statement is clear: 'a person is not justified by works of the law *but* through faith.'[20]

We agree with Dunn that:

> Paul was trying to move Peter away from . . . the ambiguity reflected in his conduct at Antioch, from the ambiguity regarding the acceptability of Gentiles who as Jews like him had 'believed' in Messiah Jesus. And that required a resolution of the possible 'both-and' (faith

and works) which Peter had practiced, into a straight 'either-or' (faith and *not* works) which his earlier experience of faith had indicated.[21]

It is not easy to know where Dunn stands on this issue. On the one hand, he muddies the waters by arguing for the exceptive meaning, 'but only', when a straightforward adversative 'but' is the only practical way of translating verse 6a. As a result, he argues that 'works of the law and faith in Jesus Christ are not necessarily being posed here as mutually exclusive antitheses'. On the other hand, however, in commenting on verse 16b he (rightly) observes that Paul is driving Peter from 'ambiguity' to adopt 'straight "either-or" (faith and *not* works)' attitude.

There is 'ambiguity' here, but it is not found in the words of Paul but in James Dunn's understanding of them.

Two other issues

Galatians 2:15–16 is a key passage in this important letter. There are three connected elements that expose weaknesses in Dunn's 'new perspective on Paul'.

One is that in reflecting on Peter's actions in Antioch Paul observes that the two men 'are Jews by birth and not Gentile sinners' (verse 15), yet who, like 'Gentile sinners' are 'not justified by works of the law but through faith in Jesus Christ'. This, however, is contrary to Dunn's argument that Jews are already 'in' the divine covenant through 'works of the law' and that being 'justified through faith' was applicable only to 'Gentile sinners'. These verses, however, indicate that the 'Jews by birth', Paul and Peter, like the Gentiles, only find justified acceptance with God in Christ crucified and risen. Paul says this directly to the Romans:

> Or is God the God of Jews only?
> Is he not the God of Gentiles also?
> Yes, of Gentiles also, since God is one.
> He will justify the circumcised by faith
> and the uncircumcised through faith. (Rom. 3:29–30)

The God who is 'one' (as in the *Shema* – 'Hear, O Israel: The LORD our God, the LORD is *one*' [Deut. 6:4, our italics]) justifies Jews and

Gentiles the 'one' way, that is, 'through/by faith'. There is but one route to righteousness, not two.

The second issue is that Dunn says very little about the passive voice of the three occurrences of the verb 'justified'. These passive voice references imply that *God* is the justifier and that the act of justifying is to 'vindicate' or 'set someone right'.

Dunn understands justification to mean the recognition or inclusion of Gentiles into the divine covenant. This, however, is a secondary benefit of justification, a 'horizontal' one. But the primary benefit of being justified is that *God* sets offenders in a right relationship with *himself*, and he does this by faith union with Christ and not by 'works of the law'.

This applies with equal force to both Gentile sinners and members of God's covenant people, including Paul and Peter.

Third, Dunn downplays the 'slavery' Paul says is true of 'the present Jerusalem', that is, the centre of law-keeping Israel ('Now Hagar is Mount Sinai in Arabia; she corresponds to the present Jerusalem, for she is in *slavery* with her children' [Gal. 4:25, our italics]). For Paul, spiritual *freedom* is a great good but *slavery* is a great evil (which reveals Paul's abhorrence of slavery). Dunn explains his awkward detail by saying, 'the items in this column need have no close relation than the fact that they belong to the same column.'[22] The fact is they are in the same column because that's where they belong!

That 'column' includes Hagar, Mt Sinai (=law), Jerusalem and slavery. In short and in spite of Dunn's argument, Jerusalem means law which means slavery, a great evil for Israel but also for Gentile believers.

A 'New Perspective'?

'Perspective' is a word used by artists, photographers and architects to describe different angles from which to view a landscape, a person or a building. The point is that the object is the same and a new perspective is just a different way of seeing it.

Dunn's reconstruction, however, does not represent another way of looking at Paul's teaching but represents a *different* teaching altogether. It's not so much a perspective of Paul as a revision of Paul, a rewriting of his theology.

Appendix 6

Paul Preaching Christ Crucified to Jews

We know that in every city Paul came to he went first to the synagogue and was given opportunity to expound the Scriptures, probably due to his eminence as a Pharisee and disciple of the famous Gamaliel. Luke in Acts indicates that Paul's method was to 'argue' and 'reason' from the Law and the Prophets that the expected Messiah was Jesus of Nazareth. According to Luke, Paul's message to Jews was scriptural and eschatological, summarized many times as the *Christ was Jesus* (e.g. Acts 18:5).

It was no different in Paul's own letters where scriptural fulfilment was fundamental. Paul himself said his Christ message was 'according to the Scriptures' and that in Christ 'all the promises of God find their "yes"' (1 Cor. 15:3; 2 Cor. 1:20).

There was just one problem that we today, whether Gentiles or Jews, can scarcely understand, something shocking about Paul's message, that was, in a nutshell, 'Christ crucified'.

Since the glory days of David and Solomon a millennium earlier God's people in God's land had lived under the heel of foreign powers, Assyrian, Babylonian, Persian, Greek, Roman. From the days of King David the prophets had kept the hopes of the people alive by repeated promises of a 'second' David, the Lord's Anointed One, his Messiah who would defeat the Gentile world-powers and establish Jerusalem as the world-centre of God's earthly kingdom. Those hopes were alive during the disappointing years of local Hasmonean and Herodian rulers who were paganizing puppets of foreign Gentile powers. The intertestamental work, the Psalms of Solomon, focuses on this David–Messiah, as do the prayers of the synagogue liturgy from that era.

Behold, O Lord, and raise up for them their king, the son of David . . .
And gird him with strength, that he may shatter unrighteous rulers,
And may cleanse Jerusalem from the Gentiles,
that trample her down in destruction . . .
Let him destroy the lawless Gentiles by the word of his mouth.
(Ps. *Solomon* 17:21–4)

A similar hope is found in a prayer in the Shemoneh 'Esreh from the era of the apostles:

May the branch of David soon spring forth,
and let his horn be exalted by thy salvation.
For we wait on thy salvation all the day.
Blessed art thou O Lord, who makest salvation spring forth.
(*Benediction* 15)[1]

It was one thing for Paul to assert that in Jesus the promises of God for the Messiah were at last fulfilled. It was another to proclaim that Jesus was Christ *crucified*. For many those words glow with evangelical fervour, evoking the idea of forgiveness of sins and justification from the hand of the merciful God.

But if we place ourselves in the shoes of a Jew in Corinth hearing Paul preach 'Christ *crucified*' what we don't pick up is the grammar implied by the passive voice, 'Christ crucified'. 'Crucified – *by whom*'? *Who* crucified this Christ? The Gentiles, that's who. Paul was saying – can it be true? – the Christ was crucified by *the very Gentiles* occupying the land whom the promised 'new David' was expected to defeat.

So Paul's un-winning message to Jews was that the Messiah had been humiliatingly defeated by the Gentiles and in the most public and shameful way.

Jean-Jacques Aubert summarizes the humiliation of those crucified:

Crucifixions were usually carried out outside the city limits, thus stressing the victim's rejection from the civic community. Because of the absence of blood shed out of an open and lethal wound, which evoked the glorious fate of warriors, this type of death was considered unclean, shameful, unmanly, and unworthy of a freeman. In addition, the victim was usually naked. Essential, too, was the fact that the victim lost contact with the ground, which was regarded as sacrilegious.[2]

The apostolic references to the crucifixion of the Messiah would have prompted that kind of reaction, including by Jewish hearers. They would have regarded the crucifixion of a messiah as unimaginable.

Do we see what else this implied? If the Messiah was defeated, then *Israel* was defeated. If Israel was defeated then the *God* of Israel was defeated. If God was defeated then all hope had gone – forever. Jews must now understand that they were *a permanently defeated* nation, and that the Gentiles will *forever* hold the power and authority, and that their understanding of a thousand years of prophecy was wrong.

So Paul's message, if true, demanded the most profound change imaginable in Jewish identity and hope.

True, Paul could point to Scriptures that spoke of the sufferings and sacrifice of the One who was to come. 'Christ died for our sins, *according to the scriptures'* could be seen to fulfil Isaiah's prophecies of a vicariously suffering Servant (Isa. 53:6,10,12). But that took some believing. To repeat: if the *Messiah* was defeated by the Gentiles, then so too was *the nation Israel* defeated by the Gentiles, and God was defeated by the Gentiles with all hope gone – forever.

Of course this Messiah had been resurrected, or so Paul of Tarsus claimed. But so shocked would they have been by his insistence on the Christ's *crucifixion* by the Romans that they would have been deaf to Paul's words about resurrection. In any case, as they knew, resurrection was to be cosmic, universal, apocalyptic – at the end of history to begin the new age. Resurrection was not something they associated with *an individual within* history. As Paul commented later to the Corinthians, the message of Christ crucified 'is a *skandalon* to Jews' (see 1 Cor. 1:23). ESV translation 'stumbling block' hardly captures the intensity of *skandalon*.

To drive home the point we must recall that when Paul came to the synagogue in Corinth and spoke about the Messiah crucified it was in the very recent past. It was *less than twenty years* since the Romans had crucified Jesus outside the city walls of Jerusalem. Over the centuries since, 'Christ crucified' has been used as a tag for theologians' various theories of the atonement. But the original Jewish hearers would not have thought about 'Christ crucified' theologically but *historically*. Corinth was a *Roman* city where people had doubtless regularly seen slaves and others crucified. Gladiatorial fights and crucifixions were part of entertainment in Roman cities[3] Paul, too, had probably seen people crucified, possibly even Jesus himself.[4] Crucifixions were by no means uncommon and the crucifixion of Jesus was a *recent historical* event.

Why Would Any Jew Believe This?

However, did Paul manage to convince *any* Jews about his message? It's true that the *archisynagōgos* Crispus was one Jew who accepted Paul's message (Acts 18:8). But, nonetheless, the synagogue as a whole 'opposed and reviled him' and drove him out and then arraigned him before the proconsul with the intention of banishing him from the city (Acts 18:6,12–13). Their charge was that Paul's message of a crucified Messiah could not be Jewish at all, and that his new group was not an alternative synagogue but therefore was an illegal association (*collegium illicitum*). Gallio, however, saw Paul's group as a second synagogue, a breakaway synagogue, yet a synagogue nonetheless. Was not the eminent Jew Crispus a member? 'Sort it out *amongst yourselves*, you Jews', said the proconsul, 'this belongs to your jurisdiction, not mine; it is not a civic matter.'

So how did Paul manage to persuade Crispus and other Jews about his contrarian message of a Messiah who had been crucified by the people the Messiah was expected to defeat?

The Something Else

It appears that Paul then did *something else* in his synagogue preaching to Jews besides point to scriptural fulfilment, *something* to convince them that the crucifixion and resurrection of Jesus was not the defeat of God, and not the defeat of Israel, but the powerful demonstration of the end-time *victory of God*.

It was that Paul introduced his *own story of conversion* as the living demonstration that, in the crucifixion and resurrection of Jesus the Christ, God had not been defeated but had *actually triumphed*.

What is the evidence? Simply this: the frequency with which Paul alludes to his Damascus Road conversion in his letters (e.g. 2 Cor. 5:15–17; Gal. 1:13–17; Phil. 3:12).[5] In the book of Acts, Luke tells Paul's Damascus Road story no less than three times, twice from speeches from Paul's own lips (Acts 9:1–19; 22:1–21; 26:2–24). We assume that Paul told his original hearers about himself and his personal conversion story. His re-echoing of that story in his letters so many times implies that his readers know that story. Paul's memoir dominates Galatians 1:11 – 2:21.

What point was Paul making? In telling of *his* persecution of the disciples of the Messiah he was identifying himself with his fellow-Jews who had rejected the Messiah and who had handed him over to the Gentiles to crucify him. In now proclaiming that the Messiah is the rejected Jesus *Paul was saying that he had been among those Jews who had rejected him*, at the very least retrospectively, by persecuting and attempting to destroy his followers and their 'faith' (Gal. 1:13,23).

Understood in this way we can see why Paul was so explicit in proclaiming the crucifixion of the Christ. Confronting and painful to Jews as this message was it was at the same time their means of escape from the holy wrath of God: the crucified Messiah had borne their sins.

The converted Paul who stood before Jews as the preacher of Christ crucified and risen as the fulfilment of the Scriptures was *himself* the living proof of the resurrection of the crucified Christ; and that God had not been defeated but had powerfully triumphed. The living evidence was the conversion of the Pharisee and persecutor who stood before them. Furthermore, Paul's micro-conversion 'in Christ' narrative corresponded with and was a demonstration of Israel's potential macro-conversion 'in Christ'. That 'conversion' had been anticipated in the prophetic promise of a 'new covenant' (Jer. 31 and Ezek. 11; 36).

New Creation and New Covenant

Paul never denied that he was a Jew although his opponents may have called that into question because of his scandalous message

of the Christ *crucified*. But to the end Paul was a Hebrew, an Israelite, a son of Abraham (2 Cor. 11:22; Rom. 9:1–5; 11:1).

We think of conversion as from (say) Hinduism to Islam, out of
one religion into another. Paul, however, lived and died as a Jew;
he was never converted *out* of Judaism. Paul's conversion was not
denominational but rather deeply personal, changing his heart
and his behaviour from the inside out (Rom. 2:28 – 'For no one is
a Jew who is merely one outwardly, nor is circumcision outward
and physical. But a Jew is one inwardly, and circumcision is a
matter of the heart, by the Spirit, not by the letter'). He lived no
longer to and for himself but for the one who died for him and
was raised alive for him (2 Cor. 5:15). It was a conversion from self
as the centre to Christ as the centre.

Paul's story was that he had attempted to 'live to God' through
law but had failed and was the 'wretched man'. His testimony
was that since Damascus he had 'lived to God' but now 'in', 'with'
and 'through' Christ crucified and risen. He now knew the God of
Israel intimately, as 'Abba, Father' (Gal. 4:6).

Paul's conversion was by no means merely private, personal
or idiosyncratic. If Paul's life was divided into two halves, before
he was 'in Christ' and after he was 'in Christ' then so too, he
said, is salvation history divided into two halves, the old covenant before Christ and new covenant since and because of Christ.
Old covenant prophets Jeremiah (31) and Ezekiel (11; 36) prophesied a new covenant to fulfil and replace the existing covenant,
when God would put his law 'within the hearts' of the people
so that each person 'knew the Lord'. The coming of Christ, his
death and resurrection and his gift of the Spirit spelt the end of
the old covenant and the beginning of the new covenant, what we
may call the (potential) macro-conversion of Israel 'in the Christ'.
Paul's personal, *micro*-conversion corresponded with and was a
demonstration of the possibility of the *macro-conversion* of Israel
'in Christ'.[6]

Figure A6.1 The Old and the New

old covenant   Christ   new covenant

Israel -------------------- | --------------------

Paul ------------------- | -------------------------

former life   new creation

In other words, Paul himself – Hebrew, Israelite, son of Abraham – as a 'new creation' and 'minister of a new covenant' was the living demonstration that the long-prophesied new covenant had come. Paul was both a minister of the new covenant and the evidence of its arrival. This was his message to Jews and this is why his own story that he frequently told was so important.

Conclusion

We are concerned to establish Paul's original message to the Jews in the synagogues of the Diaspora. From both Luke's accounts and Paul's own letters it is evident that Paul proclaimed Jesus as the Christ in fulfilment of Scriptures. Inevitably, however, this immediately raised the contentious issue that Paul's Christ had been *crucified* – by the Gentiles. In other words, this Christ had been comprehensively humiliated and defeated by the very people the Davidic Messiah was expected to overcome.

It is difficult to understand how any Jews came to accept this astonishing message. One explanation is found in the witness of Paul about himself, given in the synagogues. He, a Hebrew of Hebrews, had been radically converted in the crucified and risen Messiah. His own life was a demonstration in miniature of the expected coming of the long-prophesied new covenant. 'In Christ' Paul himself was a 'new creation'. Such was the power of Paul's own narrative that a synagogue *archisynagōgos* like Crispus was himself persuaded by the message of Paul.

Bibliography

Adamson, J.B. *The Epistle of James* New International Commentary on the New Testament (Grand Rapids: Eerdmans, 1976).

Alexander, P.S. 'Orality in Pharisaic-Rabbinic Judaism at the Turn of the Eras'. Pages 159–84 in *Jesus and the Oral Gospel Tradition* (ed. H. Wansbrough; Sheffield: JSOT Press, 1991).

Aubert, J.-J. 'A Double Standard in Roman Criminal Law?' Pages 94–133 in *Speculum Iuris: Roman Law as a Reflection of Social and Economic Life in Antiquity* (ed. J.-J. Aubert and B. Sirks; Ann Arbor: University of Michigan, 2002).

Barclay, J.M.G. *Obeying the Truth: Paul's Ethics in Galatians* (Vancouver: Regent College, 2005).

Barnett, P. *Paul: Missionary of Jesus* (Grand Rapids: Eerdmans, 2008).

Barnett, P.W. *The Birth of Christianity: The First Twenty Years* (Grand Rapids: Eerdmans, 2005).

Barnett, P.W. *The Corinthian Question* (Leicester: Inter-Varsity Press, 2011).

Barnett, P.W. *Finding the Historical Christ* (Grand Rapids: Eerdmans, 2009).

Barnett, P.W. 'The Jewish Sign Prophets AD 40–70, Their Intention and Origin'. *New Testament Studies* 27 (1980): pp. 679–97.

Barnett, Paul. *Paul Missionary of Jesus* (Grand Rapids: Eerdmans, 2008).

Barrett, C.K. 'The Allegory of Abraham, Sarah and Hagar in the Argument of Galatians' in *Essays on Paul* (London: SPCK, 1982), pp. 154–68.

Barrett, C.K. *A Commentary on the Second Epistle to the Corinthians* (London: A & C Black, 1973).

Barrett, C.K. *The New Testament Background: Selected Documents* (London: SPCK, rev. edn, 1987).

Bauckham, R. 'James and the Jerusalem Church'. Pages 415–80 in *The Book of Acts in Its First Century Setting. Vol 4 Palestinian Setting* (ed. R. Bauckham; Grand Rapids: Eerdmans, 1995).

Bauckham, R. *Jesus and the Eyewitnesses* (Grand Rapids: Eerdmans, 2006).

Bauckham, R. *The Book of Acts in Its First Century Setting. Vol 4 Palestinian Setting* (Grand Rapids: Eerdmans, 1995).

Beker, J. Christiaan. *Paul the Apostle: The Triumph of God in Life and Thought* (Edinburgh: T & T Clark, 1980).

Belleville, Linda L. ' "Under Law": Structural Analysis and the Pauline Concept of Law in Galatians 3:21–4:11'. *Journal for the Study of the New Testament* 26 (1986): pp. 59–78.

Betz, H.D. *Galatians* (Hermeneia: Philadelphia, 1979).

Bockmuehl, M. 'Antioch and James the Just'. Pages 155–98 in *James the Just and Christian Origins* Supplements to Novum Testamentum 98 (ed. B. Chilton and C.A. Evans; Leiden: Brill, 1999).

Boring, M.E., K. Berger and C. Colpe eds. *Hellenistic Commentary to the New Testament* (Nashville: Abingdon, 1995 ET).

Bornkamm, G. *Paul* (London: Hodder & Stoughton, 1971 ET).

Bruce, F.F. 'The Galatian Problem 2. North or South Galatians?' *Bulletin of the John Rylands University Library of Manchester* 52 (1970).

Bruce, F.F. 'Phrygia'. *Anchor Bible Dictionary* vol. 5 (ed. D.N. Freedman; 6 vols; New York, 1992).

Bruce, F.F. *New Testament History* (London: Oliphants, 1971).

Bruce, F.F. *Paul: Apostle of the Free Spirit* (Exeter: Paternoster, 1977).

Bruce, F.F. 'The Spirit in the Letter to the Galatians'. Pages 36–48 in *Essays on Apostolic Themes* (ed. P. Elbert; Peabody: Hendrickson, 1985).

Brunt, P.A. 'Procuratorial Jurisdiction'. *Latomus* 25 (1966), pp. 461–87.

Burton, E. de Witt, trans. *The Epistle to the Galatians*, International Critical Commentary (Edinburgh: T & T Clark, 1980).

Campbell, C.R. *Paul and Union with Christ* (Grand Rapids: Zondervan, 2012).

Campbell, Douglas A. 'An Anchor for Pauline Chronology: Paul's Flight from "the Ethnarch of King Aretas" (2 Corinthians 11:32–33)'. *Journal of Biblical Literature* 121/2 (2002): pp. 279–302.

Campbell, Douglas A. 'Galatians 5.11: Evidence of an Early Law-Observant Mission by Paul'. *NTS* 57/3 (2011).

Campbell, Douglas A. 'Paul in Pamphylia (Acts 13.13–14a; 14.24b–26): A Critical Note'. *New Testament Studies* 46.4 (2000): pp. 595–602.

Carson, D.A., P.T. O'Brien and M.A. Siefrid, eds. *Justification and Variegated Nomism 1, The Complexities of Second Temple Judaism* (Grand Rapids: Baker, 2001).

Catchpole, D.R. 'Paul, James and the Apostolic Decree'. *New Testament Studies* 23 (1977): pp. 428–44.

Cook, John Granger. 'Crucifixion as Spectacle in Roman Campania'. *Novum Testamentum* 54 (2012): pp. 68–100.

Danby, H. *The Mishnah* (Oxford: Clarendon Press, 1933).

Davids, P.H. 'Palestinian Traditions in the Epistle of James'. Pages 33–57 in *James the Just and Christian Origins* Supplements to Novum Testamentum 98 (ed. B. Chilton and C.A. Evans; Leiden: Brill, 1999).

Dessau, H. *Inscriptiones latinae selectae* (Leipzig: Weidmann, 1892–1916).

Dodd, C.H. *The Apostolic Preaching and its Development* (London: Hodder & Stoughton, 1936).

Du Toit, Andrie B. 'A Tale of Two Cities: "Tarsus or Jerusalem" Revisited', *New Testament Studies* 46/4 (2000): pp. 375–402.

Dunn, J.D.G. *Beginning from Jerusalem* (Grand Rapids: Eerdmans, 2009).

Dunn, J.D.G. *The Epistle to the Galatians* (London: A & C Black, 1993).

Dunn, J.D.G. 'The Relationship Between Paul and Jerusalem according to Galatians 1 and 2'. *New Testament Studies* 28/4 (1982): pp. 461–78.

Dunn, J.D.G. *The Theology of Paul the Apostle* (Grand Rapids: Eerdmans, 1998).

Ellis, E.E. *The Making of the New Testament Documents* (Leiden: Brill, 1999).

Elmer, Ian J. *Paul and the Judaisers*. Wissenschaftliche Untersuchungen zum Neuen Testament 258 (Tübingen: Mohr Siebeck, 2009).

Fiensy, D.A. 'The Roman Empire and Asia Minor'. Pages 48–50 in *The Face of New Testament Studies* (ed. S. McKnight and G. Osborne; Grand Rapids: Baker Academic, 2004).

Fitzmyer, J. *Luke the Theologian: Aspects of His Teaching* (London: Geoffrey Chapman, 1989).

Fitzmyer, J.A. *According to Paul* (New York: Paulist Press, 1992).

George, T. 'Modernizing Luther, Domesticating Paul: Another Perspective'. Pages 437–63 in *Justification and Variegated Nomism* (ed. D.A. Carson, P.T. O'Brien and M.A. Seifrid; Grand Rapids: Baker Academic, 2004).

Gilman, John. 'Titus', *Anchor Bible Dictionary* 6 (ed. D.N. Freedman; New York, 1992), pp. 581–2.

Goodman, M. *The Ruling Class of Judea* (Cambridge: Cambridge University Press, 1987).

Harrisville, Roy A. 'Before PISTIS CHRISTOU: The Objective Genitive as Good Greek'. *Novum Testamentum* 48/4 (2006): pp. 353–8.

Harvey, A.E. ' "Forty Strokes Save One": Social Aspects of Judaizing and Apostasy'. Pages 79–96 in *Alternative Approaches to New Testament Study* (ed. A.E. Harvey; London: SPCK, 1985).

Hays, R.B. 'PISTIS and Pauline Christology: What is at Stake?' Pages 35–60 in *Pauline Theology IV. Looking Back, Pressing On*, Symposium Series 4 (ed. E.E. Johnson and D.M. Hay; Atlanta Scholars, 1977).

Hemer, C.J. 'The Adjective "Phrygia" '. *Journal of Theological Studies* 27 (1976): pp. 122–6.

Hemer, C.J. *The Book of Acts in the Setting of Hellenistic History* Wissenschaftliche Untersuchungen zum Neuen Testament 49 (Tübingen: J.C.B. Mohr, 1989).

Hemer, C.J. 'Phrygia, a Further Note'. *Journal of Theological Studies* 28 (1977): pp. 99–101.

Hengel, M. *The Pre-Christian Paul* (London: SCM, 1991 ET).

Hengel, M. *Saint Peter: The Underestimated Apostle* (Grand Rapids: Eerdmans, 2010 ET).

Hengel, M. 'The Stance of the Apostle Paul Towards the Law in the Unknown Years Between Damascus and Antioch'. Pages 75–103 in *Justification and Variegated Nomism 2, The Paradoxes of Paul* (ed. D.A. Carson, P.T. O'Brien and M.A. Siefrid; Grand Rapids: Baker, 2004).

Hengel, Martin. *Acts and the History of Earliest Christianity* (London: SCM, 1979 ET).

Hengel, M. and A.M. Schwemer. *Paul Between Damascus and Antioch: The Unknown Years* (Louisville: Westminster John Knox Press, 1997 ET).

Hunn, Debbie. '*Ean mē* in Galatians 2:16: A Look at Greek Literature', *Novum Testamentum* 49 (2007): pp. 281–90.

Jobes, Karen H. 'Jerusalem, Our Mother: Metalepsis and Intertextuality in Galatians 4:21–31', *Westminster Theological Journal* 55/2 (1993).

Kern, P.H. *Rhetoric and Galatians: Assessing and Approach to Paul's Epistle*, Society for New Testament Studies 101 (Cambridge: Cambridge University Press, 1998).

Lightfoot, J.B. *The Epistle of St. Paul to the Galatians* (London: Macmillan, 1865).

Matlock, R. Barry. 'Detheologizing the PISTIS CHRISTOU Debate: Cautionary Remarks from a Lexical Semantic Perspective'. *Novum Testamentum* 42/1 (2000): pp. 1–23.

McDonald, L.M. and S.E. Porter. *Early Christianity and Its Sacred Literature* (Peabody: Hendrickson, 2000).

Meeks, W.A. 'Review of H.D. Betz, *A Commentary on Paul's Letter to the Churches in Galatia* (Philadelphia: Hermeneia, 1979)'. *Journal of Biblical Literature* 100 (1981): pp. 304–7.

Millar, Fergus. *The Roman Near East 31 BC – AD 337* (Cambridge, Mass.: Harvard University Press, 1993).

Mitchell, Margaret M. 'Peter's "Hypocrisy" and Paul's: Two "Hypocrites" at the Foundation of Earliest Christianity?' *New Testament Studies* 58/2 (2012): pp. 212–34.

Mitchell, S. 'Galatia'. *Anchor Bible Dictionary* vol. 2 (ed. D.N. Freedman; 6 vols; New York, 1992).

Mitchell, S. *Anatolia: Land of Men and Gods in Asia Minor II* (Oxford: Clarendon Press; 1995).

Moffatt, James. *An Introduction to the Literature of the New Testament* (Edinburgh: T & T Clark, 3rd edn, 1918).

Owen, Paul L. 'The "Works of the Law" in Romans and Galatians: A New Defense of the Subjective Genitive'. *Journal of Biblical Literature* 126/3 (2007): pp. 553–77.

Painter, J. *Just James* (Columbia: University of South Carolina, 1997).

Plummer, Alfred. *St Luke International Critical Commentary* (Edinburgh: T & T Clark, 1901).

Porter, S.E. 'The "We" Passages'. Pages 545–74 in *The Book of Acts in Its First Century Setting. Vol 2 Graeco-Roman Setting* (ed. D.W.J. Gill and C. Gempf; Grand Rapids: Eerdmans, 1994).

Ramsay, W.M. *The Church in the Roman Empire* (London: Hodder & Stoughton, 1893).

Ramsay, W.M. *St. Paul the Traveller and Roman Citizen* (Grand Rapids: Baker, 1960).

Richards, E.R. *Paul and First-Century Letter Writing* (Downers Grove: InterVarsity Press, 2004).

Riesner, R. 'Jesus as Preacher and Teacher'. Pages 185–210 in *Jesus and the Oral Gospel Tradition* (ed. H. Wansbrough; Sheffield: JSOT Press, 1991).

Riesner, R. *Paul's Early Period* (Grand Rapids: Eerdmans, 1998 ET).

Robinson, D.W.B. ' "Faith of Jesus Christ" – a New Testament Debate'. *Reformed Theological Review* 29 (1970): pp. 71–81.

Robinson, J.A.T. *Redating the New Testament* (London: SCM, 1976).

Rothschild, Clare K. 'Pisidian Antioch in Acts 13: The Denouement of the South Galatian Hypothesis'. *Novum Testamentum* 54 (2012): pp. 334–53.

Sanders, E.P. *Paul and Palestinian Judaism* (Philadelphia: Fortress Press, 1987).

Schäfer, P. 'New Testament and the Hekhalot Literature: The Journey into Heaven in Paul and Merkavah Mysticism'. *Journal of Jewish Studies* 35 (1985): pp. 19–35.

Schmidt, K.L. and M.A. Schmidt, 'Pōroō', *Theological Dictionary of the New Testament* 5 (ed. G. Kittel and G. Friedrich; trans. G.W. Bromiley; Grand Rapids, 1964–76), pp. 1025–8.

Schnabel, E. *Early Christian Mission* (Leicester: Apollos, 2004 ET).

Schnelle, U. *Apostle Paul* (Grand Rapids: Baker Academic, 2005).

Schreiner, Thomas R. *Paul Apostle of God's Glory in Christ: A Pauline Theology* (Downers Grove: InterVarsity Press, 2001).

Schürer, E. *The History of the Jewish People in the Age of Jesus Christ* (ed. G. Vermes et al.; Edinburgh: T & T Clark, rev. edn, 1979).

Sidebottom, E.M. *James, Jude and 2 Peter* New Century Bible (Nelson: London, 1967).

Silva, M. 'Galatians'. Pages 785–812 in *Commentary of New Testament Use of the Old Testament* (ed. G.K. Beale and D.A. Carson; Grand Rapids: Baker Academic, 2007).

Steinmetz, D. *Punishment and Freedom: The Rabbinic Construction of Criminal Law* (Philadelphia: University of Pennsylvania Press, 2008).

Tabor, J.D. *Things Unutterable: Paul's Ascent to Paradise in its Greco-Roman, Judaic, and Early Christian Contexts* (Lanham, MD: University Press of America, 1986).

Taylor, John W. 'Demonstrating Transgression by Building up the Faith: Argumentation in Galatians 2:17–18', *Bulletin for Biblical Research* 22/4 (2012): pp. 547–62.

Taylor, N. *Paul, Antioch and Jerusalem: A Study in Relationships and Authority in Earliest Christianity* JSNT Supplement 66 (Sheffield: JSOT Press, 1989).

Turcan, R. *The Cults of the Roman Empire* (Oxford: Blackwell, 1996).

Wansbrough, H., ed. *Jesus and the Oral Gospel Tradition* (JSOT Press, 1991).

Watson, F. 'By Faith (of Christ): An Exegetical Dilemma and Its Scriptural Solution'. Pages 147–63 in *The Faith of Jesus Christ: Exegetical, Biblical and Theological Studies* (ed. Michael E. Bird and Preston M. Sprinkle; Milton Keynes: Paternoster, 2009).

Watson, F. *Paul, Judaism and the Gentiles* (Cambridge: Cambridge University Press, 1986).

Wenham, D. 'Acts and the Pauline Corpus II: The Evidence of Parallels'. Pages 215–58 in *The Book of Acts in Its First Century Setting. Vol 1 Ancient Literary Setting* (ed. B.W. Winter and A.D. Clarke; Grand Rapids: Eerdmans, 1993).

Williams, Sam K. 'Justification and the Spirit in Galatians', *Journal for the Study of the New Testament* 29 (1987): pp. 91–100.

Witherington, B. *Grace in Galatia* (London: T & T Clark, 2004).

Wright, N.T. '4QMMT and Paul'. Pages 104–32 in *History and Exegesis: Festschrift for E.E. Ellis* (London: T & T Clark, 2006).

Endnotes

Preface

[1] Scholars are uncertain about the jurisdiction to which Damascus belonged. In AD 34 Damascus may have been assigned to Herod Antipas after being either part of the province of Syria, or alternatively a free city–state and a member of the Decapolis.

1. Paul in Syria and Cilicia (AD 37–47)

[1] Syria–Cilicia had been a single province from 38 BC but the two regions were separated under Vespasian in AD 72. While its chief cities during Paul's era were Antioch and Tarsus, it is likely that until Paul moved to Antioch he concentrated on Tarsus and the region of Cilicia. For details of settlements in Cilicia see E. Schnabel, *Early Christian Mission* (Leicester: Apollos, 2004 ET), pp. 1064–9.

Damascus was subject to different jurisdictions. It was part of Roman Syria until AD 34 (or, alternatively a free city as part of the Decapolis), under Antipas tetrarch of Galilee–Perea AD 34–6, and part of Aretas's Nabatean kingdom AD 36–40. See further Douglas A. Campbell, 'An Anchor for Pauline Chronology: Paul's Flight from "the Ethnarch of King Aretas" (2 Corinthians 11:32–33)', *JBL* 121/2 (2002): pp. 279–302.

[2] The calculation of AD 47 as Paul's second visit to Jerusalem depends on
(a) AD 33 as the date of the first Easter,
(b) AD 34 as the year of Paul's conversion (having occurred between one and two years after the first Easter), and
(c) the 'fourteen years' being calculated directly from Paul's conversion in AD 34 (33+1+14 = 47). There are other possibilities:

(i) Based on AD 30 dating for Jesus' crucifixion–resurrection
    30+1+14 = AD 45

(ii) Based on AD 30 dating for Jesus' crucifixion–resurrection
    30+1+3+14 = AD 48

(iii) Based on AD 33 dating for Jesus' crucifixion–resurrection
    33+1+3+14 = AD 51

Options (ii) and (iii) assume the 'fourteen years' should be *added* to the three years. Options (i) and (ii) are possible but option (iii) is too late since it does not allow for the mission to Galatia, and the Jerusalem Council and the travel time from Jerusalem to Corinth where Paul arrived in AD 50 (cf. Acts 18:2,12).

For discussion of the dating of Galatians see Appendix 1: Dating Galatians.

3   I have not included Paul's ministry with Barnabas in Antioch (Acts 11:25–6) in these references. For the greater part of the decade in Syria and Cilicia, Paul was not in Antioch but one supposes chiefly in Tarsus and the region of Cilicia.

4   This observation is not affected by one's opinion whether Gal. 2:1–10 and Acts 15:6–31 refer to the same or to different events. Either way the timeframe is not materially altered.

5   M. Hengel and A.M. Schwemer, *Paul Between Damascus and Antioch: The Unknown Years* (Louisville: Westminster John Knox Press, 1997 ET), p. 157.

6   Hengel and Schwemer, *Paul*, pp. 152–7 devote most effort in correcting the impression from Luke that the apostle only began his mission to Gentiles in Cyprus and Antioch in Pisidia. They appeal to the coincidence of language (*exapostellō*) in Acts 9:30 ('the brothers . . . *sent* him off to Tarsus') and Acts 22:21 ('I will *send* you far away to the Gentiles'), concluding that the divine mission to the Gentiles was to be fulfilled in Tarsus, at least initially. See also their dependence on Acts 15:22–3,41 as evidence for Paul's mission to Gentiles in Syria and Cilicia during these years (pp. 156–7).

7   F.F. Bruce, *New Testament History* (London: Oliphants, 1971), pp. 232–3; R. Riesner, *Paul's Early Period* (Grand Rapids: Eerdmans, 1998 ET), pp. 266–8; U. Schnelle, *Apostle Paul* (Grand Rapids: Baker Academic, 2005), p. 113; Schnabel, *Early Christian Mission*, pp. 1064–9; J.D.G. Dunn, *Beginning from Jerusalem* (Grand Rapids: Eerdmans, 2009), pp. 492, 721–2.

8   In the New Testament, the leading disciple of Jesus is referred to as Peter, Cephas and Simon, which is confusing. From now on we shall refer to him as Peter.

9   See Appendix 2: Luke's Acts as a Historical Source for Paul.

10 See Appendix 1: Dating Galatians.

11 It is possible that the 'Jerusalem' chapters of Mark (i.e. Mark 11 – 16) had been written quite early. Caiaphas died AD 37 and the reference to his office but absence of his name may point to a text that predated his death. Further, the creation of churches in Judea, Galilee and Samaria may indicate their need for written texts for teaching and worship (Acts 9:31–2; Gal. 1:21–4; 1 Thess. 2:14). Mark's words, 'Let the reader understand' (Mark 13:14) within the Olivet apocalypse may refer to Gaius' attempted desecration of the temple in AD 40 and indicate that this discourse was read and explained at that time.

12 Josephus observed that, 'The Pharisees have delivered to the people a great many observances by succession from their fathers, which are not written in the law of Moses' (*Jewish Antiquities* xiii.10.6; also Mishnah *Pirqe Aboth* 1:1). See P.S. Alexander, 'Orality in Pharisaic– Rabbinic Judaism at the Turn of the Eras', in *Jesus and the Oral Gospel Tradition* (ed. H. Wansbrough; Sheffield: JSOT Press, 1991), pp. 159–84.

13 See R. Riesner, 'Jesus as Preacher and Teacher', in Wansbrough, *Oral Gospel Tradition*, pp. 185–210. Cf. J. Neusner, 'No rabbi was so important to rabbinic Judaism as Jesus was to Christianity. None prophesied as an independent authority. None left a category of I–sayings, for none had the prestige to do so' (quoted in Riesner, 'Jesus as Preacher and Teacher', p. 208).

14 Such oral transmission is not the 'informal controlled' oral transmission of village raconteurs as urged by Kenneth Bailey and James Dunn, but rather the precise 'memorized' transmission of the rabbis proposed by Birger Gerhardsson. For critical discussion see R. Bauckham, *Jesus and the Eyewitnesses* (Grand Rapids: Eerdmans, 2006), pp. 249–63.

15 See Appendix 1: Dating Galatians.

16 See Appendix 1: Dating Galatians.

2. The Problem: Paul's Mission Audiences

1 While *en tois ethnesin* did not direct Paul to preach '*to* the Gentiles' it is natural to understand it that way. Had Paul been intended to preach only to Jews 'among the Gentiles' he would probably have written 'that I might preach him in the Diaspora'.

2 In light of the implied contrast with 'Jews' in Acts 11:19 it is better to translate *Hellēnistas* as 'Greeks' and not 'Hellenists' (i.e. Hellenistic Jews, as e.g., ESV does).

3 Paul's 'then after three years' (*epeita meta etē tria* – Gal. 1:18) is counted from the Damascus 'call' (Gal. 1:14–17). So is 'then after fourteen

years' (*epeita dia dekatessarōn etōn* – Gal. 2:1) to be counted (a) from the
Damascus 'call', or (b) from the visit to Jerusalem 'after three years'?
For two reasons we have opted for (a). First, because 3 + 14 (= 16 or 17
years) seems too long a period between Paul's 'call' and that second
journey to Jerusalem, and second because the preposition *dia* is better
translated 'through' rather than 'after' (as RSV). 'Through fourteen
years' is consistent with a *period* in which Paul had 'not been running
in vain' (Gal. 2:2), during which God had 'worked through him [in the
mission] to the Gentiles' (Gal. 2:8).

4   See Appendix 2: Luke's Acts as a Historical Source for Paul.
5   This dating is based on the assumptions, that (i) the first Easter was AD
    33, and (ii) the Damascus event occurred between one and two years
    later.
6   F. Watson, *Paul, Judaism and the Gentiles* (Cambridge: CUP, 1986), pp.
    29–30; N. Taylor, *Paul, Antioch and Jerusalem: A Study in Relationships
    and Authority in Earliest Christianity*, JSNT Supplement 66 (Sheffield:
    JSOT Press, 1989), pp. 29–30. G. Bornkamm, *Paul* (London: Hodder &
    Stoughton, 1971 ET), p. 27 argues that Paul engaged in mission work
    among Gentiles at Damascus.
7   M. Hengel and A.M. Schwemer, *Paul Between Damascus and Antioch:
    The Unknown Years* (Louis (Deut. 27:6) ville: Westminster John Knox
    Press, 1997 ET), p. 94.
8   Hengel and Schwemer, *Paul*, p. 107.
9   Taylor, *Paul, Antioch and Jerusalem*, pp. 82, 84–5.
10 Taylor, *Paul, Antioch and Jerusalem*, p. 84.
11 Taylor, *Paul, Antioch and Jerusalem*, pp. 143–5.
12 Taylor, *Paul, Antioch and Jerusalem*, p. 90.
13 Taylor, *Paul, Antioch and Jerusalem*, p. 122 regards Gal. 1:11 – 2:14 as
    containing 'anachronistic assertions' that have been accepted without
    'adequate scrutiny . . . statements made late in his career read back
    anachronistically and uncritically into the earlier stages'.
14 Hengel and Schwemer, *Paul*, pp. 91–105.
15 Taylor, *Paul*, p. 186.
16 Against those who refuse altogether to depend on Acts or those who
    do so with extreme scepticism the view taken here is that Luke's is a
    credible account. This author was Paul's companion and well placed
    to know the details of his life, the more so if he was indeed a member of
    the church of Antioch, as Fitzmyer and others think. Those who accept
    only the details in Paul's letters and who reject or seriously doubt the
    narrative structure of Acts have no real basis for establishing a chro-
    nology of Paul's ministry throughout those years. How does Luke get
    so much right, as comparison with Paul's autobiography in Gal. 1:13

– 2:10 and Acts 9 – 11 indicates, unless he had reliable access to Paul's own oral accounts? See Appendix 2: Luke's Acts as a Historical Source for Paul.

17 For discussion about Paul's ministry in Damascus see Douglas A. Campbell, 'An Anchor for Pauline Chronology: Paul's Flight from "the Ethnarch of King Aretas" (2 Corinthians 11:32–33)', *JBL* 121/2 (2002); pp. 279–302.

18 *War* 2.561.

19 At the outbreak of the war between the Jews and the Romans in AD 66 the people of Damascus captured and killed the entire Jewish population, 10,600 in all (*Jewish War* ii.59–60).

20 The desert kingdom of Nabatea is located on the Arabian plateau to the east of Perea and the Dead Sea. In the previous century the former nomads of this region learned how to dam, channel and even mine water and they established a series of settlements, notably their capital, the rock–city necropolis Petra, to the south. Like the people of Israel and the Idumeans the Nabateans had become deeply influenced by Hellenism, though they retained their native tongue (now transcribed in Greek script).

21 E. Schnabel, *Early Christian Mission* (Leicester: Apollos, 2004 ET), p. 1038 (following Murphy–O'Connor) argues that Paul confined his ministry to northern Nabatea, including the cities of the Decapolis east of the Jordan (p. 1043). Hengel and Schwemer, *Paul*, p. 184 contend that Paul travelled as far south as the capital, Petra. In reality, we do not have sufficient evidence to do more than guess where Paul went in Arabia.

22 Cf. Hengel and Schwemer, *Paul*, p. 113.

23 The Nabateans had dynastic connections with the Idumean Herods: (i) Herod's mother Cypros was from an aristocratic Nabatean family in Petra; (ii) Herod Antipas, tetrarch of Galilee and Perea from 4 BC, son of Herod the King, married Phasaelis, the daughter of Aretas IV, Nabatea's most famous king (9 BC – AD 40). Antipas' shabby treatment of the Nabatean princess provoked the implacable hatred of her father who bided his time to inflict vengeance. Various clashes *c.*34–6 erupted into open war when the Nabateans decimated the army of the tetrarch of Galilee and Perea (Josephus, *Jewish Antiquities* xviii.111–114).

24 E. Schürer, *The History of the Jewish People in the Age of Jesus Christ* II (T & T Clark: Edinburgh, 1979), p. 129.

25 R. Riesner, *Paul's Early Period* (Grand Rapids: Eerdmans, 1994), pp. 70–79 believes Damascus was an independent city–state, based on the reference in 2 Cor. 11:32 to 'the *city* of Damascus'.

26 Fergus Millar, *The Roman Near East 31 BC — AD 337* (Cambridge, Mass.: Harvard University Press, 1993), pp. 56–7 states that Damascus was under Nabatean control at the time. Campbell, 'An Anchor', pp. 279–302 argues that Aretas had seized Damascus following his defeat of Antipas in *c*. 36 and appointed an ethnarch to govern it (cf. 'An Anchor', p. 281).

27 Luke's use of imperfective verb tenses for Paul's ministry in Jerusalem (Acts 9:28–9) suggests a rather protracted period of time there.

28 In their Chronological Table (xi) Hengel and Schwemer, *Paul*, allocate about five years for Paul's ministry in Tarsus and Cilicia. Schnabel, *Early Christian Mission*, p. 1056 indicates a period of about nine years.

29 See further Hengel and Schwemer, *Paul*, pp. 151–61; Schnabel, *Early Christian Mission*, p. 1058.

30 Substantial wealth, property worth 500 drachmae (equivalent to two years' wages), was fixed as a qualification for enrolment as a citizen of Tarsus (Dio Chrysostom, *Orations* 34.23). Tarsus appears to have been unusual in regard to individual citizenship for Jews. Full citizenship on an individual basis was typically disallowed to Jews living in Greek cities who only enjoyed a corporate citizenship, in order freely to practise their ancestral religion.

31 Hengel and Schwemer, *Paul*, pp. 158–67.

32 D.R.Catchpole, 'Paul, James and the Apostolic Decree', *NTS* 23 (1977), p. 436. Although Luke doesn't say Paul founded these churches it is reasonable to conclude that he did.

33 See Appendix 1: Dating Galatians.

3. Paul in Tarsus and Cilicia (c. AD 37–45)

1 Various descriptions of Tarsus have survived from those times. Paul himself described Tarsus as a 'no mean city' (Acts 21:39). Strabo wrote that 'Tarsus lies in a plain . . . and it is intersected by the Cydnus River . . . [whose] source is not very far away and its stream passes through a deep ravine and then empties immediately into the city; its discharge is both cold and swift' (*Geography* 14.5.12–13).

The fertile plain of Cilicia is hemmed in by the Mediterranean to the south and the Taurus Mountains which encircle the region from the north to the west where they come down to the sea. The trade route from the east crosses eastern Cilicia through Tarsus before striking north through the Cilician Gates, the main access through the Taurus range. The city of Tarsus is located about ten miles from the coast.

Originally Hittite but more recently Persian, Tarsus had been refounded as a Greek city following Alexander's conquests of that region; Alexander won the battle of Issus at the gateway to Syria in 333 BC. Tarsus was among the cities that Alexander refounded as a Greek city.

> Alexander established more than seventy cities among savage tribes
> and sowed all Asia with Grecian magistracies
> and thus overcame its uncivilized and brutish manner of living
> . . . for by the founding of cities in these places
> savagery was extinguished and the worst element gaining familiarity with the better,
> changed under its influence. (Plutarch, *Alexander*, 328)

As part of the Seleucid kingdom, whose capital was Antioch in Syria, Tarsus became a noted Hellenistic city with a reputation for scholarship. According to Strabo, Tarsus was famous for various schools of rhetoric, in particular for the teaching of Stoic philosophy (*Geography* 14.5.12–13).

More recently the Romans had expanded their empire eastwards under the leadership of Pompey. In 67 BC Cilicia had been annexed as a province to Rome. Dio Chrysostom described the political significance of Tarsus as 'the greatest of all the cities of Cilicia and a metropolis from the start' (*Orations* 37.7–8).

In c.44 BC Augustus rewarded the city for its support for him against Cassius with tax exemptions, by enlarging the territory of their city so as to be coterminous with Cilicia itself and bestowing on it the status of a 'free city'. These measures led to the city's burgeoning prosperity so that it soon was second in that region only to Antioch of Syria. In 38 BC eastern Cilicia was joined administratively to Syria as the province of 'Syria and Cilicia', the title by which Paul correctly refers to it (Gal. 1:21; cf. Acts 15:23,41).

From early in the second century BC large numbers of Jews settled in Cilicia where they are known to have been powerful and influential. It is likely that the hostility Antiochus IV showed towards Jews in Judea he also showed to Jews in other parts of his empire, including to a region like Cilicia that was close to Antioch. Numbers of Jews appear to have succumbed to syncretism under the pressure of Antiochus' aggressive Hellenism. Others were seduced by the gentle influences of Greek culture – the theatre, the gymnasia, the games and the philosophic academies. Therefore Jews like Paul's parents who retained intact their integrity under the covenant must have exercised considerable determination to do so. Paul's strictness of Jewish upbringing, as described beforehand, demands that his family were among those who retained their distinctive Jewishness against the powerful influence of Hellenism.

2 F.F. Bruce, *Paul: Apostle of the Free Spirit* (Exeter: Paternoster, 1977), p. 132 called it 'the largely unchronicled interval between Paul's return to Tarsus and his call to Antioch'.

3 See e.g. C.K. Barrett, *A Commentary on the Second Epistle to the Corinthians* (London: A & C Black, 1973), 'the floggings will probably go back to the earliest period of his apostolic work' (p. 297). M. Hengel, 'The Stance of the Apostle Paul Towards the Law in the Unknown Years Between Damascus and Antioch' in D.A. Carson, P.T. O'Brien and M.A. Siefrid (eds), *Justification and Variegated Nomism 2, The Paradoxes of Paul* (Grand Rapids: Baker, 2004), pp. 75–103 suggests that these beatings began in Syria (i.e. Damascus). See also M. Hengel and A.M. Schwemer, *Paul Between Damascus and Antioch: The Unknown Years* (Louisville: Westminster John Knox: ET 1997), p. 464 n. 1261.

4 Josephus, *Jewish Antiquities* iv. 238.

5 Quoted in H. Danby, *The Mishnah* (Oxford: Clarendon Press, 1933), pp. 460 and 408. For general discussion see D.A. Carson, P.T. O'Brien and M.A. Siefrid, *Justification and Variegated Nomism 1, The Complexities of Second Temple Judaism* (Grand Rapids: Baker, 2001).

6 Gal. 3:6–21 reflects Paul's standard scriptural argument in the synagogues against those who claimed that the keeping of the law was effective in securing 'life'. In fact, argued Paul, the failure to 'abide by everything written in the Book of the Law, and do them' attracted only the curse of God. That curse, said Paul, Christ endured vicariously. It is my understanding that Paul wrote Galatians, including Gal. 3:1–21, soon after his years in 'the regions of Syria and Cilicia' reflecting the outlines of his exegetical apologetic exegesis that he developed at that time. See Appendix 1: Dating Galatians.

7 So Hengel, 'Stance of the Apostle Paul', p. 84.

8 Appendix 6: Paul Preaching Christ Crucified to Jews.

9 Ironically, in effect the scourging was a 'work' that the tractate claimed was meritorious that restored the transgressor to life!

10 See D. Steinmetz, *Punishment and Freedom: The Rabbinic Construction of Criminal Law* (Philadelphia: University of Pennsylvania Press, 2008), pp. 70–77.

11 A.E. Harvey, '"Forty Strokes Save One": Social Aspects of Judaizing and Apostasy' in *Alternative Approaches to New Testament Study* (ed. A.E. Harvey; London: SPCK, 1985), p. 93.

12 See e.g. J.D. Tabor, *Things Unutterable: Paul's Ascent to Paradise in its Greco–Roman, Judaic, and Early Christian Contexts* (Lanham, MD:

University Press of America, 1986); P. Schäfer, 'New Testament and the Hekhalot Literature: The Journey into Heaven in Paul and Merkavah Mysticism', *JJS* 35 (1985): pp. 19–35.

13 Their keyword for themselves is 'superior' and for Paul it is 'inferior' (2 Cor. 11:5; 12:11). Paul picks up on their self–description as 'superior' and parodies them. He attaches the prefix *super* to a number of words to describe them, for instance, they have '*over*extended' themselves into 'lands *beyond*' (10:14,16) and they boast in an *abundance* of revelations with resulting '*super*–elation' (12:7), where the words in italics each render their keyword 'super' (Greek, *hyper*). Most biting of all is Paul's reference to them as '*superlative* apostles' (*hyperlian apostoloi*), where Paul seems to have invented a word (*hyperlian* – 'exceedingly super') to mock them (11:5; 12:11).

14 1 Enoch 12:1 – 16:4; cf. 71:1–17.

15 Bruce, *Paul: Apostle of the Free Spirit*, p. 137 following A. Schweitzer, helpfully points out that Paul's 'mysticism' was not undifferentiated God–mysticism but a Christ–mysticism.

16 Based on the view that Paul wrote to the Galatians soon after his missionary visit to them (see Appendix 1: Dating Galatians).

17 Cilicia is a boomerang–shaped region that wrapped around the northeast corner of the Mediterranean. The large coastal plain ('flat Cilicia' – *Kilikia Pedias*) is hedged in at the east and north by the Taurus Mountains ('rugged Cilicia' – *Kilikia Tracheia*) and to the east by the Syrian desert. Three rivers – the Cydnus, the Sarus and the Pyramus – water the Cilician plain. Pompey's military expedition in 67–64 BC began the process of Romanization when Cilicia with parts of Phrygia were formed into a province. From the time of Paul's birth and throughout his years of return to Tarsus Cilicia had been joined to Syria as a province, whose capital was Antioch. Vespasian later made Cilicia a separate province (in AD 72).

18 Paul usually speaks about geography in terms of Roman jurisdictions. Cilicia and Syria, which had been combined as a province since 38 BC, was large and significant. It boasted as its capital, Antioch, the third city of the empire and Rome's military bastion against incursions from the east and it extended from Tarsus in the northwest to or near Damascus in the south.

19 The grammar is unusual: referring to 'the regions of Syria and *of* Cilicia' (*ta klimata tēs Syrias kai tēs Kilikias*), suggesting separate 'regions'. See further E. de Witt Burton, *The Epistle to the Galatians* ICC (Edinburgh: T & T Clark, 1980), p. 62, who questions the accurate transmission of the text.

20 It is a moot point whether Paul confined himself more or less to the region of Cilicia or travelled throughout the whole province of Syria–

Cilicia, including south to Damascus. The fact that Barnabas has to bring Paul from Tarsus to Antioch suggests that Paul had more or less limited his ministry to Cilicia before he came to Antioch.

21 See Burton, *Galatians*, pp. 62–4.

22 *From whom* did 'the churches of Judea' hear of Paul's radical conversion from persecutor and attempted destroyer of the faith to preacher of the faith? While the believers in Jerusalem knew Paul 'by face' (or 'in person' – *tō prosōpō*) those numerous ones outside the holy city only knew him by his evil reputation, as 'the persecutor'. The main possibilities reporting Paul's amazing volte–face to the churches in Judea are (i) the formerly persecuted Christians of Jerusalem, or (ii) the *Hellenists* (Greek–speaking Jewish disciples) who had fled from Paul's persecutions in Jerusalem to Syria and Cilicia (Acts 11:19). On balance, option (ii) is to be preferred. Paul is narrating his years in Syria and Cilicia so it is most natural to identify the reports of his preaching as coming from those regions.

23 H.D. Betz, *Galatians* (Hermeneia: Philadelphia, 1979).

24 See Appendix 1: Dating Galatians.

25 Betz's rhetorical approach for Galatians has been followed (more generally) by others, for example, by Witherington (1 and 2 Corinthians), Fee (Philippians) and Jewett (Romans).

26 Contra Andrie B. Du Toit 'A Tale of Two Cities: "Tarsus or Jerusalem" Revisited', *NTS* 46/4 (2000): pp. 375–402, who contends that it was from the philosophical schools in Tarsus that Paul learned rhetorical elements lie the epistolary paraenesis, the *Haustafeln*, the diatribe, the *peristasis* catalogues, and the list of virtues and vices that appear in his letters. Du Toit thinks Paul migrated to Jerusalem aged about fifteen. It is, however, not easy to imagine a boy so young mastering such rhetorical skills to say nothing of the elements of speech rhetoric. Nonetheless, given Tarsus' reputation for scholarship (Strabo, *Geography* 14.5–13) and Paul's decade in 'the regions of Syria and Cilicia' it is reasonable to suppose that Paul learned some of these literary skills during those years.

27 M. Hengel, *The Pre–Christian Paul* (London: SCM, 1991 ET), pp. 40–62.

28 See the review of texts in M.E. Boring, K. Berger and C. Colpe eds. *Hellenistic Commentary to the New Testament* (Nashville: Abingdon, 1995 ET), pp. 459–75 where no Hellenistic text among those cited has a clear connection to Galatians.

29 W.A. Meeks, 'Review of H.D. Betz, *A Commentary on Paul's Letter to the Churches in Galatia* (Philadelphia: Hermeneia, 1979), *JBL* 100 (1981): pp. 304–7; P.H. Kern, *Rhetoric and Galatians: Assessing and Approach to Paul's Epistle*, SNTS 101 (Cambridge: CUP, 1998), pp. 256–9.

³⁰ See Appendix 5: The 'New Perspective on Paul' According to James Dunn.

4. Paul in Antioch–on–the Orontes and Syria (AD *c*.45–7)

¹ Antioch was a new city founded along Greek lines in 300 BC following Alexander's conquests. Located on the Orontes River about fifteen miles from the sea and in a large fertile plain, Antioch became the capital of the Seleucid Empire, a city that at its height is estimated to have had a population of about 300,000 (M. Hengel and A.M. Schwemer, *Paul Between Damascus and Antioch: The Unknown Years* [Louisville: Westminster John Knox Press, 1997 ET], p 186).

Pompey captured Antioch in 66 BC making it capital of the province of Syria. So began Antioch's history as a great Roman city with considerable extension and beautification of the city from that time. Antioch became Rome's military sentinel guarding the eastern frontier's formidable enemies like the Parthians. Judea, too, came under the administrative supervision as well as the military protection of Antioch. After the death of Herod in 4 BC and at the outbreak of war in AD 66 the legions were periodically marched south from Antioch to restore peace to Judea. By New Testament times Antioch was the third city in the empire, after Rome and Alexandria.

Greek–Jew relationships had a troubled history in Antioch from 175 BC when Antiochus IV attempted to Hellenize Jerusalem and Judea, leading to the outbreak of the Maccabean revolt and the eventual loss of Judea from the Graeco–Syrian kingdom. From its inception Jews formed a significant proportion of its population; the numbers have been estimated as high as 50,000. There was an ongoing dispute with the Greek community over Jewish citizenship rights. The available evidence suggests that, as in most other places, Jews enjoyed a corporate, but not an individual citizenship, allowing them to pursue their religion unhindered (Josephus, *Jewish War* vii. 43). However, Jews periodically agitated for individual citizenship rights leading to serious tension between the two communities.

At the same time, Jews who upheld strict standards held a certain attraction to numbers of Gentiles, based on the monotheism of the covenant of Israel and the superior ethical and family values practised by Jews. Josephus commented: 'through their worship [the Jews] attracted a large number of Greeks and in a way made them part of themselves' (*Jewish War* vii.450).

These 'Greeks' (= Gentiles) were 'God–fearers' who had become part of the synagogue congregations. Others, however, became proselytes accepting baptism and circumcision as members of the covenant people. Nicolaus the 'proselyte of Antioch' was one of the seven almoners, chosen to serve the widows of the Hellenist community in Jerusalem (Acts 6:5). It is reasonable to believe that Nicolaus returned to Antioch following the scattering of the Hellenists during Paul's attacks.

The immediate background to the rise of Christianity in Antioch was the turbulent years of Caligula (AD 37–41) and the furore among Jews created by his policies that threatened to erupt into open war in the Greek cities of the eastern Mediterranean, including Antioch.

Simmering hostility in Alexandria broke out into a bloody pogrom against Jews in 38. Significantly, Antioch held Caligula, and his father Germanicus who had died in the city, in particular honour. There are medieval accounts of a Greek assault of Jews in Antioch, including the burning of their major synagogue (see Hengel and Schwemer, *Paul,* pp. 183–91).

Clearly, cities like Antioch in the late thirties and early forties witnessed severe hostility by Greeks against Jews (and by Jews against Greeks). It is against this background that we must understand how alarmed the Greeks and Romans of Antioch must have been on hearing the reports that a Messiah/Christ of Israel was being proclaimed in the synagogues by recently arrived Jews. Jews everywhere might be united under this leader, who would even rival the emperor himself. This explains why these preachers and their supporters were called *Christianoi,* that is, 'supporters of the Christ'. At the same time we can only reflect on the turmoil within the synagogues of Antioch in the knowledge that these preachers, fellow–Jews as they were, were offering the salvation of the God of Israel *free* to *Greeks!* We cannot easily imagine how explosive for Greeks and Romans and Jews the arrival in Antioch of these preachers of the Christ must have been.

[2] Jews and God–fearers who became *Christianoi* may have continued as members of the synagogues.

[3] This word, like *Hērōdianoi* (Mark 3:6; 12:13 par.), is political in nature and points to those who were publicly known followers of a noted leader, and who took their faction name from their leader's name.

[4] For a magisterial review of this question, which emphatically argues for Damascus in the early thirties see Hengel and Schwemer, *Paul,* pp. 268–310.

[5] See e.g., 2 Cor. 6:11–13; 11:1 – 12:13 *passim;* Gal. 3:1.

[6] P. Barnett, *Paul: Missionary of Jesus* (Grand Rapids: Eerdmans, 2008), pp. 57–70.

7 For examples of present–tense verbs following aorist or perfect–tense verbs, Barnett, *Paul*, pp. 57–70.

8 See e.g. Acts 22:17; 2 Cor. 12:1–4; Acts 16:9; 18:9.

9 See J.D.G. Dunn, 'The Relationship Between Paul and Jerusalem according to Galatians 1 and 2', *NTS* 28/4 (1982): pp. 461–78.

10 Hengel and Schwemer, *Paul*, pp. 279–86.

11 Hengel and Schwemer, *Paul*, pp. 268–79.

12 According to R. Turcan, *The Cults of the Roman Empire* (Oxford: Blackwell, 1996), pp. 131–2, the cults from Syria did not have the same impact on outsiders as those from Egypt. While this observation is made regarding the influence of expatriate Syrians, the comment likely applies also to minimal impact of Syrian cults on Jews resident in Antioch.

13 Cf. F. Millar, *The Roman Near East 31 BC–AD 337* (Harvard: Harvard University Press, 1993), pp. 460–67.

14 Appendix 2: Luke's Acts as a Historical Source for Paul.

15 See Hengel and Schwemer, *Paul*, pp. 183–91.

16 See Hengel and Schwemer, *Paul*, *passim*.

17 Hengel and Schwemer, *Paul*, pp. 180–91.

18 See P.A. Brunt, 'Procuratorial Jurisdiction', *Latomus* 25 (1966): pp. 461–87.

19 For a general account of the instability of Judea during this period see M. Goodman, *The Ruling Class of Judea* (Cambridge: CUP, 1987), pp. 5–14.

20 Josephus, *Jewish Antiquities* xx.13.

21 Josephus, *Jewish Antiquities* xx.2–4.

22 Josephus, *Jewish Antiquities* xx.97–9.

23 P.W. Barnett, 'The Jewish Sign Prophets AD 40–70, Their Intention and Origin'. *NTS* 27 (1980), pp. 679–97.

24 Other references to the 'hardening' of Israel include: Mark 6:52 ('[F]or they did not understand about the loaves, but their hearts were hardened'); cf. 4:11–13 ('for those outside everything is in parables so that "they may indeed see but not perceive, and may indeed hear but not understand, lest they should turn and be forgiven"'); cf. 8:17; John 12:40 ('[God] has blinded their eyes and hardened their heart'); 2 Cor. 3:14 ('But their minds were hardened. For to this day, when they read the old covenant, that same veil remains unlifted'); see K.L. and M.A. Schmidt, 'Pōroō', *TDNT* 5, pp. 1025–8.

25 See e.g. Mark 9:43,45,47; 10:15,23,24,25; Matt. 5:20; 7:13,14,21; 18:3; 19:17; John 3:5).

26 See also Isa. 60:3,4,5,6,7,14.

27 See also Zech. 8:20.

[28] See R. Riesner, *Paul's Early Period* (Grand Rapids: Eerdmans, 1998), pp. 241–56 for argument that Paul followed a travel itinerary foreshadowed in Isa. 66:19 and P.W. Barnett, *The Birth of Christianity: The First Twenty Years* (Grand Rapids: Eerdmans, 2005), pp. 267–9 for a contrary view.

[29] 1 Thess. 1:10; 4:13 – 5:11; 2 Thess. 1:9; 2:1–12; 1 Cor. 7:29; 15:23.

[30] See Appendix 1: Dating Galatians.

5. Jerusalem, Antioch and Galatia (AD 47–8)

[1] The view taken here is that Paul dates the 'fourteen years' from the time of the Damascus event and not from his earlier visit to Jerusalem (Gal. 1:18). See Appendix 1: Dating Galatians.

[2] Douglas A. Campbell, 'Galatians 5.11: Evidence of an Early Law–observant Mission by Paul', *NTS* 57/3 (2011) argues for post–call construal of Gal. 5:11 against Donaldson's proposition of Paul's pre-call circumcision mission to the uncircumcised. The understanding of this passage remains elusive. Paul makes it clear, however, that he had preached the circumcision–free gospel throughout the fourteen years between Damascus and his second visit to Jerusalem (Gal. 2:1–2).

[3] John Gilman, 'Titus' in *ABD* 6 (1992); pp. 581–2.

[4] Later Paul will refer to 'false brothers' as a source of danger to him (2 Cor. 11:26).

[5] James D.G. Dunn, *The Epistle to the Galatians* (London: A & C Black, 1993), p. 98, helpfully observes, 'whereas baptism in Christ's name had meant a complete about–face in Paul's understanding of God's promise and purpose, for the "false brothers" it had meant simply an extension of their faith and *halakhah* as Pharisees.'

[6] The 'truth of the gospel' is that Christ alone, apart from 'works', is the sole basis of justification with God. Dunn, *Galatians*, p. 101, weakens the force of this by saying that here Paul 'appeals to the reality of his readers' own experience as an experience of liberation'. Paul, however, is not speaking about human experience but the ways of God in accepting people as justified.

[7] The verb 'force' (*anangkazō*) is prominent in Galatians – 2:3 ('Titus was not *forced* – by the false brothers – to be circumcised'); 2:14 ('How can you [Peter] *force* the Gentiles to live like Jews?'); 6:12 ('It is those who would make a good showing in the flesh who would *force* you to be circumcised').

[8] Paul only travelled on to Derbe to escape the dangers in Lystra (see Appendix 2: Luke's Acts as a Historical Source for Paul).

9   Dunn, *Galatians*, p. 11.

10 Some argue that Paul came to hear of the problems in Galatia during one or other of his known *subsequent* visits, and that he wrote to the Galatians from Corinth either after the second visit (Acts 16:6), or from Ephesus after the third visit (Acts 18:23). Gal. 4:13 ('You know it was because of a bodily ailment that I came to you *at first'* – *to proteron*) is taken by some to support the writing of the epistle following one or other of the *later* visits. On the other hand, however, Paul may simply be reminding the Galatians that he came to them during his first visit – at the beginning – for health reasons. Two reasons at least support the writing of Galatians from Antioch soon after the first visit: (i) the passionate urgency of the letter ('so quickly' – Gal. 1:6) does not fit with the Corinth hypothesis; and (ii) the proximity of Galatia to Antioch and its relative remoteness from either Corinth (in particular) or Ephesus (see further Appendix 1: Dating Galatians).

11 Luke's account of the Incident in Antioch (Acts 15:1–2) sits awkwardly alongside Paul's version in Gal. 2:11–14: (i) there is no indication that these men from Judea 'came from James'; (ii) Peter is not mentioned; (iii) Barnabas was in agreement with Paul; and (iv) the issue was not table–fellowship and schism but circumcision and salvation. Yet Acts 15:1–2 appears to be referring to the same incident. Typical of Luke's style he tends to gloss over differences between the apostles.

12 This is well understood by D.R. Catchpole, 'Paul, James and the Apostolic Decree', *NTS* 23 (1977): pp. 428–44, who observed that 'the presupposition of this whole situation [where Cephas ate with Gentile believers in Antioch] and of terminology employed is, of course, that Gentiles remain Gentiles, that is, that circumcision is not treated as obligatory' (p. 440). According to Catchpole (p. 441) the term ' "compel to Judaize (*anangkazeis Ioudaizein* – 2:14)" . . . must be taken seriously', just as much as the [words] ' "Titus was not compelled to be circumcised (*oude . . . ēnankasthē peritmēthēnai* – 2:3)" and the "they compel you to be circumcised (*anangkousin humas peritemnesthai* – 6:12)". In all three cases a demand is being made . . . Peter aligns himself with the demand by changing his own conduct and he thus intensifies the pressure upon the Gentiles to come into line . . . which is intended by [the term] "to live like a Jew (*Ioudaikōs zēs*)".'

This is a more reasonable reading of Galatians than M. Bockmuehl, 'Antioch and James the Just', in *James the Just and Christian Origins* NovTSup 98 (ed. B. Chilton and C.A. Evans; Leiden: Brill, 1999), pp. 155–98. It may be agreed that James saw Antioch as within the aegis of the promised land but to argue that his emissaries were pressing Peter to separate over a matter of purity *halahka* merely begs the question:

what next? This does not understand the two–pronged approach of the circumcision party to compel Gentiles to be circumcised – (i) the direct approach to compel them to be circumcised (Titus in Jerusalem; members in the churches of Galatia); and (ii) the indirect pressure on Peter and the Jewish believers in Antioch forcing them to separate from Gentiles in table–fellowship, implying their need to be circumcised.

For the argument that the dispute began and ended over the necessity to break table–fellowship with Gentiles and did not impinge on the necessity for them to be circumcised see J.D.G Dunn, *Beginning from Jerusalem* (Grand Rapids: Eerdmans, 2009), pp. 470–94. For Dunn, the issue was about table–fellowship pure and simple, the demand that Gentiles become more Jewish. This, however, is unlikely since (i) the issue in Galatians *overall* is Paul's passionate resistance to the *necessity* of the circumcision of Gentiles; and (ii) those who came from James are called 'the circumcision party' (*tous ek peritomnēs* – Gal. 2:12). Accordingly, Catchpole's arguments noted above are more convincing than those of Bockmuehl or Dunn.

6. James and Paul (AD 34–49)

[1] For a comprehensive account of the life and achievement of James see R. Bauckham, 'James and the Jerusalem Church' in *The Book of Acts in Its First Century Setting. Vol 4 Palestinian Setting* (ed. R. Bauckham; Grand Rapids: Eerdmans, 1995): pp. 415–480.

[2] The biblical records do not explain why James replaced Peter as leader. The most likely possibility is that, once Peter had departed from Jerusalem, the faith community looked to James because he was *the brother* of the Messiah, Jesus. Also possible, but less likely – at least initially – was that James, as a more conservative figure than Peter, enjoyed the support of the wider and increasingly nationalistic Jewish community in Jerusalem. See further, Ian J. Elmer, *Paul and the Judaisers* WUNT 258 (Tübingen: Mohr Siebeck, 2009), p. 84.

[3] See M. Bockmuehl, 'Antioch and James the Just' in *James the Just and Christian Origins* NovTSup 98 (ed. B. Chilton and C.A. Evans; Leiden: Brill, 1999): pp. 155–98.

[4] See P.W. Barnett, *The Corinthian Question* (Leicester: IVP, 2011), pp. 155–177.

[5] See Appendix 1: Dating Galatians.

[6] Following the Damascus christophany, Paul punctuates his memoir with critical movements, each introduced by 'then' (*epeita*): 'Then

after (*meta*) three years I went up to Jerusalem' (1:18); '*Then epeita* I went into the regions of Syria–Cilicia' (1:21); '*Then epeita* after (*dia*) fourteen years I went up again to Jerusalem' (2:1). See Ch. 1, n. 2.

7 Elmer, *Paul and the Judaisers*, speaks for many in finding 'difficulties in ascribing historical reliability to Luke's version of events' (p. 111), a view he expresses throughout his monograph. Yet he makes repeated use of the book of Acts as, indeed, he must since from Paul's letters alone it is impossible to establish a global chronology for the life and missionary vocation of Paul or a sequence in which he wrote his letters. J.A. Fitzmyer, *According to Paul* (New York: Paulist Press, 1992), pp. 36–46, correlates many chronological aspects relating to Paul using his letters and the Acts. Yet he could not do this without an overall confidence in the Acts of the Apostles. Furthermore, (i) the 'we'/'us' passages in Acts 21 – 28 indicate that Luke was Paul's close companion for about five years affording him the opportunity to narrate Paul's life within the wider narrative of Luke–Acts. In any case (ii) who else but Paul could have been the source of the huge volume of detail about Paul that we find in Luke's text? Accordingly, it is inconsistent selectively to 'cherry–pick' only those texts in Acts that suit particular idiosyncratic theories. See Appendix 2: Luke's Acts as a Historical Source for Paul.

8 So Bauckham, 'James and the Jerusalem Church', pp. 468–70. However, Elmer, *Paul and the Judaisers*, pp. 87–9, is among those who equate Gal. 2:1–10 with Acts 15:6–21 (the Jerusalem Council). His principal reason against equating Acts 11:27–30 = Gal. 2:1–10 (the famine visit) is that Luke locates Agrippa's persecution (AD 42?) in Acts 12 *after* the famine visit (AD 47). But the Agrippa passage begins 'About that time', that is, vaguely. After all, Luke is attempting to weave together disparate strands: Paul's persecutions, his return to Jerusalem and journey to Tarsus (8:1–3; 9:1–30); Peter's ministry in Judea, Galilee and Samaria culminating in the baptism of the Gentiles in Caesarea (9:31 – 11:18); the northward scattering of the Hellenists issuing in the formation of the church in Antioch, led by Barnabas and Saul and their famine visit to Jerusalem (11:19–30); the persecutions of 'King Herod' and the flight of Peter (12:1–24); the return of Barnabas and Saul to Antioch as the prelude to missions in Cyprus and Galatia (12:25). Luke's use of the 'flashback' passage 'out of sequence' (12:1–24) is awkward but is not evidence of serious inaccuracy, as Elmer proposes.

9 Elmer, *Paul and the Judaisers*, asserts that James 'did not agree carte blanche in Jerusalem' (p. 111) and that 'the rise of Jesus' brother James to a position of authority at Jerusalem . . . signalled the beginning of a

new offensive on the part of the Law–observant faction to gain control of the situation in Antioch' (p. 116).

[10] So Bockmuehl, 'Antioch and James the Just', pp. 165, 178–9, who regards James' motivation as 'in part political' as influences by Caligula's intended desecration of the temple (p. 182).

[11] So Elmer, *Paul and the Judaisers*, pp. 111, 116.

[12] Bockmuehl, 'Antioch and James the Just', p. 179.

[13] Josephus, *Jewish Antiquities* xx.100–102.

[14] M. Hengel, *Saint Peter: The Underestimated Apostle* (Grand Rapids: Eerdmans, 2010 ET), p. 61, suggests that Peter's action in Antioch was designed to avert persecution in Jerusalem, contra Elmer, *Paul and the Judaisers*, p. 106.

[15] See Elmer, *Paul and the Judaisers*, pp. 41, 85–6, 108–9, 111, 116, 162; Hengel, Saint Peter, pp. 57–65.

[16] So Elmer, *Paul and the Judaisers*, p. 116.

[17] See Appendix 2: Luke's Acts as a Historical Source for Paul.

[18] See Bauckham, 'James and the Jerusalem Church', pp. 459–62, who argues that the four requirements of the 'Jerusalem Decree' to the Gentiles relate to the four commandments for 'the alien who sojourns in your midst', as in Lev. 17 – 18.

[19] See Chapter 10. See Appendix 2: Luke's Acts as a Historical Source for Paul.

[20] In support of the prominence of oral use see J.D.G. Dunn, *Beginning from Jerusalem* (Grand Rapids: Eerdmans, 2009), pp. 1132–6.

[21] See Appendix 4: James' Encyclical to 'the Twelve Tribes of the Diaspora'.

7. Peter and Paul AD 34–49

[1] For details of Paul's influence as rabbi in the synagogue address in Acts 13 see P.W. Barnett, *Finding the Historical Christ* (Grand Rapids: Eerdmans, 2009), pp. 69–71.

[2] C.H. Dodd, *The Apostolic Preaching and its Development* (London: Hodder & Stoughton, 1936).

[3] Whereas the passages in Mark 1 – 10 are mostly shorter units those in Mark 11 – 16 are generally longer and are organically part of a tightly connected, sequential story. It seems that Mark 11 – 16 (or 14 – 16) originated as a separate entity, most likely as a *written* text. Mark 11 – 16 does not supply the name of the high priest, whereas lesser figures are named (e.g. the two Marys and Salome and Joseph). The high priest was the most prominent person in Jerusalem and the chief offender in the mistrial of Jesus and the subsequent transference of the prisoner

to Pilate for crucifixion (14:53,54,60,61,63; cf. 15:1). Yet Mark does not name the high priest. This is the more striking since Matthew in a parallel passage does name him (Matt. 26:57). This omission would be explained if the early composition of Mark 11 – 16 were allowed. That is to say, if Mark 11 – 16 were composed before Caiaphas was deposed (as he was in AD 37) there would be no need to mention him by name since everyone would know his name. Based on these considerations there is a compelling case that a narrative of Jesus' last days in Jerusalem was created quite early. Based on Mark 13:14 ('let the reader – i.e. lector – understand') this account was designed for church reading, perhaps in a liturgical setting.

4   M. Hengel, *Saint Peter: The Underestimated Apostle* (Grand Rapids: Eerdmans, 2010 ET), pp. 39–42.

5   R. Bauckham, *Jesus and the Eyewitnesses* (Grand Rapids: Eerdmans, 2006), pp. 124–7; 132–47; 155–6.

6   Bauckham, *Eyewitnesses*, p. 126.

7   Hengel, *Saint Peter*, p. 39; Bauckham, *Eyewitnesses*, pp. 131–3.

8   Acts 8:1,3; 9:1–2; 26:9–11.

9   Acts 8:14–25; 9:31–2; cf. Acts 15:3; 1 Thess. 2:14; Gal. 1:21.

10 Josephus, *Jewish Antiquities* xx.97–98.

11 Paul mentions two groups: 'certain men who came from James' and 'those of the circumcision party' (Gal. 2:12). While some commentators think these are different groups it is more logical to regard them as one. In fact, it is most probable that they represent the same viewpoint as the 'false brothers' in Jerusalem who attempted to 'force' Titus to be circumcised (2:3) and the counter–mission who travelled to Galatia to 'force' Gentiles to be circumcised (6:12). Luke's parallel passage is clear: 'some men came down from Judea and were teaching the brothers, "Unless you are *circumcised* according to the custom of Moses, you cannot be saved"' (Acts 15:1, our italics).

12 See Margaret M. Mitchell, 'Peter's "Hypocrisy" and Paul's: Two "Hypocrites" at the Foundation of Earliest Christianity?' *NTS* 58/2 (2012): pp. 212–34, for an examination of Gal. 2:11–14 in relationship to 1 Cor. 9:19–23 where Paul made himself 'all things to all people'. Mitchell also reviews the patristic discussion of this issue.

13 See Chapter 5.

14 J.D.G. Dunn, *The Epistle to the Galatians* (London: A & C Black, 1993), p. 127, observes: 'Paul understood that agreement (see 2:5) as safeguarding the reality of the gospel as one of liberation and its trustworthiness as ensuring participation in the blessing of Abraham without requiring Gentiles to judaize.' This, however, considerably weakens the force of Paul's argument that *compulsion* to 'judaize' (= live like

a Jew; *do* the works of the law) destroys the 'truth of the gospel', the gospel of grace that declares that sinners are 'justified by God by faith alone' (2:15–16). The 'truth of the gospel' is that Christ and faith in him is the only source of justification. 'Faith' and 'works of the law' are stark, mutually antithetical alternatives and cannot be complements. J.M.G. Barclay, *Obeying the Truth: Paul's Ethics in Galatians* (Vancouver: Regent College, 2005), argues that 'the truth of the gospel' are the 'basic facts of the gospel' (p. 77). He underplays the element of 'force' or 'compulsion' that is implied requiring Gentiles to observe Jewish dietary rules, submit to circumcision (i.e. to 'judaize') that overturns the 'truth of the gospel' (p. 81).

[15] Despite their strong earlier relationships in Antioch (Acts 11:23–6), Jerusalem (Gal. 2:1,9) and mission journeys to Cyprus and southern Galatia (Acts 13 – 14), it does not appear that Paul and Barnabas worked in close association after the schism in Antioch in *c.*48. There was already tension over Barnabas' cousin, John Mark (Acts 13:13; 15:36–9). Barnabas was pointedly not a co–sender with Paul in the letter to the Galatian churches. Nonetheless, while the one subsequent reference Paul makes to Barnabas is not negative (1 Cor. 9:6), the schism in Antioch effectively spelled the end of their partnership.

[16] See Appendix 3: Barnabas and Peter after the Incident in Antioch.

[17] See Appendix 3: Barnabas and Peter after the Incident in Antioch.

8. Paul, Christ and the Law (Gal. 2:15–21)

[1] Prominent among those who have attempted to identify the centre of Paul's theology is J. Christiaan Beker, *Paul the Apostle: The Triumph of God in Life and Thought* (Edinburgh: T & T Clark, 1980). After reviewing the views of other scholars Beker concluded that, 'Paul's centre is located in the lordship of Christ as it anticipates the final triumph of God' (p. 260). According to Beker, Paul is an apocalyptic thinker who saw the life, death and resurrection of Christ as the inauguration of the age that will be climaxed by the Parousia. The difficulty with this view is that it sees Paul as primarily a 'future' thinker whereas he actually located himself 'in' the One who was crucified and raised for him. For Thomas R. Schreiner, *Paul Apostle of God's Glory in Christ: A Pauline Theology* (Downers Grove: IVP, 2001), that centre is the glory of God in Christ.

[2] While Paul may be writing 'as if' the conversation occurred, I am taking it to be a version of the actual conversation. Nonetheless, he is actually addressing the Galatians.

3 Contra J.D.G. Dunn, *The Epistle to the Galatians* (London: A & C Black, 1993), p. 141, who argued that the 'discovery' that 'Paul (and Peter)' were 'eating with Gentiles caused them to be regarded as "sinners"'. Even less likely is his suggestion that calling Christ a 'servant' = 'table waiter' was because the Lord had metaphorically served the meals to these Jews in the presence of Gentiles (pp. 141–2).

4 John W. Taylor, 'Demonstrating Transgression by Building up the Faith: Argumentation in Galatians 2:17–18', *BBR* 22/4 (2012): pp. 547–62, argues that Paul meant that he had previously transgressed the law as persecutor and lawbreaker.

5 According to Acts 22:16 Ananias said to Paul, 'Rise and be baptized, and wash away your sins, calling on his name.'

6 It is striking that the gospels employ the verb *systauroō* for the literal simultaneous crucifixion of those crucified with Jesus (Matt. 27:44; Mark 15:32; John 19:32).

7 According to Acts 9:17 Ananias laid hands on Paul and said, 'Be filled with the Holy Spirit.'

8 The emotional force of *hyper* is not captured by the notion of 'representation'. A substitutionary understanding of *hyper* is also clear from a non–soteriological usage (2 Cor. 5:20 – 'We implore you on behalf of – *hyper* – Christ'). For further comment on substitution and representation see C.R. Campbell, *Paul and Union with Christ* (Grand Rapids: Zondervan, 2012), pp. 350–51.

9 See Appendix 1: Dating Galatians.

10 Dunn, *Galatians*, p. 137, argues that in the statement ' "a person is *not* justified by works of the law *but* (*ean mē*) through faith in Jesus Christ" the translation "but" is not adversative but *exceptive*' (italics added). Understood thus it would mean that ' "faith in Jesus Christ" [is] the one *exception* to the rule that "no one is justified by works of the law"'. But this hardly makes sense since 'except' (*ean mē*) in this sentence effectively has the force of the adversative, 'but'. Dunn says that ' "works of the law" and "faith in Jesus Christ" are not necessarily being posed here as mutually exclusive antitheses' when Paul is making the exactly opposite point that 'Christ' and 'law' *are* 'mutually exclusive antitheses'. For a view contra to Dunn see Debbie Hunn, '*Ean mē* in Galatians 2:16: A Look at Greek Literature' *NovT* 49 (2007): pp. 281–90.

11 *dia pisteōs Iēsou Christou* has been understood in the objective sense ('through faith *in* Jesus Christ'), and in the subjective sense ('through the faith[fullness] *of* Jesus Christ', or in both senses. There is an exhaustive literature on this question based on comparative linguistic considerations. On argument for the objective genitive see Roy A.

Harrisville, 'Before PISTIS CHRISTOU: The Objective genitive as Good Greek', *NovT* 48/4 (2006): pp. 353–8; R. Barry Matlock, 'Detheologizing the PISTIS CHRISTOU Debate: Cautionary Remarks from a Lexical Semantic Perspective', *NovT* 42/1 (2000): pp. 1–23; F. Watson, 'By Faith (of Christ): an Exegetical Dilemma and its Scriptural Solution' in *The Faith of Jesus Christ: Exegetical, Biblical and Theological Studies* (ed. Michael E. Bird and Preston M. Sprinkle; Milton Keynes: Paternoster, 2009), pp. 147–63; and for the subjectivist viewpoint see D.W.B. Robinson, ' "Faith of Jesus Christ" – a New Testament Debate', *RTR* 29 (1970): pp. 71–81; R.B. Hays, 'PISTIS and Pauline Christology: What is at Stake?' in *Pauline Theology IV. Looking Back, Pressing On*, Symposium Series 4; (ed. E.E. Johnson and D.M. Hay; Atlanta Scholars, 1977), pp. 35–60; Paul L. Owen, 'The "Works of the Law" in Romans and Galatians: A New Defense of the Subjective Genitive', *JBL* 126/3 (2007): pp. 553–77. In favour of the objective reading we note (a) the passage itself that states 'we have believed in (*eis*) Christ Jesus' supporting an objective meaning; (b) Paul's words 'we know that a man (*anthrōpos*) is not justified from works of the law but through faith in Jesus Christ' refer to individuals like himself and Peter being 'justified' by *their* faith. Furthermore (c), balancing references to *ek pisteōs* and *ex ergōn nomou* contrasts 'faith' (as a *human* activity) with 'works of the law' (as a *human* activity), especially since *ek* is used in an instrumental sense. The instrumental sense of *ek* is also evident in the antithetical statements – *ex ergōn nomou* and *ex akoēs pisteōs* – where God gives his Spirit to the latter but not the former (Gal. 3:5). There is also a connection between *ex ergōn nomou* (2:16; 3:2,5,10) and *ta erga tēs sarkos* (Gal. 5:19) where both 'works' are *human* activities, reinforcing the impression that the balancing reference *ek pisteōs* is a human activity, supporting the objectivist understanding. The changing references 'through (*dia*)', 'towards (*eis*)' and 'out of (*ek*)' are for literary variation.

12 The verbs in v. 16 are each passive (*dikaioutai, dikaiōthōmen, dikaiothesetai*) expressive of the divine or reverential passive.

13 For two reasons Dunn, *Galatians*, p. 149, is wide of the mark in saying, 'Paul's object here is not the law per se, but the law as preventing Gentiles' full and free participation in the grace of God as Gentiles.' First, Paul does not distinguish between 'the law' (i.e. the Decalogue) and 'works of the law' (Gal. 2:16 – 'by works of the law no one will be justified'; Gal. 3:11 – 'no one is justified before God by law'). Second, in Gal. 2:20 Paul is speaking about *himself* and his relationship with God and not the separation of the Gentiles from the Jews.

14 F.F. Bruce, 'The Spirit in the Letter to the Galatians', in *Essays on Apostolic Themes* (ed. P. Elbert; Peabody: Hendrickson, 1985), p. 36.

9. Christ Crucified, the Spirit and Scripture (Gal. 3:1–14)

1. Gal. 2:16 (x 4); 3:2; 3:5 (x 2); 3:7,8,9,10,11,12.
2. Gal. 2:16; 3:7,8,9,11,12.
3. Gal. 2:16 (x 3); 3:2,5,10.
4. See Gal. 3:11,12.
5. Greek, *kathōs* is an abbreviation of the formulaic, 'Even as it is written' (cf. Rom. 2:24). Contra Sam K. Williams, 'Justification and the Spirit in Galatians', *JSNT* 29 (1987): pp. 91–100, who sees *kathōs* as joining 3:5 with 3:6, the sense of 'so too' or 'in the same way', arguing that as the Galatians heard (= heeded) the word of God, so too did Abraham. Williams also contends that 'throughout vv. 13–14 Paul has in mind all Christians. Those whom Christ has redeemed from the curse of the Law are not only Jews but also Gentiles, who apart from Christ would have had to live "under the Law" in order to belong to the people of God' (pp. 91–2). It is more likely, however, that in 3:6 – 4:7 Paul is addressing Jews whom he is challenging to find their redemption in Christ which of course is an indirect encouragement to Gentile believers not to forgo their new freedom.
6. Rom. 4 is Paul's expansive exposition of the importance of Gen. 15:6 to Gentile believers. No less than eleven times in Rom. 4 does Paul say that God 'imputes righteousness' to those who have faith, first to the uncircumcised Abraham and then to uncircumcised Gentiles.
7. We must not miss Paul's threefold repetition of the words 'those of faith' (*ek pisteōs*), in these verses, which clearly relate back to a key passage (2:16):
    a person is not *justified* by works of the law
    but through faith in Jesus Christ,
    so we [Jews like Peter and Paul] also have believed in Christ Jesus,
    in order to be *justified* by faith (*ek pisteōs*) in Christ
    and not by works of the law (*ex ergōn nomou*),
    because by works of the law (*ex ergōn nomou*), no one will be *justified*.
8. Paul uses the words 'live' (and 'life') in a layered way, to mean (a) the *way* one lives now, but also (b) life with God *eternally*. However, J.D.G. Dunn, *The Epistle to the Galatians* (London: A & C Black, 1993), p. 175, argues (wrongly in our view) that it refers 'to life in the covenant . . . and not just to life after death'.
9. A man who committed a capital crime was to be 'hanged on a tree' but his body might not remain there all night lest the whole land be defiled because a 'hanged' man was 'cursed by God' (Deut. 21:23; Josh. 8:29). Each gospel indicates the disciples' concern to remove the body of Jesus from the cross for burial before sunset, especially since

that sunset would begin the Sabbath when no work could be done to remove the body (cf. John 19:31). The 'curse' on a 'hanged man' implied rejection from inheritance in the covenant of the Lord and expulsion from the land (Deut. 29:27–8; 30:1). Accordingly, 'the cursed Israelite is like the uncovenanted Gentile . . . therefore . . . the cursed Christ has been in effect put out of the covenant' (Dunn, *Galatians*, p. 226).

[10] See generally M. Silva, 'Galatians' in *Commentary of New Testament Use of the Old Testament* (ed. G.K. Beale and D.A. Carson; Grand Rapids: Baker Academic, 2007), pp. 785–812.

[11] Contra Dunn, *Galatians*, pp. 170–174, who argues that Israel was practically able to fulfil God's covenant ('covenantal nomism') and that the curse here was directed at Israel's over–confidence in the law as marking her 'distinctiveness from and advantage over those outside the law' that 'blinds "the Jew" to the seriousness of his sin' (p. 173), that is, 'her "favoured nation" status' (p. 172). The fundamental problem here is that we need to depend on *Paul's* adapted use of OT texts, seen through the eyes of eschatological and christological fulfilment.

[12] The MT, however, has 'but the righteous by *his* faithfulness will live'.

10. Freedom and Slavery: Two Jerusalems

[1] Freedom (*eleutheria* – 2:4; 5:1,13); free (*eleutheros* – 3:28; 4:22,23,26,30); to set free (*eleutheroō* – 5:1); slavery (*douleia* – 4:24; 5:1); slave (*doulos* – 1:10; 3:28; 4:1,7); to be a slave (*douleuō* – 4:8,9,25; 5:13); to enslave (*douloō* – 4:3).

[2] See C.K. Barrett, 'The Allegory of Abraham, Sarah and Hagar in the Argument of Galatians' in *Essays on Paul* (London: SPCK, 1982), pp. 154–68; Karen H. Jobes, 'Jerusalem, our Mother: Metalepsis and Intertexuality in Galatians 4:21–31', *WTJ* 55/2 (1993): p. 305, argues that Paul's use of Isa. 54:1 evokes a 'rippling pool of promises' in Isaiah upon which, it is inferred, Paul was depending in Gal. 4:21–31.

[3] There is no biblical warrant for Ishmael persecuting Isaac.

[4] It is uncertain whether Paul intends 'born according to the Spirit' to connect with himself and others who are people 'of the Spirit' and not 'of the flesh'.

[5] 'Sin indeed was in the world before the law was given, but sin is not counted – *ellogeitai* – where there is no law' (Rom. 5:13).

[6] However J.D.G. Dunn, *The Epistle to the Galatians* (London: A & C Black, 1993), p. 189, understands this to be 'a positive description of

the role of the law in the period prior to the coming of Christ' which
was not 'in order to provoke (or prevent) transgressions' but 'in order
to provide a way of dealing with, in order to provide some sort of
remedy for transgressions . . . viz. the sacrificial system, whereby transgressions could be dealt with, whereby atonement was provided'. He
adds, 'For an interim measure which went on provoking transgressions for more than a millennium, without providing a remedy for
all that time, would imply a remarkably heartless picture of the God
who so failed to provide. The more natural sense is that the law was
provided as an interim measure precisely to deal with the problem of
transgression, until it could be dealt with definitively and finally in
the cross of Christ.' Against this view, however, it is pointed out that
Old Testament sacrifice did not atone for breaches of the Decalogue,
but only minor ritual breaches (Acts 13:38–9).

7 In v. 24 Paul changes the image from prison with a jailer to the home–
based 'guardian' (*paidagōgos* – literally, 'boy–leader'). Today pedagogue is a positive word meaning 'teacher' or 'mentor', but it had
a negative meaning then. A pedagogue was not a teacher but a carer
of children, and often semiliterate and harsh. See further Linda L.
Belleville, ' "Under Law": Structural Analysis and the Pauline Concept
of Law in Galatians 3:21–4:11', *JSNT* 26 (1986): pp. 59–63.

8 Dunn, *Galatians*, regards the epoch of law positively, protecting Israel
from idolatry and the Gentiles' low moral standards (p. 199), as Israel's
'guardian angel' (p. 198). But while historically law had this role it is
not the point Paul is making here. Paul's argument in Gal. 3:22–5 is
that Israel 'under' law was Israel 'under' sin, in captivity and subject
to harsh guardians.

9 Belleville, 'Under Law', pp. 53–78 provides an analysis of Gal. 3:22 –
4:3 to arrive at an understanding of *hypo nomon* (3:23). Her conclusion
is that these verses point to 'a single function of the Law', to act as
'a custodian who closely regulates and supervises God's people in
a period of spiritual minority . . . [that] functions as a "bridle" for a
people who are prone to sin' (p. 70). Against this view, however, we
note that Paul employs the language of 'redemption' from law (3:13;
4:5) – from (i) its 'curse' upon the non–compliant (3:10,13), and (ii) its
consequent 'captivity' and 'imprisonment' for transgressors (3:23; cf.
3:19). In Paul's account of the Damascus encounter he states that he
'died to law' at the time he exercised 'faith' in the 'Son of God who
loved him and gave himself for him' (2:19–20). In the complex allegory
(4:21–31) Paul portrays 'the present (*nun*) Jerusalem' as 'from Mount
Sinai [i.e. law] bearing children for slavery . . . [being] in slavery with
her children' (4:24,25). In brief, the understanding of *hypo nomon* is

to be found within the narrow band of texts Gal. 3:22 – 4:3, but also within a wider angle of references within the letter, especially considering the key vocabulary of 'slavery', 'freedom' and 'redemption'.

[10] Paul's word 'turning back' (*epistrephō*) was used in the Old Testament for apostasy, for turning away from God (e.g. Num. 14:43; 1 Sam. 15:11; 1 Kgs 9:6; Jer. 3:19). Ironically these Gentiles who *turned to* the 'works of the law' were *turning back* from the God who gave the law. The present tense of this verb indicates that the 'turning back' was a process that was still happening but which could still be averted (so Dunn, *Galatians*, pp. 225–6).

[11] See Chapters 5, 6 and 7.

[12] See Chapter 7.

[13] Given the prominence of 'Jerusalem' in Galatians (1:17,18; 2:1; 4:25,26), especially in the 'allegory' (4:21–3), it can scarcely be doubted that the 'agitators' in Galatia had come from Jerusalem. See further Dunn, *Galatians*, p. 10.

[14] For discussion, see Chapter 5.

[15] M. Bockmuehl, 'Antioch and James the Just' in *James the Just and Christian Origins* NovTSup 98 (ed. B. Chilton and C.A. Evans; Leiden: Brill, 1999): pp. 155–98; and Dunn, *Galatians*, who regard the Incident in Antioch as related to dietary *halakha*, tend to ignore the parallel passage in Acts 15:1 where the issue is the demand for circumcision. See Chapter 5.

[16] Josephus, *Jewish Antiquities* xx.201.

[17] Josephus, *Jewish War* ii.254–57.

[18] Josephus, *Jewish War* ii.258, 261–3; Acts 21:38.

[19] See further Appendix 4: James' Encyclical to the 'Twelve Tribes of the Diaspora'.

[20] To 'fulfil the gospel' would include declaring Christ as the fulfilment of the promises, the gathering of and careful instruction of the congregation in the basics of belief and behaviour, the appointment of leaders, and the identification of local evangelists for establishing new congregations.

11. Syria and Cilicia as the Background to Galatians

[1] According to Acts 9:17 Ananias laid hands on Paul and said, 'Be filled with the Holy Spirit.'

Appendix 1: Dating Galatians

1. Towards the end of the third century the Romans detached the southern area and reduced the province to the northern sector. Accordingly, it was this later, diminished northern part that was called 'Galatia' and this became the traditional understanding of the location of the recipients of Paul's letter. According to W.M. Ramsay, *The Church in the Roman Empire* (London: Hodder & Stoughton, 1893), pp. 13–15, the churches were established along the great lines of Roman administration and these were located in the southern parts of Galatia, not the north. The labours and writings of Ramsay, explorer and scholar, questioned the 'northern' consensus and argued instead for a 'southerly' hypothesis, which is now widely, although not universally held.

2. The 'northern' Galatian hypothesis has been supported by many scholars including the noted historian, Mommsen, and the renowned biblical scholars, J.B. Lightfoot and W.G. Kümmel. The 'northern' case against the 'southern' alternative, as vigorously argued by James Moffatt, *An Introduction to the Literature of the New Testament* (Edinburgh: T & T Clark, 3rd edn, 1918), esp. pp. 90–101, has found a detailed response in C.J. Hemer, *The Book of Acts in the Setting of Hellenistic History* WUNT 49 (Tübingen: J.C.B. Mohr, 1989), pp. 280–89. It should be noted that Lightfoot adopted the 'northern' solution before the epochal argument of Ramsay for the 'southern' hypothesis. Among the advocates of the 'southern' hypothesis are biblical scholars Burton, Duncan and Bruce and classical historians Hemer and Mitchell who follow Ramsay's reconstructions. It is noteworthy that Ramsay, Hemer and Mitchell are first-hand experts through their travels in the topography of central Anatolia, as well as in the history of the region.

3. For discussion with references see D.A. Fiensy, 'The Roman Empire and Asia Minor' in *The Face of New Testament Studies* (ed. S. McKnight and G. Osborne; Grand Rapids: Baker Academic, 2004): pp. 48–50.

4. F.F. Bruce, 'The Galatian Problem 2. North or South Galatians?' *BJRL* 52 (1970): p. 258.

5. S. Mitchell, 'Galatia', *ABD* 2, p. 871.

6. Mitchell, 'Galatia', p. 871. I have driven from Ankara to Konya where the landscape is still essentially uninhabited due to its flatness and relative aridity. That journey through mile upon mile of steppe country was sufficient in itself for me to reject the 'northern' hypothesis. How different once we left Konya and rose up from the plain to the fertile lands of the high country en route to Yalvaç (Antioch of Pisidia), the region of Paul's Galatian churches.

7 C.J. Hemer, 'The Adjective "Phrygia"'. *JTS* 27 (1976): pp. 122–6; C.J. Hemer, 'Phrygia, a Further Note'. *JTS* 28 (1977): pp. 99–101; F.F. Bruce, 'Phrygia', *ABD* 5, p. 367.

8 While it is true that Paul did not personally know the believers in Colossae and Laodicea (Col. 2:1), it is possible – even likely – that he passed through that region en route to Ephesus.

9 Lystra, Iconium and Antioch in Pisidia were Roman colonies and connected by a network of Roman roads, including the *Via Sebaste*. Initially Paul and Barnabas appeared to have travelled to Derbe only because of the danger to Paul in Lystra (Acts 16:20–21).

10 Item 1017 in H. Dessau, *Inscriptiones latinae selectae* (Leipzig: Weidmann, 1892–1916) cited in L.M. McDonald and S.E. Porter, *Early Christianity and its Sacred Literature* (Peabody: Hendrickson, 2000), p. 413.

11 Hemer, *Book of Acts*, p. 301.

12 W.M. Ramsay, *St. Paul the Traveller and Roman Citizen* (Grand Rapids: Baker, 1960).

13 Mitchell, 'Galatia', p. 871.

14 According to Rom. 15:26 Achaia did contribute to the collection but Acts 20:4 does not mention an Achaian delegate. Did the Corinthians nominate Paul as the Achaian delegate?

15 So also McDonald and Porter, *Early Christianity*, pp. 412–13.

16 The dating of Galatians has attracted extensive commentary over many decades. For more recent opinion see e.g. Ian J. Elmer, *Paul and the Judaisers* WUNT 258 (Tübingen, Mohr Siebeck, 2009), who supports the 'southern' hypothesis and proposes that Paul wrote Galatians from Corinth or Ephesus during the years AD 50–51 (p. 128).

17 While recognizing that Luke is selective in his presentation in Acts, and tends to gloss over the conflicts between leaders, there is a strong argument for the historicity of his overall narrative. Elmer, *Paul and the Judaisers*, is generally dismissive of the Acts as late and so tendentious as to be unreliable. Nonetheless, of necessity, he is forced to depend on Luke's detail at many points; the letters of Paul provide no sense of sequence and chronology apart from the book of Acts. Logically speaking, if the Acts is so remotely late and basically unreliable it begs the question by what criteria one is able to employ this text at all. The question must be asked, however, where did Luke get his information about Paul if it wasn't from Paul? The 'we' and 'us' narratives that dominate Acts 21 – 28 logically locate the author as Paul's companion for at least five years (57–62), thereby providing the author with first-hand information about the apostle to the Gentiles and the capacity to get the overall chronology right. While Acts is a secondary authority it does not follow that it is intrinsically unreliable. See further J.A. Fitzmyer, *According to Paul* (New

York: Paulist Press, 1992), pp. 36–46; R. Riesner, *Paul's Early Period* (Grand Rapids: Eerdmans, 1998), pp. 3–28; P.W. Barnett, *The Birth of Christianity* (Grand Rapids: Eerdmans, 2005), pp. 187–206.

[18] According to S. Mitchell, *Anatolia: Land of Men and Gods in Asia Minor II* (Oxford: Clarendon Press, 1995), p. 5, '[Galatians] thereby becomes, by a margin of several years, the earliest document of the Christian church'.

[19] These dates depend on (i) AD 33 as the date of the first Easter, and (ii) the references to '*Then* after (*meta*) three years' (Gal. 1:18) and '*Then* after (*dia*) fourteen years' (2:1) are measured from the dramatic event at Damascus (Gal. 1:15–16) in *c*.34.

[20] J.D.G. Dunn, *The Epistle to the Galatians* (London: A & C Black, 1993), p. 88, and many others think that Paul's meeting with the 'pillars' James, Peter and John (Gal. 2:1–10) = the Jerusalem Council meeting (Acts 15:4–29). A major obstacle to this view is that the Gal. 2:1–10 visit was 'private' and small (Gal. 2:2) whereas the council meeting involved 'the church . . . apostles and elders' (Acts 15:4,6). It is more likely that the permission of the 'pillars' for Paul to 'go' to the Gentiles in Visit II (Gal. 2:9) did not anticipate the significant numbers of Gentiles who would respond to the circumcision–free gospel so that the Jerusalem Council – Visit III – was needed to address this unexpected situation.

[21] See Dunn, *Galatians*, pp. 13–14.

[22] M. Bockmuehl, 'Antioch and James the Just', in *James the Just and Christian Origins* NovTSup 98 (ed. B. Chilton and C.A. Evans; Leiden: Brill, 1999): pp. 155–98. Bockmuehl dates Galatians early, 'possibly in the near aftermath of the Antioch Incident itself', p. 183.

[23] Curiously Dunn, *Galatians*, p. 7, makes no reference to the account of the Incident in Antioch recorded in Acts 15:1–2.

[24] See. pp. XXX–XXX.

[25] B. Witherington, *Grace in Galatia* (London: T & T Clark, 2004), p. 10, suggests that the lack of personal greetings in Galatians or of appeals to local officials to address the issues points to a letter written in the early life of these congregations. This, however, does not necessarily point to an early *dating* of the epistle.

[26] Theories for a later dating of Galatians are sometimes associated with a minimal view of the chronological accuracy of the book of Acts. See Appendix 2: Luke's Acts as a Historical Source for Paul.

[27] See e.g. Dunn, *Galatians*, pp. 7–8, who supports the 'south' Galatian theory but who argues that the letter was less likely written from Antioch in 48 than from Corinth or Ephesus in the mid–fifties.

[28] For J.B. Lightfoot, *The Epistle of St. Paul to the Galatians* (London: Macmillan, 1865), the later dating of the letter and the 'north' Galatian

hypothesis go together. It is noteworthy, however, that Lightfoot wrote his Galatians commentary before Ramsay publicised his arguments for the 'south' Galatians hypothesis.

29 E.R. Richards, *Paul and First–Century Letter Writing* (Downers Grove: IVP, 2004), pp. 210–23.

30 Bockmuehl, 'Antioch and James', p. 183, observes that 'I think it likely [that] Galatians must be dated considerably earlier than the usual assumption of AD 54 or 57, quite possibly in the near aftermath of the Antioch incident itself'. In n. 110 on p. 183 he notes that 'Paul's angry account in Galatians suggests that his memory of these events is still quite vivid; his reproachful description of Peter here contrasts with the far more respectful picture in 1 Corinthians. Paul also seems to look back on the foundation of the (south) Galatian churches in AD 47–48 as relatively recent.'

Appendix 2: Luke's Acts as a Historical Source for Paul

1 For a detailed review of scholarly attempts to establish a Pauline chronology, dependent on or independent of the book of Acts see R. Riesner, *Paul's Early Period* (Grand Rapids: Eerdmans, 1998), pp. 3–28.

2 This view is especially connected with J. Knox but has become critical orthodoxy for many (as in U. Schnelle, *Apostle Paul* [Grand Rapids: Baker Academic, 2005], pp. 48, 51–4, 94, 112 n. 44). For critical comment see C.J. Hemer, *The Book of Acts in the Setting of Hellenistic History* WUNT 49 (Tübingen: J.B. Mohr, 1989), pp. 244–5.

3 Some acknowledge using Acts only for the reason that there is a dearth of other information. For example, on the one hand, K. Donfried insists 'on the radical priority of the Pauline letters' while on the other conceding 'when all is said and done, Paul gives us not one specific date. Inevitably, if one is to establish a possible chronology of this period, there will have to be some dependence on Acts' (Quoted in Riesner, *Paul's Early Period*, p. 24 n. 93, 94).

4 Advocates point to the anachronism of the 'King Herod' passage in Acts 12 that covers the period from 41 (his accession in Judea) to his death (in Caesarea in 44). Since this sequence clearly predates the events of Acts 11:27–30 (the famine relief visit to Jerusalem in the mid–to–late forties) it raises doubts about Luke's accuracy overall. This is not a fatal defect, however, since Luke is attempting concurrently to narrate a number of disparate story strands – from Saul's conversion at Damascus to his journey to Tarsus (9:1–30), from Peter's journeys in Judea, Galilee and Samaria to his preaching to Gentiles in Caesarea

(9:31–48), from the scattering of the Hellenists from Jerusalem through to the formation of the church in Antioch to the famine relief journey of Barnabas and Saul to Jerusalem (11:19–27), from Peter's escape in Jerusalem from King Herod to 'another place' and the rise of James (12:1–24), and the return of Barnabas and Saul from Jerusalem to Antioch as the prelude to the mission journeys (12:25). To accommodate this complex of events Luke employs a 'flashback' in Acts 12:1–24 to explain the removal of Peter as leader and the rise of James (upon which the later narrative of Acts depends – Acts 15:13–21; 21:17–26). Luke's sequence is awkward rather than erroneous.

5 Josephus states that Theudas led his insurrection in the mid–forties, *forty or so years after* the uprising of Judas the Galilean (*Jewish Antiquities*, xviii.3; xx.97–99). It is no less serious that the Theudas incident occurred between AD 44–6 whereas Luke quotes Gamaliel speaking to the Sanhedrin about Theudas in *c*.34, about twelve years earlier.

6 Contra S.E. Porter, 'The "We" Passages', in *The Book of Acts in its First Century Setting. Vol 2 Graeco–Roman Setting* (ed. D.W.J. Gill and C. Gempf, Grand Rapids: Eerdmans, 1994): pp. 545–74, who rejects theories that the 'we' and 'us' motif was dependent on contemporary literary models (p. 561), but who suggests 'that these sections seem to have come from an author other than the author of Luke–Acts' (p. 572). Porter adopts this view despite his conviction that the literary style of these chapters is generally consistent with the earlier chapters of Luke–Acts (p. 567). Not least he leaves open the question of the identity of the author who accompanied Paul on the sea voyage to Rome. The only other on–board disciple mentioned was 'Aristarchus a Macedonian from Thessalonica' (Acts 27:2), but his reference is in the third not the first person and to our knowledge he was not present during the earlier 'we' and 'us' passages.

7 Hemer, *Book of Acts*, pp. 329–33, 388–90.

8 J. Fitzmyer, *Luke the Theologian: Aspects of His Teaching* (London: Geoffrey Chapman, 1989), p. 22.

9 As well, Luke was attempting concurrently to relate the narratives about both Peter and Paul, a difficult task. On the basis that Paul was converted in 34, and depending on information in Galatians, it would mean that Paul made his first return visit to Jerusalem in 36/37 (Gal. 1:18) and his second return visit in *c*.47 (Gal. 2:1). But Luke locates Peter's flight to 'another place' following Herod Agrippa's death (Acts 12:17,23) *after* Paul's second visit to Jerusalem (Acts 11:30). This is chronologically incorrect because Agrippa died in AD 44 and Paul's return visit to Jerusalem 'after fourteen years' occurred in *c*.47. Clearly Luke's narrative about Paul's visit to Jerusalem and Peter's flight

from Jerusalem is technically incorrect but the error is probably due to his attempt to weave into one the complex chronologies of Peter and Paul.

10 In defence of Gal. 2:1–10 = Acts 11:27–30 as Visit II see D. Wenham, 'Acts and the Pauline Corpus II: The Evidence of Parallels', in *The Book of Acts in Its First Century Setting. Vol 1 Ancient Literary Setting* (ed. B.W. Winter and A.D. Clarke; Grand Rapids: Eerdmans, 1993), pp. 215–58 (34–43). Cf. also D.R. Catchpole, 'Paul, James and the Apostolic Decree', *NTS* 23 (1977): pp. 428–44.

11 As translated by E. de Witt Burton, *The Epistle to the Galatians*, ICC (Edinburgh: T & T Clark, 1980), p. 99.

12 For extensive discussion in favour of Gal. 2:1–10 and Acts 11:27–30 as Visit II see Richard Bauckham, *The Book of Acts in Its First Century Setting. Vol 4 Palestinian Setting* (Grand Rapids: Eerdmans, 1995), pp. 467–72.

13 See further Appendix 1: Dating Galatians.

14 Clare K. Rothschild, 'Pisidian Antioch in Acts 13. The Denouement of the South Galatian Hypothesis', *NovT* 54 (2012): 334–353 assumes a second century writing of Acts based on a reconstruction of the course of Paul's travels from the corpus of Paul's letters that had been assembled by that time.

Rothschild argues that Pisidian Antioch in Acts 13 (which she calls 'little Rome') typologically anticipates Paul's arrival in Rome proper (which she calls 'big Rome'). This is a confusion of categories. Modern archaeologists indeed know what the people of Antioch in Pisidia then knew, that *Colonia Antiocheia* was a 'little' Rome. Luke may or may not have known this, but either way it is not the point he is making in Acts 13.

In the overall structure of Acts, Pisidian Antioch does indeed begin an *inclusio* that is concluded by Paul's arrival in Rome, but it is a *Gentile*–focused *inclusio* (Acts 13:46; 28:29), not a *Rome*–focused *inclusio*. While Rothchild claims that 'Pisidian Antioch affords Luke an attractively Romanesque departure point for his Roman–born, Roman–named, Rome–bound missionary' (p. 348), the fact is Acts 13:14–52 nowhere mentions 'Rome'. The 'little Rome'/'big Rome' typology that Rothchild finds is true historically, but it is not the point Luke is making.

Rothschild (following Pervo and Betz) is unreasonably critical of Luke. With Betz she asserts that 'Acts is not historically accurate' (p. 339) and that 'the author knows little more about Paul in the region of Galatia than the duty to place him there' (p. 340). She adds, 'A writer in possession of a map or even just a list of the cities on this road might easily have selected them as an itinerant missionary's (or other traveller's) choices *in lieu of sources*' (p. 341). In short, according to her, Luke's narrative detail in Acts

13 – 14 is an invention and it does not correspond to what happened, apart from the names of the places visited.

Some responses are appropriate. First, the creation of a Pauline corpus may or may not have occurred within the first part of the second century, but in any case it would not have been possible for 'Luke' to recreate his narrative for Paul, based on a list of Paul's letters. Is Rothschild really saying that Luke's detail in Acts 13 – 14 is fiction, pure and simple?

Second, the actual routes that Paul took would not necessarily have been as predictable as Rothschild assumes. When Paul departed for Syria he re–embarked in Attalia where he would have been expected to arrive. Attalia was a major harbour city whereas Perga was a river port twenty kilometres inland. Regarding the accuracy of Luke for Paul's arrival in and departure from Pamphylia, Douglas A. Campbell comments, 'In my judgement the author of Acts at these two junctures is, quite simply, spot on' ('Paul in Pamphylia (Acts 13.13–14a; 14.24b–26): A Critical Note', *NTS* 46.4 (2000): p. 602 (595–602). Further, the journey from Lystra on to Derbe (a minor settlement, not on the *Via Sebaste*) is inexplicable except to escape from the problems in Iconium and Lystra from which Paul had fled. Luke's reference to such an unimportant place as Derbe simply doesn't make sense unless Paul actually went there.

Third, it is not appropriate to dismiss Luke's narrative about Paul's direct journey from Cyprus to Pisidia as due to 'the connection, unifying Cyprus and Pisidian Antioch' (Rothschild, 'Pisidian Antioch', p. 345). Through the discovery of the 'Sergius Paulus' inscription in Pisidian Antioch we may now guess that Paul was keen to arrive in a region where there were relatives of the proconsul of Cyprus. But if Luke knew this he doesn't say so. It is quite likely that this was, indeed, Paul's motive but it cannot be discerned from the text of Acts. Alternatively, a health issue may have been the reason (cf. Gal. 4:13–14). Arguably Luke was faithfully narrating the expeditious journey from Cyprus to Antioch based on what he had been told without knowing the reason for the haste.

Finally, we ask: how much detail does Rothschild reasonably expect in a third–person narrative within a scroll of limited length that spans the first thirty years of Christian history? The author doesn't claim to have travelled with Paul so that he is dependent on sources for this information, the most likely of which was Paul himself, an option Rothschild does not explore. Given that scenario, and mindful of Luke's 'Jerusalem to the end of the earth' thrust, it is not surprising that he expands on some details (e.g. the lengthy synagogue speech and the hostile reaction) while passing over others more briefly. Put simply, this is just what Luke repeatedly does throughout his Acts narrative, which although occasionally frustrating, is nonetheless the one text that connects Jesus with the early church and the key role Paul played in his witness to the Gentiles at 'the end of the earth'.

[15] The inscription with the words [PAULLISER] was discovered in Antioch of Pisidia and is now displayed in the museum of its modern town, Yalvaç. It is too much of a coincidence that Paul travelled so directly from Cyprus (where Sergius Paulus was proconsul) to Antioch (where his family was prominent). It is possible that Paul had letters of introduction from the proconsul of Cyprus to relatives in Pisidia.

[16] Martin Hengel, *Acts and the History of Earliest Christianity* (London: SCM, 1979, ET), p. 66.

[17] Alfred Plummer, *St Luke* ICC (Edinburgh: T & T Clark, 1901), p. xii.

Appendix 3: Barnabas and Peter after the Incident in Antioch

[1] J.D.G. Dunn, *Beginning from Jerusalem* (Grand Rapids: Eerdmans, 2009), pp. 1062–8; M. Hengel, *Saint Peter: The Underestimated Apostle* (Grand Rapids: Eerdmans, 2010 ET), pp. 79–89.

[2] Hengel, *Saint Peter*, p. 94.

[3] Josephus, *Jewish War* ii.254–265; Jewish Antiqities xx.160–172.

[4] Josephus, *Jewish Antiquities* xx.200–203 (LCL., trans. L.H. Feldman).

[5] This view broadly depends on the analysis of E.E. Ellis, *The Making of the New Testament Documents* (Leiden: Brill, 1999), pp. 32–6, 251–66, 307–14. Ellis draws attention to the comment of Clement of Alexandria on 'the true tradition of the blessed teaching in direct line from Peter, James, John and Paul, the holy apostles' (p. 309).

[6] Irenaeus, *Against the Heresies* III.1.1.

[7] The anonymous Letter to the Hebrews, an early work, may have been written by a known associate of Paul's, perhaps Apollos or Barnabas.

Appendix 4: James' Encyclical to the 'Twelve Tribes of the Diaspora'

[1] Had the letter been pseudonymous, as many hold it to have been, we would have expected the writer overtly to claim to be 'the brother of Jesus' or 'first pillar in Jerusalem'.

2 So J.D.G. Dunn, *Beginning from Jerusalem* (Grand Rapids: Eerdmans, 2009), pp. 1123–9.

3 J.A.T. Robinson, *Redating the New Testament* (London: SCM, 1976), pp. 131–4, effectively responds to objections to James, brother of Jesus, as author of this letter. Included among the objections is the linguistic consideration that James is written in 'high *koine*' where Robinson appeals to the writings of Sevenster, Argyle and Zahn in defence of Jacobean authorship.

4 James was executed under the high priest Annas II during the interregnum between the death in office of Festus and the arrival of Albinus (Josephus, *Jewish Antiquties* xx.200).

5 Dunn, *Beginning from Jerusalem*, p. 1143, believes James is responding to Paul, but to his Letter to the Romans, suggesting a later dating for James.

6 P.H. Davids, 'Palestinian Traditions in the Epistle of James', in *James the Just and Christian Origins* NovTSup 98 (ed. B. Chilton and C.A. Evans; Leiden: Brill, 1999), pp. 51–2. Unfortunately we have no details about how Paul's teaching, or a skewed version of Paul's teaching, came to the attention of James. Yet there is the evidence of other reports of Paul's activities in the Diaspora reaching the attention of people in Jerusalem. Prominent among the reports was the information about Paul's about–face preaching in Syria–Cilicia of the faith he had previously attempted to destroy (Gal. 1:23). News of his missionary foray into Pisidia and Lycaonia with Barnabas also came to the notice of Christians in Jerusalem, attracting a counter–mission by those 'troublers' that he writes against in Galatians (Gal. 1:7; 5:7–12). Likewise Peter's table–fellowship with Gentiles in Antioch became known in Jerusalem where it provoked a disciplinary embassy from Jerusalem, sent by James (Gal. 2:11–14). It is reasonable, therefore, to believe that Paul's teaching about being 'justified' and 'saved' and the role of 'faith' and 'works' during his decade in Syria and Cilicia had also reached James in the Holy City, provoking him to write his encyclical letter.

7 See Chapter 2.

8 See e.g. C.K. Barrett, *A Commentary on the Second Epistle to the Corinthians* (London: A & C Black, 1973), p. 297: 'the floggings will probably go back to the earliest period of his apostolic work.' M. Hengel, 'The Stance of the Apostle Paul Towards the Law in the Unknown Years Between Damascus and Antioch', in *Justification and Variegated Nomism 2, The Paradoxes of Paul* (ed. D.A. Carson, P.T. O'Brien and M.A. Siefrid; Grand Rapids: Baker, 2004), pp. 75–103, suggests that these beatings began in Syria (i.e. Damascus). See also M. Hengel and

A.M. Schwemer, *Paul Between Damascus and Antioch: The Unknown Years* (Louisville: Westminster John Knox: ET 1997), p. 464 n. 1261.

9 According to Deut. 25:1–3 this punishment was for the wrongdoer in a dispute, on the verdict of a judge. Writing during the New Testament era Josephus observed that this public punishment, which was most disgraceful to the offender, was for someone who had acted 'contrary to the law' (*Jewish Antiquites* iv.238).

10 Such teaching was antithetical to Jewish theology. Mishnah *Aboth* 6:7 asserts, 'Great is the Law, for it gives life to them that practice it both in this world and in the world to come.' According to R. Hananiah b. Akasya, 'The Holy One, blessed is he, was minded to grant merit to Israel; therefore hath he multiplied for them the Law and commandments, as it is written, *It pleased the Lord for his righteousness' sake to magnify the Law and make it honourable*' (*Makk.* 3.16; Isa. 42:21).

11 Mishnah *Makkot* provided relief from 'extirpation' if one submitted to the scourging of the forty lashes less one. The tractate decreed, 'when he is scourged then he is thy brother' adding, 'and his soul shall be restored to him' (*Makk.* 3.15). In other words, the Mishnah mandated this beating in order to enable the violator of the law to be accepted back within Judaism. The scourging effectively absolved the perpetrator from 'extirpation'. See D. Steinmetz, *Punishment and Freedom: The Rabbinic Construction of Criminal Law* (Philadelphia: University of Pennsylvania Press, 2008), pp. 70–77.

12 The coincidence of language is considerable. By 'faith' Paul understands a faith commitment to Christ crucified and risen whereas James meant creedal assent to the *Shema*'. Paul's dependence on Gen. 15:6 was to demonstrate that God counted Abraham's faith in God's promise of innumerable descendants as righteousness. James' example of Abraham's faith relates to his obedience in the binding of Isaac (Gen. 22:1–14). Despite their apparently divergent understandings of Gen. 15:6 Paul and James may actually have broadly agreed about its meaning and application. Paul understood Gen. 15:6 in its immediate context of God's promise of innumerable descendants to the aged man whereas James connected it with Abraham's faith expressed in his obedience in offering up Isaac, the one who would make it possible for the patriarch to have innumerable descendants. For both Paul and James faith was important, but according to James Abraham showed his faith 'by his works' (Jas. 2:28).

13 Davids, 'Palestinian Traditions', pp. 33–57.

14 James' apparently developed ecclesiology is not necessarily an argument for a later dating. True, James discouraged 'many' from becoming

teachers (*didaskaloi* – 3:1) and assumed the existence of 'elders of the church (*presbyteroi tēs ekklēsias* – 5:14). Yet Paul and Barnabas appointed 'elders in every church' during the Galatian mission (Acts 14:23) in *c*.47 and referred to 'those who *teach*' (Gal. 6:6) in *c*.48. By *c*.49, and most probably sooner, there were 'elders' in the church of Jerusalem (Acts 15:6).

15 For a complete list see J.B. Adamson, *The Epistle of James* NICNT (Grand Rapids: Eerdmans, 1976), p. 188.

16 Davids, 'Palestinian Traditions', pp. 33–57.

17 J. Painter, *Just James* (Columbia: University of South Carolina, ????), pp. 261–2.

18 Robinson, *Redating*, p. 123, quoting E.M. Sidebottom, *James, Jude and 2 Peter* New Century Bible (Nelson: London, 1967), p. 14.

19 Josephus, *Jewish Antiquities* x.201.

20 Suetonius, *Claudius* 5.4.

21 According to Benediction 12: 'For the renegades let there be no hope, and may the arrogant kingdom soon be rooted out in our days, and the Nazarenes and the minim perish as in a moment and be blotted out from the book of life and with the righteous may they not be inscribed. Blessed art thou, O Lord, who humblest the arrogant' (C.K. Barrett, *The New Testament Background: Selected Documents* [London: SPCK, rev. edn, 1987], p. 211).

22 See further P.W. Barnett, *The Corinthian Question* (Leicester: IVP, 2011), pp. 34–52.

Appendix 5: The 'New Perspective on Paul' According to James Dunn

1 J.D.G. Dunn, *The Theology of Paul the Apostle* (Grand Rapids: Eerdmans, 1998); J.D.G. Dunn, *The Epistle to the Galatians* (London: A & C Black, 1993).

2 Dunn, *Theology of Paul*, p. 338.

3 E.P. Sanders, *Paul and Palestinian Judaism* (Philadelphia: Fortress Press, 1987).

4 Dunn, *Theology of Paul*, p. 348.

5 Quoted in N.T. Wright, '4QMMT and Paul', in *History and Exegesis: FS for E.E. Ellis* (ed. San–Won Son; London: T & T Clark, 2006), pp. 104–32.

6 Dunn, *Theology of Paul*, p. 352.

7 Dunn, *Theology of Paul*, p. 352.

8 Dunn, *Theology of Paul*, p. 353.

9   Dunn, *Theology of Paul*, p. 353.
10 Dunn, *Theology of Paul*, pp. 354–5.
11 *Luther's Works* 26:122 quoted in T. George, 'Modernizing Luther, Domesticating Paul: Another Perspective', in *Justification and Variegated Nomism* (ed. D.A. Carson, P.T. O'Brien and M.A. Seifrid; Grand Rapids: Baker Academic, 2004), p. 457.
12 Commenting on Rom. 4:4–5 Dunn, *Theology of Paul*, p. 367, says, 'There is of course some play between 'works' (*erga*) and 'the one who works/does not work (*ergazomenō*). But the precise character of the wordplay remains unclear.'
13 Dunn, *Theology of Paul*, p. 361.
14 George, 'Modernizing Luther', p. 454.
15 Dunn, *Theology of Paul*, p. 227.
16 Dunn, *Theology of Paul*, p. 227.
17 Dunn, *Theology of Paul*, p. 344.
18 Dunn, *Galatians*, p. 137.
19 Dunn, *Galatians*, p. 140.
20 See further, Debbie Hunn, '*Ean mē* in Galatians 2:16: A Look at Greek Literature', *NovT* 49 (2007): pp. 281–290.
21 Dunn, *Galatians*, p. 140.
22 Dunn, *Galatians*, p. 252.

Appendix 6: Paul Preaching Christ Crucified to Jews

1   *Benediction* 15 (quoted in E. Schürer, *The History of the Jewish People in the Age of Jesus Christ* (ed. G. Vermes et al.; Edinburgh: T & T Clark, rev. edn, 1979), p. 458.
2   J.–J. Aubert, 'A Double Standard in Roman Criminal Law?', in *Speculum Iuris: Roman Law as a Reflection of Social and Economic Life in Antiquity* (ed. J.–J. Aubert and B. Sirks; Ann Arbor: University of Michigan, 2002), pp. 94–133, esp. p. 113 (with reference to supporting literature).
3   John Granger Cook, 'Crucifixion as Spectacle in Roman Campania', *NovT* 54 (2012), pp. 68–100.
4   Particularly significant is Paul's reminder to the Galatians that before their 'eyes' Christ had been 'publicly portrayed (*proegraphē*) crucified' (Gal. 3:1). The imagery of 'bewitchment' (necessarily through the eyes) connected with 'before whose eyes' he had *placarded* Christ as crucified suggests that Paul's preaching of 'Christ crucified' was *strikingly visual*. This probably means one of two things, either (i) that Paul had not witnessed the crucifixion of Jesus but described it in his preaching based on crucifixions he had witnessed in his travels in

the Roman east, or (ii) he had actually witnessed the crucifixion of Jesus in Jerusalem. The horrific character of crucifixion is set out in Cook, 'Crucifixion as Spectacle', pp. 68–100. Crucifixions would have occurred in Roman colonies Antioch in Pisidia, Iconium and Lystra.

5 Paul Barnett, *Paul Missionary of Jesus* (Grand Rapids: Eerdmans, 2008), pp. 54–75.

6 For another example of Paul speaking of himself as Israel in miniature see Gal. 3:23–9 where Paul can speak representatively of previously being imprisoned under law/under a pedagogue before faith/justification came.

Author Index

Subject Index

Scriptural References

Quotations from Josephus are from the Loeb Classical Library texts and from the Mishnah are from H. Danby, *The Mishnah* (Oxford, Clarendon Press, 1933).

Following Jesus to Jerusalem

Luke 9–19

Paul Barnett

Taking the metaphor of life as a journey, Paul Barnett follows the journey of Jesus to Jerusalem and suggests that we journey with him. Barnett stresses the important place of kingdom in this and the ethics of Christian living which naturally follow from being in the presence of a humble saviour. More than a commentary, then, this important book challenges the way we live in the light of Jesus' last days and self-sacrifice. Paul Barnett expounds Luke, chapters 9–19, with the intention of provoking faith and faithulness in the lives of Jesus' followers today.

Paul Barnett is the former Bishop of North Sydney and lecturer in New Testament, Moore College, Syndey, Ausralia.

978-1-84227-767-6 (e-book 978-1-84227-859-8)